June 1984

Dear Joseph,

I hope that these writings will give you some insight into the field of polygraphy.

Hopefully, we'll have the opportunity of discussing it someday soon.

My very best,

Stan

A Polygraph Handbook
for Attorneys

A Polygraph Handbook for Attorneys

Stanley Abrams

Lexington Books
D.C. Heath and Company
Lexington, Massachusetts
Toronto

Library of Congress Cataloging in Publication Data

Abrams, Stanley.
  A polygraph handbook for attorneys.

  Includes index.
  1. Lie detectors and detection. I. Title.
HV8078.A23   364.12'8   77-6074
ISBN 0-669-01598-9

Third printing, February 1981.

Published simultaneously in Canada.

Printed in the United States of America.

International Standard Book Number: 0-669-01598-9

Library of Congress Catalog Card Number: 77-6074

Contents

List of Figures

List of Tables

Preface

During the times of the ancient Greeks, Diogenes is said to have wandered about the land in search of an honest man. The quest for truth has continued throughout the ages with reliance first placed on mysticism, then religion, and finally science. In the latter, attempts were made to achieve this goal through hypnosis, truth serums, word-association tests, and polygraphy. In the end, however, it only has been through the polygraph technique that any significant degree of success has been attained in differentiating truth from deception.

In spite of this and its rather consistent demonstration of high validity, the polygraph was not ruled admissible in a higher court until 1948. Primarily, this was due to the fact that the approach had to reach a higher set of standards than other scientific procedures. But now, after over eighty years of development and continued experimentation, it has attained a status in which it is routinely admitted into evidence on a stipulated basis in many jurisdictions. Moreover, since the seventies, there has been a growing trend toward the admission of polygraph testimony over the objection of prosecution. It is anticipated that in the near future a much greater use will be made of this technique and that it will no longer be necessary to establish a foundation for admission into court.

While the polygraph procedure is now experiencing a rather wide usage, there are still a large number of attorneys who do not have sufficient familiarity with it to employ it to its full potential. This book was specifically written for lawyers to answer this need. It will provide them with the research findings to enable them to establish a foundation and the transcripts from the Medina trial presented in the Appendix will serve as a model for this procedure. The description of the actual polygraph technique and the methods of interpretation will make available the data necessary to determine whether the test has been properly conducted. Criticisms against the use of polygraphy are also dealt with in detail to provide an argument for or against its admission into evidence. Finally, a series of court cases is described to indicate those in which polygraph testimony has been accepted, and in some instances, the reasons for which it has been rejected. All of this information should be of real practical value and add to the attorney's armamentarium regardless of whether he is in the public or private sphere.

There has been a tendency to emphasize the value of polygraphy in the realm of criminal law, but this is rather unfortunate considering its great worth in civil cases. In all too many instances, the opposing statements of the claimant and the defendant are so equally believable that a stalemate results, and the decision is made based on factors other than the evidence presented in court. It is quite obvious that the jury's decision is frequently biased by such extraneous factors as the witness's demeanor, intelligence, dress, or station in life. The old adage that a jury is composed of a group of people deciding who has the better attorney could certainly be extended to include witnesses who can present their testimony most effectively. In these situations, when the polygraph is administered to both parties, it has definite probative value, for the examiner reaches his conclusion by an objective analysis of the charts and not the behavior of the subject. Thus, the most effective method yet devised can ascertain the truth. It is hoped that this book will assist the attorney to do likewise.

1 Polygraphy Today

In May of 1973, David Wise published his book, *The Politics of Lying*, which he introduced with a quote from Herbert Klein who said ". . . there has been this feeling that perhaps the government is lying."[1] Coincidentally, at the same time the Senate Watergate hearings began an attempt to search for the truth. It is most appropriate that during the 1970s, polygraphy, after years of exceedingly slow progress in gaining acceptance, was now achieving its goal: It, too, now could fulfill its purpose of seeking truth.

During these years, there has been a greater utilization of the polygraph approach as an investigative tool in law enforcement and as a means for reducing employee theft in business. In both of these realms, it was so effective as to result in a greater demand for the use of the technique. In government, however, efforts were made to reduce its employment as a device for screening out possible security risks at the behest of the labor unions. Despite this fact, many courts were routinely admitting polygraph testimony into evidence on a stipulated basis, and some federal and state courts have ruled it admissible over the objection of prosecution. Perhaps it is here that polygraphy can be of most benefit. As far back as 1906 Sigmund Freud pointed out: "There is a growing recognition of the untrustworthiness of statements made by witnesses. . . ."[2] Larson also emphasized that ". . . the amount of deliberate false swearing in our criminal courts would be inadequately described as shocking."[3]

It is quite evident that neither the taking of an oath nor cross-examination by a competent trial attorney has achieved any great amount of success in eliminating perjury. Perjury has been described as most easy to commit, but very difficult to prove. Like lying itself, it is extremely common and takes place in all people regardless of such factors as nationality, race, age, religion, or sex. It can be expected that friends and relatives of the accused will perjure themselves to help the defendant. Certainly, accused persons often will lie or try to place the blame on someone in order to protect themselves. Witnesses will perjure themselves out of loyalty, fear of reprisal, or even in an effort to get revenge. Whatever the motivation, a considerable degree of deception occurs in the courtroom, and the polygraph approach is by far the most effective means of disclosing it.

Because of this fact and the increased utilization of polygraphy in the courts, it is almost imperative for the counsel, whether involved in civil or criminal cases, to become more knowledgeable about this technique. Counsel must have a sufficient understanding of the test in order to argue to have the results admitted or to keep the test out if it has been improperly conducted.[4] Moreover, for the lawyer, it is a most useful method for ascertaining whether the client's statements are truthful so as to avoid what Rapaport described as the bane of all attorneys: not knowing the facts.[5]

When the facts are known and corroborated by the polygraph findings, the technique becomes a powerful tool. In accident claims, for example, it could readily be determined whether the individual is malingering or if his symptoms, which cannot be authenticated by medical findings, are really being experienced. Differentiating between a conversion reaction in an hysteric and a person who is attempting to defraud an insurance carrier is an often difficult task for a psychologist or psychiatrist. A differential diagnosis can be made much more easily with the aid of a polygraph test. Other insurance claims ranging from theft losses to possible arson can be confirmed by this approach. Instances involving one person's word against another's—that is, where the evidence is so balanced that it almost only can be decided by a toss of a coin—can be settled by examining both parties. These include paternity cases or automobile accidents in which both persons disclaim blame. The list of uses for polygraphy can go on interminably, with only the counsel's lack of imagination setting the limits.·

With the growing recognition of the validity of polygraphy, prosecutors can often be persuaded to drop the charges against a suspect who has been found truthful in his denial of the accusation against him, even when no stipulation has been entered.[6] In those instances in which an agreement has been made to a stipulated examination, defense attorneys often have their clients take an ex parte test prior to the stipulated examination, to be assured that their clients are being truthful. If their clients are found deceptive, they can then consider entering into a plea-bargaining arrangement.

The attorney must employ considerable care in selecting a polygraphist in recognition of the fact that the accuracy of the findings are intimately related to the expertise of the examiner. In accomplishing this, the attorney protects the conclusions from the attack of the opposing counsel and reduces the likelihood of contradictory results being obtained by another examiner.[7] The polygraphist chosen should be experienced and have graduated from an accredited polygraph school as well as having a college degree, preferably with a major in psychology. His education should have continued through regular attendance at professional seminars, and ideally, he should have presented papers at these meetings himself. A familiarity with the literature is quite important so that he can readily cope with cross-examination by being able to quote the research that has been conducted. Obviously, it would be valuable if he also had published reports of investigations that he had conducted.

The examiner should be a member of the local and national societies and licensed in his state, if such legislation has been passed. He should utilize a technique that is accepted by those in his profession, and the test should have been administered and numerically scored in a manner that would allow other examiners to verify his findings. Obviously, considerable advantages result if the polygraphist is also experienced in courtroom testimony and is able to present his data in a professional manner that was clearly understandable to a jury.

The lawyer should supply the examiner with all of the appropriate data pertinent to the case including the witnesses' statements, police reports, the charges against the individual, and such background information as his medical, psychiatric, and educational background. In order to avoid the "friendly examiner syndrome," it is extremely important for the subject who is being tested by a private polygraphist to recognize that the results, regardless of the outcome, will be utilized in some manner. If he believes that the findings will be discarded if they are not to his advantage, it is conceivable that he will be so unconcerned about the results that deception may not be detected. This would be an obvious disadvantage if he were to be reexamined and a definite weakness in the test procedure that could be pointed out during the cross-examination.

There are two ways in which the polygraph examination can be made more meaningful to the subject. The first technique is to emphasize that the charges against him could be dropped if he were to be found nondeceptive in his denial of the accusation against him. Since this is a frequent occurrence, it is a perfectly acceptable approach. The second method, however, requires the use of a subterfuge, which many attorneys would not find acceptable, even though it is to their client's advantage. It simply requires that the subject be informed that the results will be used regardless of the outcome. This approach is the more desirable one since it would most closely resemble an examination administered by a law enforcement polygraphist and thus assure that comparable results would be obtained on reexamination.

To further assure that there will be no areas of vulnerability during cross-examination, the entire test process should be taped. If there is any question as to the emotional or intellectual state of the subject, he should be interviewed by a psychologist or psychiatrist who can testify that he was not suffering from any mental defect that might preclude the attainment of accurate results. While the use of drugs would at the most only cause an inconclusive finding, it would strengthen the test findings if a urine sample were taken at the time of the examination to demonstrate that no pharmaceutical agents were used to "beat the test." In addition, all of the polygrams should be properly identified and signed by the subject. The polygraphist should maintain custody of the charts, but copies should be available so at least one other examiner can verify the test findings.[8] Finally, the examiner should be able to document that his instrument had been recently calibrated to attest to the fact that it was operating up to the manufacturer's standards.

The subject himself should be in good physical condition at the time of the testing and not overly fatigued, hungry, or having been just subjected to a long interrogation. It should be clear that he is taking the test voluntarily and that the procedure has been thoroughly explained and every question used has been discussed with him.[9]

A proper foundation must be established, and it is often advantageous to utilize expert opinion from individuals in other professions such as psychology or physiology to accomplish this. The testimony should include an explanation of the psychophysiologic basis underlying polygraphy along with a review of the research findings summarizing the validity and reliability of the approach. It is also important to indicate the results of the surveys that have demonstrated that the polygraph technique has been accepted by behavioral scientists and the law profession. A brief account of the historical background should be reported and a description of the considerable usage made of polygraphy in law enforcement, business, government, and its status insofar as admissibility into court is concerned. Both the instrumentation and the technique should be discussed in detail, with particular emphasis upon the control question technique that is so difficult for a layman to comprehend. The standards developed by the American Polygraph Association and the state of polygraphy in general should be outlined to assure recognition that it has attained the status of a profession.

The examiner himself should be qualified, and he should present in detail the procedures that he employed. His charts should be available for cross-examination, and he should be able to demonstrate how he reached his conclusions based on the polygraph tracings. A second polygraphist might also testify as to his interpretation of the same charts.

Scientific attempts at lie detection had its beginnings as far back as 1895 and a considerable amount of research has been accumulated over the years. Polygraph validity, however, has been most difficult to ascertain because complete verification in actual cases has been obtained only rarely. Experimentation in a laboratory situation is quite dissimilar from the use made of the polygraph in real investigations. The major difference lies in the fact that a volunteer subject in a simulated crime responds in a very different manner than an actual criminal suspect. In the case of the former, he has little or nothing to lose if his lie is detected. Therefore, his emotional reaction is not at all like that of the criminal suspect who faces imprisonment, embarrassment, and financial loss if his deception is discovered. Because of this factor, researchers have been most hesitant to generalize from the findings in the laboratory to actual life situations. In both settings, high levels of accuracy have been reported in the range of 90 to 100 percent when competent and experienced examiners are employed.

Polygraphy is a psychophysiologic approach with the emphasis on the psychologic aspects. If a subject lies in response to a question, it engenders an emotional reaction that in turn creates a variation in his physiologic functioning. These physical changes are recorded by the polygraph and interpreted by the polygraphist as being indicative of truth or deception. The physical reactions are a natural response of the organism to assist it in dealing with a threat situation. When intimidation of any nature occurs, a series of physical changes take place that enable the organism to deal more effectively with the threat through the utilization of all of its resources. A wide range of changes occur, including the pupils of the eyes dilating so that perception is improved and the palms of the hands growing moist to aid in locomotion or grasping. The blood vessels in the skin constrict resulting in a lesser loss of blood should an injury occur. Stronger contractions of the heart send more oxygenated blood through the body and an additional blood supply is directed to the skeletal muscles allowing for a more effective utilization of the arms and legs. In this way, the body is more able to deal with the threat in what Cannon described as a flight or fight reaction.[10] These and many other physiologic changes act to assist the individual in coping with the situation. What the threat is matters relatively little, for the body will respond in a like manner regardless of what is creating the stress. Therefore, whether a person is facing a possible fight or lying during a polygraph examination, his physical responses will be essentially the same. Ironically, those same responses that typically serve to get the individual out of trouble get him into difficulty if he is deceptive during a polygraph test situation.

The polygraph records some of the individual's physical responses—namely, blood volume and relative blood pressure, heart rate, respiration, and the skin's resistance to electricity. The changes in reactions that are recorded on the chart are sufficiently measurable to enable the examiner to assign a numerical weight to each response. These scores are reliable to the extent that a number of polygraphists can draw identical conclusions through their interpretations of the same chart.

A number of theories exist that explain the efficacy of the polygraph approach. Marston hypothesized that anger was one of the emotions elicited during deception while being tested.[11] Since this particular affective state does create the changes in physiologic functioning characteristic of the response seen in one who is deceiving, this hypothesis is a plausible explanation, but Marston also indicated that there must be a consciousness of lying for these reactions to be demonstrated, which is only partially true. Weinstein et al., Germann, and Bittermann and Marcuse utilized hypnosis to create an amnesia for a particular act, but in spite of this state, various degrees of awareness were later disclosed through polygraphy.[12] It can be assumed that if an individual commits a crime and then represses any conscious awareness of it, he may still be seen as deceptive if he were to deny it.

Davis presented three theories in an explanation for the means by which this technique can differentiate truth from deception.[13] The concept that is most accepted at the present time was described in terms of the threat of punishment or fear of the consequences. The subject, recognizing that severe consequences may result if his untruthfulness is discovered, becomes fearful each time he lies to a question. This emotional reaction, perhaps more than any other, causes the characteristic physiologic signs of deception. It can be assumed that the more intense the fear, the greater will be the degree of physiologic change demonstrated. Generally, the deception then will be more easily interpreted. The role of the examiner is to develop the test so that the guilty become more fearful of detection, while the innocent are reassured that their truthfulness will be recognized. This goal is accomplished in a great many ways, all of which relate to a demonstration that the instrument can definitely differentiate truth from deception, and much of the effectiveness of the technique is dependent upon the ability of the polygraphist to accomplish just that.

Directly related to the fear of detection is the desire to successfully deceive. Gustafson and Orne in their research demonstrated that the deception of the more motivated subjects was more readily detected.[14]

There are, however, sound arguments against the consequence theory. Thackray and Orne reported that the lies of subjects who were unaware that they were being tested were as easily determined as those of individuals who were cognizant of the examination's being administered.[15] In addition to these findings, high accuracy is obtained in laboratory experimentation in which there is little fear and no punishment if the deception is discovered. This finding indicates that the fear of punishment theory is not the whole explanation for the effectiveness of the technique.

A second theory postulated by Davis relates to the emotional state associated with conflict.[16] He assumed that habit, or what might be more meaningfully described as learning, disposed a person to be truthful. If, however, deceiving reduces a threat, then a conflict between the two would result. He theorized that a large physiologic disturbance would occur when the two incompatible reactions were aroused at the same time. While this hypothesis is quite reasonable, it does not account for those individuals such as psychopaths, who have no qualms at all about lying. Since individuals within this diagnostic category have recently been studied and found to be as easily detected in their deception as others, the conflict theory is also not in itself a complete explanation for the effectiveness of the polygraph.

Davis' final explanation, the conditioned response theory, is based on his view that the critical questions were the conditioned stimuli and that they produced an emotional response (conditioned response) comparable to one with which they have been associated in the past. The criminal act then would be the unconditioned stimulus and the emotional state at that time would be the unconditioned response. Therefore, asking a suspect about his involvement in a murder would be expected to arouse an affective state similar to the one that had been stimulated during the act itself. The weakness of this supposition is that laboratory subjects can demonstrate a large physiologic response to deception, despite the fact there is little emotion involved in the task of selecting one of four numbered cards and then denying doing so. Moreover, critical questions can cause a large reaction in an innocent subject as well as in one who is guilty. As was the case with the other theories, the conditioned response is not a sufficient answer.

A deceptive response is not a necessary requirement to determining whether the individual has guilty knowledge or has actually been involved in a crime. The subject can answer truthfully or not at all, and a physiologic response will occur. If, for example, a robbery had taken place in a shopping center and the suspect denied any knowledge of it, even to the extent of stating that he did not know which store was involved, the polygraphist would have only to read off the names of a number of the stores and if the subject reacted to the one in which the robbery had occurred, guilty knowledge could be discerned. In this situation, though no deception was involved, the presence of fear could be assumed. In a laboratory setting, using the same design in which the subject had selected a number from a series, a similar physiologic response would be demonstrated at the key number without any verbal response or deception being necessary. This suggests the presence of an emotional response similar to generalized excitement, which would account for the high level of accuracy obtained in laboratory studies.

None of the theories set forth is a sufficient explanation in itself for the varying kinds of lie detection that take place; thus we can assume that they are all applicable to some degree. Emotional responses vary with different situations and different individuals and a number of these affective states may be operating at the same time. Generalized excitement may be more prominent in laboratory investigations while fear and the consequence theory play a more significant role in actual criminal cases. It is quite likely that in some circumstances, conflict and even guilt may play a role in altering the physiologic response pattern.

The literature relating to polygraphy and many of the statements made by the courts in rejecting polygraph testimony are replete with fallacies. Having once been written, they are quoted and repeated so that many of the same misconceptions live on. Over the years, the technique has been described as unreliable, unaccepted by the scientific community, easily "beaten" by psychopaths, hearsay evidence, usurping the role of the jury, and a violation of the civil rights of the individual. A large number of the population was described as being untestable, including children, psychopaths, retardates, psychotics, neurotics, those on drugs, and individuals with cardiovascular and respiratory disorders. From this list, we would wonder whether there were any people who could be accurately examined. Of all of those listed, only the psychotics and retardates cannot be tested with any high degree of accuracy, and none of the arguments listed for refusing to admit polygraph testimony are felt to be legitimate at this time.

A final criticism that has been leveled against polygraphy is that sufficient standardization does not exist. In contrast to this statement, the technique, instrumentation, school curriculums, and requirements for acceptance into the various professional organizations have been standardized. By 1976, statutes for polygraph licensure had been passed in nineteen states, and polygraphy had taken on the trappings of a profession. There were accredited schools, national and local societies, annual seminars, a code of ethics, and a journal. Research was being expanded and improvements in the technique and instrumentation were being made.

Polygraphy is continuing to serve many needs in law enforcement. Innocent suspects are cleared without having to face the stress associated with investigation, interrogations, and the costs of attorney's fees. There have been large savings of both money and manpower in police work through the elimination of many of the suspects so that they can concentrate their efforts on those who are more likely to be guilty. Large amounts of money and merchandise have been recovered, and the losses in business and industry due to employee theft have been greatly reduced when this approach is utilized. It has also been proved to be of great worth for attorneys and has been shown to have probative value in the courts.

It seems quite evident that there will be a continued expansion of polygraph usage, particularly in the courtroom. Therefore, it behooves the lawyer to understand this approach. The purpose of this book is not to attempt to make the reader a polygraphist, but only to present a firm explanation of the principles and techniques involved. Both the strengths and the weaknesses will be discussed in what is hoped will be a fairly unbiased presentation of the facts.

Notes

1. Wise, D., *The Politics of Lying* (N.Y.: Random House, 1973).

2. Freud, S., "Psycho-analysis and the Ascertaining of Truth in Courts of Law," in E. Jones (ed.), *Sigmund Freud Collected Papers*, Vol. 2 (N.Y.: Basic Books, 1959), pp. 13-24.

3. Larson, J.A., *Lying and Its Detection* (Montclair, N.J.: Patterson Smith, 1962).

4. Bailey, F.L., and Rothblatt, H.B., *Investigation and Preparation of Criminal Cases Federal and State* (San Francisco: Bancroft-Whitney Co., 1970).

5. Rapaport, D., "The Greening of the Lie Detector," *The Washington Post*, April 15, 1973.

6. Bailey and Rothblatt, *Investigation and Preparation*.

7. Ibid.

8. Sevilla, C.M., "Should Polygraph Evidence Be Admissible at Trial?" *Criminal Defense* 2 (1975): 4-14.

9. Bailey and Rothblatt, *Investigation and Preparation*.

10. Cannon, W.B. *Bodily Changes in Pain, Horror, Fear and Rage* (N.Y.: Appleton-Century-Crofts, 1929).

11. Marston, W.M., "Systolic Blood Pressure Symptoms of Deception," *J. Exp. Psych.* 2 (1917): 117-63.

12. Weinstein, E., Abrams, S., and Gibbons, D., "The Validity of the Polygraph with Hypnotically Induced Repression and Guilt," *Amer. J. Psychtr* 126 (1970): 1159-62; Germann, A.C., "Hypnosis as Related to the Scientific Detection of Deception by Polygraph Examination: A Pilot Study," *Interntl. J. Clin. Exper. Hypn.* 9 (1961): 309-11; and Bitterman, M.E., and Marcuse, F.L., "Autonomic Response in Post-hypnotic Amnesia," *J. Exp. Psych.* 35 (1945): 248-52.

13. Davis, R.C., "Physiological Responses as a Means of Evaluating Information," in A.D. Biderman and H. Zimmer (eds.), *The Manipulation of Human Behavior* (New York: Wiley, 1961).

14. Gustafson, L.A., and Orne, M.T., "Effects of Heightened Motivation on the Detection of Deception," *J. Appl. Psych.* 47 (1963): 408-11.

15. Thackray, R.I., and Orne, M.T., "A Comparison of Physiological Indices in Detection of Deception," *Psychophysiology* 4 (1968): 329-39.

16. Davis, "Physiological Responses."

2 The History of Polygraphy

The search for truth and attempts at uncovering falsehood has been a universal and almost constant endeavor that has dated back to ancient times. At times, it seems almost to have become a preoccupation as lying, guilt, and sorcery became intermingled. Primitive societies developed complex procedures founded on magic and mysticism in their attempt to discover deception. Divine creatures sent messages through their devices of fire, boiling waters, and torture to open the doors to the truth, and faith in these powerful mechanisms miraculously, at least in some instances, allowed the innocent to go unscathed while the guilty bore the mark of guilt. Some of the rituals had a foundation based on sound physiologic principles, probably learned by observation.

Oriental people, for example, distinguished truth from lying by having all of the accused chew dry rice and then spit it out. While this was a simple task for the honest, those who were deceiving had difficulty in accomplishing it and were then judged to be guilty and punished accordingly. This practice recognized that fear slows the digestive processes, including salivation. Thus, the deceptive were unable to spit out the dry rice, while the innocent, having faith in the power of their deity to clear them of the unjust accusation, felt little fear in contrast to the guilty who knew they would be discovered.

In a similar vein, the Arabs applied a hot iron to the tongue of the accused, and probably for the same physiologic reasons, the truthful were not injured. Other ordeals, however, seem to have no logical basis. In India, suspects were required to hold fire in their hands and were considered innocent if they remained unburned. Both the accused and the accuser were made to withdraw a stone from a boiling cauldron of water as a means of determining truthfulness in Tibet. The people were so influenced by their beliefs that they themselves requested the trial of the ordeals in order to prove their innocence. In Africa, the suspects willingly placed their arms in boiling water, and reportedly only the guilty evidenced blisters or burned skin. While this result is difficult to comprehend, there have been demonstrations using hypnosis in which the converse has been shown. Subjects are informed, while in a hypnotic state, that they will be burned, and this has resulted in a blister being formed.[1] An explanation for some of these unusual physical reactions obviously lies in the usual mind-body interaction, but our inability to explain them does not mean that they do not occur.

A second early means of distinguishing truth from deception and innocence from guilt was the trial by combat. A duel would be fought, and the vanquished was considered to have been deceitful. Since the guilty person failed to establish his innocence in this test, further punishment, if he in fact were still alive, was meted out. Nielson described the hapless loser of a contest having his eyes gouged out and being left to rot in public display as a warning to other wrongdoers.[2]

Trial by tortures was, in medieval times, viewed as one of the best proofs of guilt. Trovillo provides a description that exemplifies both the barbarism as well as the futility of ever obtaining any meaningful admission: "If . . . the prisoner persistently denied his guilt there was no limit to the repetitions of the torture, and yet, even when no confession could be extracted, the failure did not always exempt the prisoner from punishment. If he retracted the confession extorted from him, he was tortured again and again until he ceased to assert his innocence, for it was a positive necessity for convictions that the confession under torture should be confirmed by the prisoner without constraint. . . . If again, the luckless prisoner freely confessed the crime of which he stood accused, he was likewise promptly tortured to find out what other offenses he might at some previous time have committed."[3]

Toward the end of the eighteenth century, it became obvious that a confession attained through such means was of little value. Although torturous practices were discontinued in the more "civilized" countries, it should be recognized that in many primitive societies they persist even today. For example, Chief Inspector Roberts of the Calgary Police in Canada visited law enforcement agencies throughout the world in recent years and reported that such brutal methods as crushing the suspects limbs and restraining the accused while snakes are allowed to enter the various orifices of the body are still practiced to obtain a confession.[4]

In less primitive societies and more modern times, the "third degree" replaced the trial by torture: Admissions were elicited through sleep and food deprivation, bright lights, and general brutality. More recently, brainwashing has been the result of combining these techniques with more sophisticated and insidious measures to exact a confession or convert the subject to a different political philosophy.[5] While humanitarianism and the recognition of the likelihood of attaining a false confession has fostered legislation to ban the use of the third degree, only in the future will the power and dangers of brainwashing be learned.

In contemporary times scientific attempts have been made to discover measures that would be successful in uncovering deception. Hypnosis and the so-called truth serums showed early promise, and there have been claims of their effectiveness. In the former, the concept often held, even by those in the professions, is of an individual in a sleep-like state under the control of the hypnotist who has induced a condition of heightened suggestibility. From this description, the assumption can readily be made that the subject is incapable of lying.

In three cases reported by Beigel, those subjects who had lied prior to hypnosis became truthful when they were placed in a hypnotic state, in spite of the fact that the truth was personally disadvantageous to them.[6] Beigel admits, however, that "In spite of the results achieved it was evident that the subject had retained some control over his utterances." It should also be apparent that it is not possible, in these instances, to determine whether these same individuals would have been just as truthful if other procedures had been applied. Bryan describes a number of cases in which he was able to attain truthful statements and admissions that were to the detriment of the subjects.[7]

Arons, a lay hypnotist, published a series of cases in which he applied hypnotic procedures in the investigation of criminal cases.[8] A more accurate description and a greater number of details were obtained from witnesses and suspects who were later found to be innocent. These, quite obviously, were willing subjects who were not motivated to be deceitful for self-protective reasons. While Arons admitted it was not feasible to attempt to evoke an honest response from a guilty person, he did report a case in which this was accomplished.

Experts in the field of hypnosis have generally agreed over the years that the subject can lie as effectively under the hypnotic state as when he is fully conscious.[9] Kubis, in investigating techniques for eliciting valid information from witnesses, concluded that this procedure would have limited value with individuals who are unwilling to reveal information.[10] After reviewing the literature, Orne indicated that even the induction of a trance state would be difficult and highly unlikely in a resistant subject.[11]

This author has never achieved any clear indication of either a dramatic or consistent degree of success in attempting to obtain an honest response through hypnosis from a subject who is unwilling to give one. In criminal investigations, the subjects who were later found to be guilty appeared to act out their version of what they felt a hypnotic state should be. When this acting out is performed by a sophisticated subject, it is not possible to determine whether he is actually in a hypnotic state, and therefore, his denial of guilt at this time only serves to cloud the issue. In those instances in which suspects had admitted their guilt under hypnosis, on awakening they claimed to have had amnesia for the criminal act. Although this explanation was a possibility, it was felt that the hypnotic procedures simply allowed these individuals to admit their guilt and have a rationalization for their action through the claim of amnesia.

One final risk in employing hypnotic techniques in attempting to elicit an admission is associated with the possibility of obtaining a false confession from a highly suggestible person. Because of this factor as well as the ability of the individual to lie under hypnosis and the inability to determine whether a subject is feigning this state, hypnosis has not been proven to be a valid means of detecting deception.

The use of drugs, notably the various truth serums, like hypnosis, has been considered an effective means for reaching the truth. The subject, seen in a sleep-like state, speaking quietly or at times imperceptively or incoherently, appeared to have little control over his statements. For example, in 1922 House attempted to "... extract from the subconscious mind the stored content of the mind called memory" and believed not only that the procedure's "... value lies in the fact that it can be done without the consent of the subject," but also that by using Scapolomine, the subject was not capable of resisting the drug because "... it is difficult to lie and recall what is said when one is oblivious to his existence [and has] no appreciation of his environment, and will power [is] non-existent."[12]

Inbau, however, reported that while this approach had been successful in experimental cases, only 50 percent accuracy is reached in actual investigations.[13] Attaining similar findings, Wolfle, in a memorandum to the Armed Services as a member of the Emergency Committee of the National Council, recommended against the use of the truth serums as a means of lie detection by saying in regard to Scapolomine, Sodium Amytal, and Sodium Pentathal: "The enthusiasm of the advocates of these truth serums is not well founded and their use is not recommended."[14] Eliasberg also criticized the use of these drugs as a means of detecting lies because of the legal and psychological problems that would be inevitably associated with their utilization.[15] As was found with hypnosis, the validity would have to be questioned on the grounds of the subject feigning a state in which he could not control his statements and the probability of an individual becoming hypersuggestible and confessing to a crime he did not commit. In agreement with this finding, Kubis stated that "... the 'facts' elicited may only reflect the suggestions of the examiner. Needs, fantasies and wishful thinking may so contaminate the findings that it is difficult to discriminate fact from fancy. It is the conviction of a number of investigators that a deceptive witness will continue to lie under narcosis while repressed material can be retrieved from an individual who does not intend to lie and has nothing to lose in being truthful."[16]

Thus, with hypnosis and the truth serums, the examiner can never be certain of the meaning of his results. The subject who appears nondeceptive may only have accomplished a persuasive enactment of the truth, while the individual who admits his guilt could conceivably only be demonstrating his suggestibility or proneness to experience guilt.

During the process of psychotherapy, a constant attempt is made to gain insight into the individual's conscious and unconscious functioning. To accomplish this, the therapist must become aware of the patient's needs, wishes, and fears. While these motivations often become obvious through the individual's verbalizations, there are other means of achieving a broader concept of the person. One of these techniques is through his expressive movements.[17] Movements, facial expressions, and inflection all provide some clue as to what the individual thinks and feels at both a conscious and unconscious level. A very obvious difference exists in the therapeutic relationship of a patient who looks directly at the therapist and is bent towards him in contrast to the person who sits in the far corner of his chair with his arms wrapped around himself. Some nonverbal communication exists in all aspects of life, and people interpret, make judgments, and respond to these messages. Bryan has claimed that an evaluation of expressive movements can be applied with a great deal of efficiency in the court during voir dire as a means of predicting in which direction a juror will decide.[18]

In much the same manner, through an evaluation of nonverbal communication, truth and deception are evaluated. Parents so often feel they know when their children lie, as do spouses who after years of living together are accustomed to their mate's embarrassed blush. Inevitably, the same decisions are made by the same cues in the courtroom. Wigmore has pointed out that "... judges and juries habitually and with sanction of law consider and give weight to their interpretations of these changes of appearance, expression, voice, respiration, etc. in passing judgment of truth or falsity upon the witness' testimony."[19] In an attempt at isolating those signs of lying that could be observed, Reid and Arther characterized the deceptive individual as manifesting aggressiveness, blocking, evasiveness, sighing, avoidance of eye contact, and a dry mouth.[20] Confidence in the examiner and an interest in the procedure were thought to be indicative of truthfulness. Unfortunately, many of the symptoms of deception are only signs of anxiety, which thus suggests that the more stable the individual, the more likely it is that he will be labeled as truthful. There would seem to be a considerable degree of risk in differentiating truth from deception on the basis of the individual's voice, demeanor, dress, or expressive movements. Eliasberg also views this type of evidence as being highly unreliable.[21]

Another psychologic approach that had demonstrated some degree of validity in the detection of deception and guilt is the word-association test combined with a measure of reaction time. This procedure is described by Munsterberg in the following way:

Our purpose may be to find out whether a suspected person has really participated in a certain crime. He declares that he is innocent, that he was not present when the outrage occurred, and that he is not even familiar with the locality. An innocent man will not object to our proposing a series of one hundred associations to demonstrate his innocence. A guilty man, of course, will not object, either, as a declination would indicate a fear of betraying himself; he cannot refuse, and yet affirm his innocence. Moreover, he will feel sure that no questions can bring out any facts which he wants to keep hidden in his soul; he will be on the lookout. As long as nothing more is demanded than that he speak the first word that comes to his mind, when another is spoken to him, there is indeed no legal and no practical reason for declining, as long as innocence is professed. Such an experiment will at once become interesting in three different directions as soon as we mix into our list of one hundred words a number, perhaps thirty, which stand in more or less close connection to the crime in question-words which refer to the details of the locality, or to the persons present at the crime, or to the probable motive, or to the professed alibi, and so on. The first direction of our interest is toward the choice of the associations. Of course, everyone believes that he would be sure to admit only harmless words to his lips; but the conditions of the experiment quickly destroy that feeling of safety. As soon as a dangerous association rushes to the consciousness, it tries to push its way out. It may, indeed, need some skill to discover the physical influence, as the suspected person may have self-control enough not to give away the dangerous idea directly; but the suppressed idea remains in consciousness, and taints the next association, or perhaps the next but one, without his knowledge.

He has, perhaps, slain a woman in her room, and yet protests that he has never been in her house. By the side of her body was a cage with a canary-bird. I therefore mix into my list of words also "bird." His mind is full of the gruesome memory of his heinous deed. The word "bird," therefore, at once awakens the association "canary-bird" in his consciousness; yet he is immediately aware that this would be suspicious, and he succeeds, before the dangerous word comes to his lips, in substituting the harmless word "sparrow." Yet my next word, or perhaps my second or third next, is "color," and his prompt association is "yellow"; the canary-bird is still in his mind, and shows its betraying influence. The preparation of the list of words to be called thus needs psychological judgment and insight if a man with quick self-control is to be trapped. In most cases, however, there is hardly any need of relying on the next and following words, as the primary associations for the critical words unveil themselves for important evidence directly enough.

Yet not only the first associations are interesting. There is interest in another direction in the associations which result from a second and third repetition of the series. Perhaps after half an hour, I go once more through the whole list. The subject gives once more his hundred replies. An analysis of the results will show that most of the words which he now gives are the same which he gave the first time; pronouncing the words has merely accentuated his tendency to associate them in the same connection as before. If it was "house"-"window" first, then it will probably be "house"-"window" again. But a number of associations have been changed, and a careful analysis will show that these are first of all the suspicious ones. Those words which by their connection with the crime stir up deep emotional complexes of ideas will throw ever new associations into consciousness, while the indifferent ones will link themselves in a superficial way without change. To a certain degree, this variation of the dangerous associations is reinforced by the intentional effort of the suspected. He does not feel satisfied with his first words, and hopes that other words may better hide his real thoughts, not knowing that just this change is to betray him.

But most important is the third direction of inquiry; more characteristic than the choice and the constancy of the associations is their involuntary retardation by emotional influence. A word which stirs emotional memories will show an association-time twice or three times as long as a commonplace idea. It may be said at once that it is not ordinarily necessary, even for legal purposes, that the described measurement be in thousandths of a second; the differences of time which betray a bad conscience or a guilty knowledge of certain facts are large enough to be easily measured in hundredths or even in tenths of a second. . . .[22]

Jung found that subjects responded at an average of 1.6 seconds to neutral stimuli but approximately three seconds longer to key words.[23] This was corroborated by Crosland who demonstrated that experimentally "guilty" subjects reacted more slowly to both significant words and the word that immediately followed it.[24] These subjects gave twice as many guilty knowledge responses and failed to respond or to hear the stimuli more frequently.

It is quite conceivable that this approach could have considerable value in some instances, but its worth is limited because it is a test of guilty knowledge rather than lie detection per se. For this reason, it can only be utilized in those cases in which the subjects have no awareness of some of the pertinent details of the crime. If, for example, entry in a theft had been through a side door and this information had not been made available through the news media, attorneys, or investigating officers, then none of the suspects except the thief should respond to stimuli associated with that means of entry. The innocent should not respond to "side door" anymore than they would to "front window" or "cellar door." Unfortunately, in most criminal acts, the suspects have all of the significant crime data. Thus, Marston believed that this approach had little practical value.[25] Crane, in addition, found in an experimental situation that he was unable to differentiate his "guilty" subjects from the "innocent" with any degree of accuracy.[26] Findings of this nature have resulted in the gradual disuse of this approach so that there is little or no application of it in criminal investigation at this time.

None of the four psychological techniques described thus far—hypnosis, truth serum, word association, or expressive movements—have been proven to be sufficiently valid in the detection of deception. In contrast, the polygraph has literally withstood the test of time. Experimentation of its various measures—the pneumograph, galvanometer, and sphygmograph—and its use in actual criminal investigation began over eighty years ago and is continuing today. Polygraphy was not developed with any goal of measuring truthfulness, but rather, it evolved from developments in medicine, physiology and psychology. While the scientists in these fields did the early research, for some reason they lost interest and the later development was carried out by the practitioners involved in criminal investigation. The result is that at the present time only a relatively small number of scientists are knowledgable insofar as the advances that have been made, and only a handful are actually involved with the polygraph as a means of lie detection.

While research with the various sensors began before 1898, Cesare Lombroso, an Italian physiologist, is credited with being the first to scientifically attempt to diagnose lying through a measure of physiologic functioning.[27] Utilizing a hydrosphygmograph that measured the pulse rate and the blood volume as it was effected by emotional responses, he examined actual criminal suspects. The subject held a rod that was sealed in a rubber tank while the variations in the pulse raised and lowered the water level in a glass bulb which was in turn transposed to a recording device. In this manner, he examined Bersone Pierre:

Bersone Pierre, 37 years of age, well known as a thief, had been arrested under charge of having stolen 20,000 francs upon the railroad. In person he feigned madness, pretending that someone had poisoned him. It was soon plain that he had committed many other thefts, since he was in possession of a number of documents and passports, among others that of a certain Torelli . . . . investigation with the hydrosphygmograph confirmed me in my observation of his great insensitivity to pain, which did not change the sphygmographic lines. The same apathy persisted when he was spoken to of the robbery on the railroad, while there was an enormous depression—a fall of 14 mm—when the Torelli theft was mentioned. I concluded, therefore, that he had had no part in the railway robbery, but that he had certainly participated in the Torelli affair; and my conclusions were completely verified.[28]

In 1914, Vittorio Benussi reported success in detecting deception by comparing the subject's duration of inspiration and expiration. His procedure involved strapping rubber tubes around the subject's chest with one end sealed and the other leading into a hose connected into a recording mechanism, which allowed him to reflect both inspiration and expiration in graphic form.[29] Benussi demonstrated that the duration of the inspiration increased following a lie so that the inspiration expiration rate (I/E) is larger after lying than it was before. The opposite effect occurred after a truthful response. Benussi instructed the subject to lie regarding the pattern of numbers or letters on a card while observers attempted to assess the credibility of his response. The judges were successful in 50 percent of the cases, while the accuracy of the pneumograph was close to 100 percent.

Marston, an American, who was both a psychologist and an attorney, conducted a considerable amount of meaningful research in the use of blood pressure to differentiate an honest from a lying response.[30] In 1917, he developed a procedure in which he applied a "Tycos" sphygmomanometer at the left brachial artery and found that ". . . the behavior of the blood pressure . . . constitutes a practically infallible test of the consciousness of an attitude of deception." His technique consisted of pumping up the bladder in the blood pressure cuff and then releasing it to allow circulation to continue. After a brief pause, he would again inflate the cuff. This took place throughout the period in which the subject was being "cross-examined." Neutral material was introjected at times to ascertain the subject's normal state. The subject essentially "told his story" and answered questions, while the sphygmomanometer measured the subject's systolic blood pressure, which in turn evaluated ". . . the fluctuation of the witness' emotions . . . ."

This discontinuous measure of blood pressure inevitably resulted in the loss of some data.[31] Nevertheless, Marston's results were dramatically impressive. In October of 1917, at the request of the Psychological Committee of the National

Research Council, he studied the effectiveness of his approach to determine its value for use during the First World War. He reported achieving 100 percent accuracy. Burtt, studying the value of lie detection possibilities for use by the Army, compared the effectiveness of Benussi's measure of respiration with Marston's discontinuous blood pressure techniques.[32] He reported 73 percent accuracy for the former and 91 percent for Marston's approach. His conclusion was that the most effective lie detection procedures should be composed of a combination of a number of sensors including measures of respiration and blood pressure.

Marston compared the responses attained in systolic blood pressure readings with those at the diastolic level and found that a measure of the latter was less valid in determining truthfulness.[33] Diastolic blood pressure was significantly altered by minor affective states, by pain, and by intellectual activity. All of these factors could serve to distort the results. The systolic measure, on the other hand, was effected by fear and anger, both of which Marston felt were associated with lying and the concerns of the lie being detected. Because of these findings, he utilized a systolic measure of blood pressure and ignored the diastolic. He interpreted what he called the deceptive curve that resulted as ". . . a function of the struggle between the involuntary impulse to express fear in response to an an awareness of danger, and the voluntary focusing of attention to exclude the fear from consciousness." Thus, in his thinking, the fear of the lie's being detected and the conflict associated with its expression caused the change in blood pressure.

In 1923, Marston reported that, in the last ten years, he had obtained an accuracy of over 95 percent and that "few psychological tests, if any, can show as high an index of efficiency . . . ."[34] In that same year, Marston attempted to have the discontinuous measure of blood pressure test of deception admitted into court as evidence. In this precedent-setting case, *Frye* v. *U.S.*, Marston examined Frye, who had been accused of murder and reported him to be nondeceptive in his denial of this charge. The court ruled against admitting the test as evidence:

Just when a scientific principle or discovery crosses the line between the experimental and demonstrable stages is difficult to define. Somewhere in the twilight zone the evidential forces of the principle must be recognized, and while courts will go a long way in admitting expert testimony deduced from a well-recognized scientific principle or discovery, the thing from which the deduction is made must be sufficiently established to have gained general acceptance in the particular field in which it belongs.

We think the systolic blood pressure deception test has not yet gained such standing and scientific recognition among physiological and psychological authorities as would justify the court in admitting expert testimony deduced from the discovery, development and experiments thus far made.[35]

The jury went on to find Frye guilty of second degree murder, and he was imprisoned—only to be released three years later when additional evidence was found that cleared him. It is of note that Marston's rather primitive approach by today's standards demonstrated a considerable degree of accuracy. It is also important to recognize that the precedent set for admissibility was not based on a polygraph test, but rather on a much more primitive measure consisting of only a single sensor.

After the Frye decision, McCormick in 1927 attempted to determine whether the scientific community viewed the blood pressure test of deception as the court had found.[36] Eighty-eight members of the American Psychological Association were selected by a psychologist as likely to be interested in the field. They were asked whether the lie detection approach furnished results of sufficient accuracy to warrant consideration by judges and jurors in determining the credibility of witnesses testifying in court. Of the thirty-nine replies recorded, eighteen responded affirmatively, but with qualifications, while another thirteen reacted negatively. The remaining respondents could not be classified. McCormick concluded that the courts should wait for further verification and wider acceptance before relying on this technique as evidence. He did find, however, that psychologists accepted the lie detection approach as being based on a sound underlying theory.

Becoming aware of the successes of Marston and Benussi, John Larson developed his own instrument in 1921 by combining some of the features of both.[37] He also borrowed from the "ink polygraph" developed by cardiologist James MacKenzie in 1908, which, like Larson's instrument, consisted of sensors to measure blood pressure, pulse, and respiration.[38] In contrast to Marston's instrument, Larson's polygraph recorded a continuous measure of cardiovascular activity, but he utilized an occlusion plethysmograph rather than an actual measure of blood pressure so that he measured relative blood pressure and blood volume. Larson indicated that he employed a pneumograph ". . . if for no other reason that to determine the effect of respiration on heart rate."

In Marston's procedure, the subject reported his version of the events while being questioned. Larson, instead, employed a word association technique and inserted a crime word at every third word. Later, he reported that more meaningful results were attained when direct questions were asked with the subject responding only with a "yes" or "no."[39] The questions also had to be presented in a monotone so that a reaction would not occur simply in response to the examiner's inflection. Larson also studied the efficiency of the galvanometer, but he viewed it as being impractical as a test of deception and felt it would not be a valid measure during situations in which an extreme emotional reaction was aroused, such as the affective state that accompanied deception. Moreover, he saw it only as a duplication of information already being attained through the sphygmograph.

Some of Larson's critics argued that the accuracy achieved was a direct result of behavioral cues that experienced examiners were able to observe in the subjects rather than due to interpretable changes in the tracings. Larson, however, was able to demonstrate through a blind interpretation of the charts alone that a high degree of validity could be achieved.[40] He also reported that the error of interpretation in a laboratory situation can be quite large in contrast to an actual criminal investigation. He saw the laboratory subject as having little or nothing to lose if his lie were detected, while in a real situation, the suspect risks imprisonment, disgrace, and a financial loss. One must be wary, therefore, in generalizing from the findings of the laboratory to actual criminal investigation.[41] Larson also investigated the effects of fear and anger present in the innocent individual to determine whether these factors could result in inaccurately labeling the truthful as deceptive. In his first investigation, a store clerk had indicated that one, in a group of thirty-eight women, had been shoplifting, but she only knew that she lived in a particular college boarding house. Larson examined all thirty-eight subjects; thirty-seven were found to be honest, while one was judged to be deceptive. An admission was attained demonstrating complete accuracy. In a somewhat similar case, ninety girls in a college dormitory complained of a series of thefts ranging from underwear to a diamond ring. Once again he was able to eliminate all of the nondeceptive subjects and determine who was not truthful. In questioning the innocent suspects who were examined in both studies, he was informed that some of them experienced feelings of both fear and anger, which he reported, did not vitiate the effectiveness of the polygraph techniques.

In another area, Larson found that the testing of recidivists was no more difficult than other subjects. While these individuals cannot necessarily be classified as psychopaths, it can be assumed that his sample was at least partly composed of this diagnostic category. Later studies by Barland and Raskin found no difference in ability to detect deception in psychopaths.[42] Raskin obtained 95 percent accuracy, thereby demonstrating that these individuals can be accurately examined.[43] While they may be lacking in conscience and guilt, it is logical to assume that they too are fearful of their lie's being discovered because of the consequences. Therefore, their responses would be expected to be essentially the same as the nonpsychopathic population.

At the time that Marston was attempting to have his systolic blood pressure test admitted into court, Larson clearly indicated that in his view the effort was premature. He stated that ". . . it will only be by the correlation and standardization of thousands of cases by experts using uniform techniques that it will be time to present in court."[44]

During Larson's research at Berkeley, he had a high school student assist him, Leonarde Keeler. While Larson had continued his studies and attained a degree in medicine, specializing in psychiatry, Keeler later trained in psychology. Like his predecessor, he made many lasting contributions to the field. In 1926 he altered Larson's polygraph so that it was compact enough to be portable. He went on to manufacture this instrument and founded a training program, thereby starting the first polygraph school. In expanding the technique he introduced the peak of tension test and the stimulation test.[45] The former, like the word-association test, requires a situation in which certain details of the crime have not been made available to the suspects so that only the guilty person would have access to that information. Employing the same, previously used example relating to a burglary, each subject would be asked: "Do you know whether the house was entered through the front door?" The following four or five questions would use the same wording, but would indicate different possible points of entry, including the actual point of entrance. The innocent suspect, having no awareness as to where the house was entered, should respond to each question in the same manner. This would be in direct contrast to the guilty suspect who would react to the correct point of entry each time the test was repeated.

In the stimulation test, the subject is given a situation in which he lies and thus allows the examiner to demonstrate how easily a lie can be detected. This test serves to reduce the fears of the innocent and assumedly causes the guilty to be more reactive. Research by Gustafson and Orne, Barland, and Ellson et al., however, has not corroborated these results.[46] Their separate findings indicated that a demonstration of accuracy or inaccuracy did not significantly effect the accuracy of the tests that followed the stimulation test. Examiners in the field tend to disagree with these findings and cite the change in the subject's physiologic reactivity after the administration of this test.

Another contribution of Keeler's was to clearly define what a polygraph test was. The term *lie detector*, which has unfortunately become associated with it is a misnomer, and in Keeler's terms ". . . there is no such thing as a 'lie detector'. There are no instruments recording bodily changes, such as blood pressure, pulse, respiration, or galvanic reflex, that deserve the name 'lie detector' anymore than a stethoscope, a chemical thermometer, or a blood count apparatus with a microscope can be called an "appendicitis detector'."[47]

In 1931, Wilson developed a galvanometer and collaborated with Keeler in adding it to Keeler's instrument.[48] In his research with the galvanometer, Wilson reported 95 percent accuracy in the detection of lies in laboratory studies, but he attained a lower degree of validity in actual criminal investigations. While for many years, this appraisal was the stand of most field polygraphists,[49] recent investigations have demonstrated that the galvonometer is one of the most accurate of the sensors.[50]

While Larson and Marston both judged the psychogalvanometer to be an ineffectual means of detecting falsehood, it has had a long history of investigation in the fields of physiology and psychology. The galvanic response was first reported by Galvani in 1791 when he described his work in animal electricity.[51] Virgaguth combined the psychogalvanometer with a word-association test and demonstrated that words eliciting an emotional response, in contrast to neutral stimuli, caused a change that could be registered by the galvanometer.[52] Walter Summers reported that he had carried out thousands of tests of deception with the galvanometer in a laboratory setting and obtained 98 to 100 percent accuracy.[53] It was his belief that if he were working with actual criminal subjects, he would achieve complete accuracy. In 1938, Summers findings were admitted into court as evidence in *People* v. *Kenny* with Kenny being acquitted.[54]

In 1941, as in 1917, a request was made of the American Psychological Association to evaluate the validity of the polygraph for use by the government during the war. Wolfle, a member of the investigating committee, based his findings on a review of the literature and discussion with individuals who have had extensive experience with the polygraph in business, law enforcement, and research.[55] In addition, he observed the work of the Chicago Police Scientific Crime Laboratory as well as private examiners. His findings were ". . . that the methods for the detection of deception have been adequately worked out, that the necessary recording devices have been developed and that a few adequately trained men were available. Of these three factors, the man is by far the most important in determining the success or failure of attempts to detect deception. Whenever thoroughly competent investigators are available, the results will be highly useful. When such men are not available there should be no use of the apparatus and methods."

In another investigation of the polygraph, Eliasberg on May 15, 1944, presented a resolution to the Forensic Section of the American Psychiatric Association that was adopted:

Whereas, modern psychopathology has discovered the nature of the feelings of guilt;

Whereas, the defendent may legally refuse to submit to any of the lie detection tests, and his enforced cooperation, as in other tests, e.g., intoxication tests, may in some states, be held to violate the constitutional guarantee against self-incrimination;

Whereas, the hardened criminal is more immune to lie detector tests than to the free interview and other recognized methods of clinical criminal investigation;

Whereas, the much vaunted confessions after the administration of the lie detector tests are (a) by no means particularly conclusive; (b) are by no means more reliable than the ordinary confession and (c) are not free from possible objections on the grounds of admissibility and voluntariness;

Whereas, the pathological confession (confession of the pathological innocent man) is likely to occur with the lie detector more often than with other methods;

Whereas, the popular belief in the infallibility of the lie detector is apt to prevail unduly upon jurors and to lead to a belief in the machine rather than in conscientious deliberation;

Whereas, there is no conscience-robot and no diagnosis-robot;

Now, therefore, we the Forensic Section of the A.P.A., want to go on record as cautioning against advertising of the lie detector device.

The section wants to point out that the machine can give valuable results only in the hands of thoroughly trained physicians and psychologists who will evaluate the data derived by applying other available methods and making use of all independently obtainable evidence.[56]

Eliasberg's recommendation must be considered in keeping with the history of polygraphy. While the approach had its beginnings in the research of scientists, for some reason, they lost interest and discontinued their involvement. This occurrence may have been related to the expense of the instrumentation or the unavailability of actual criminal subjects. The void was filled by practioners who improved on the technique and instrumentation, and one might wonder whether present day physicians and psychologists have either sufficient knowledge of the procedure or the right to dictate who should be administering polygraph examinations. John Reid, an attorney and polygraphist, was one of the leaders in the field, and with Fred Inbau he has written the only text in the field and has developed a training program for polygraphists.[57] In 1945 Reid developed a measure of muscular movements that served to detect purposeful movements that were designed to distort the polygraph tracings.[58] In 1947 he also developed a procedure to reduce the risk of diagnosing a nondeceptive subject as deceptive. Reid recognized that while there were relatively few, there were nevertheless some individuals who, because of a proclivity toward guilt or anxiety, responded physiologically to any accusatory question, which could result in a misdiagnosis—that is, labeling a truthful person deceptive. Accordingly, Reid developed the "guilt complex test":

The "guilt complex" question is based upon an entirely fictitious crime of the same type as the actual crime under investigation, but one which is made to appear very realistic to the subject. . . . The purpose of the "guilt complex" or fictitious crime question is to determine if the subject, although innocent, is unduly apprehensive because of the fact that he is suspected and interrogated about the crime under investigation. A reaction to the fictitious crime question which is greater than or about the same as that to the actual crime question would be indicative of truthtelling and innocence respecting the real offense. On the other hand, however, a response to the actual crime questions, coupled with the absence of a response to the fictitious crime question, or by one considerably less than that to the actual crime questions, would be strongly indicative of lying regarding the offense under investigation.[59]

Reid and Inbau's 1969 edition of *Truth and Deception* described a somewhat different approach in which the subject was questioned only about the fictitious crime after three tests were administered:

If the subject responds to the fictitious incident questions to a degree comparable to that on the earlier tests relating to the actual occurrence, that fact is indicative of the subject's truthfulness. Nevertheless, it is advisable to administer a fifth test in which there is a mixture of the questions about both the real and the fictitious case. If the subject still responds to the fictitious incident questions to the same or similar degree as he did to the actual case questions, that is further suggestive of truth-telling about the actual case incident.

In instances where a seemingly "overly responsive" subject does not respond to any of the guilt complex questions on test four or five, this fact is strongly indicative of deception regarding the actual occurrence.

This guilt complex test for the overly responsive subject usually will resolve the issue as to the subject's truthfulness or deception with respect to the matter under investigation. In those instances where it does not, the examiner should arrange for a reexamination at a later date.[60]

Of much greater importance than the guilt complex test was Reid's "comparative response" question, which is now referred to as the control question. This technique has dramatically altered the test procedure and probably greatly enhanced the test's validity. He described this approach in the following manner:

Special consideration must be given to the selection of Question 6, the "comparative response" question, because the magnitude of the response to that question is to be compared with responses to questions pertaining to the actual crime, and it may therefore serve to include or exclude definitely the subject as a suspect in the crime under investigation. If the examiner is fortunate enough to have in his possession certain information concerning a situation or offense involving the subject (but of less importance than the actual crime being investigated) which the examiner knows or feels reasonably sure the subject will lie about, a question based upon such information and actually lied to will serve very well to indicate the subject's responsiveness when lying. Such a question thereby affords a basis for evaluating the nature of the response to the questions pertinent to the offense under investigation. For instance, when it is a known fact as indicated in the police records that the subject had been previously arrested but he denies ever having been arrested, a question should be framed about the prior arrest, such as, "Have you ever been arrested before?" When, however, a known lie control question is lacking, as is usually the case, a short preliminary interrogation of the subject regarding other crimes or happenings should precede the preparation of the "comparative response" question in order to ascertain the specific question to be used which may offer the best possibility of a deception response. For example, if John "Red" Brown in the foregoing case illustration is a known burglar and now suspected of the murder of John Jones, he may be asked, as a "comparative response" question, "Since you got out of the penitentiary have you committed any burglaries?" A response to that question which is greater than whatever response may be present at the point where the murder questions were asked, offers a reliable indication that the subject is innocent of the murder. As an alternative "comparative response" question for subjects such as John "Red" Brown, who have probably committed perjury in some of their previous trials, they may be asked, "Have you ever lied on the witness stand?" If the subject is a suspected first offender any one of several types of questions may be asked for comparative response purposes: for example, "Have you ever stolen anything?" "Have you ever cheated on your income tax returns?" If the subject upon preliminary interrogation states that he once stole five dollars, the question must be rephrased and asked, "Besides that five dollars you told me about, have you stolen any other money?" (Questions regarding sex offenses or irregularities should be avoided for comparative response purposes, except in a sex case itself, because the very nature of the inquiry tends to cause some emotional disturbance.)

The examiner must feel reasonably sure, as the result of his preliminary interrogation, that the subject will answer "no" to any of the above suggested questions used for "comparative response" purposes. The examiner must also convey the impression in his pre-test interview with the subject that the "comparative response" questions are of real significance and importance.[61]

Backster refined the control question and explained it in terms of a psychological set.[62] "A subject establishes a psychological set for a given situation of significant importance to himself when his attention is involuntarily channeled toward that which holds the greater immediate threat to his well being."[63] In addition, Backster has fostered a more scientific approach to polygraphy by emphasizing a standardized testing technique and principles of scoring. He developed the first numerical scoring system, which has greatly enhanced both objective scoring and polygraph reliability. Utilizing this approach, different examiners scoring the same chart should reach the same conclusion. With changes of this nature, polygraphy had achieved the goal set by Larson as necessary for admissibility into court.

Twenty-six years after McCormick's survey of the opinions of psychologists regarding the polygraph, Cureton conducted a second poll in 1953. Questionnaires were sent to all groups and individuals known to be competent at polygraph procedures. This included psychologists, polygraphists, and criminologists. Of the 1,682 individuals contacted, the analysis was based on the 711 completed questionnaires. The results of the survey indicated that:

(1) Of the 199 Examiners, 83 percent believe the polygraph is highly valid for recording physiological reactions, 47 percent recommend court testimony by competent examiners, and 83 percent recommend periodic examination of certain personnel in business and industry.

(2) Of the 230 psychologists who have conducted polygraphic tests of deception in experimental situations or observed or conducted such tests on criminal suspects, employed personnel, or applicants, 63 percent consider the polygraph highly valid for recording physiological reactions, 51 percent recommend court testimony, and 28 percent recommend use in business and industry.

(3) Of the small group of 35 psychologists who are also Examiners, 63 percent think the polygraph is highly valid for recording physiological reactions, 60 percent recommend court testimony, and 51 percent recommend use in business and industry.

(4) No appreciable proportion of any group considers the polygraph invalid and useless when in competent hands.[64]

The results of this survey indicated that the use of the polygraph in lie detection was expanding and that it was generally more accepted. Law enforcement agencies found it an efficient means of reducing the number of suspects of a specific crime and thus allowed them to concentrate their efforts and time on the more likely suspects. Obviously, such use of the polygraph was also an advantage to the innocent who were relieved of the stress, embarrassment, and costs that might have been entailed in extended investigations.

Attorneys were more frequently having their clients examined to ascertain whether they were truthful in order that they might better defend them. The government also made wider use of this approach in screening out possible security risks. Business and industry also rushed to make use of a technique that had been dramatically demonstrated to reduce their losses due to employee theft.[65] Through preemployment testing, they were able to eliminate undesirable job applicants by determining who had past histories of theft, absenteeism, and alcohol and drug use. Repeated testing of employees at six-month intervals acted as a deterrant to employee theft and saved business literally millions of dollars. While this practice was a boon to business, it was also of value to the consumer who had been paying for the losses attributable to theft. The unions and the American Civil Liberties Union, however, became highly critical of this procedure and fostered antipolygraph legislation.

Growing out of claims of unfair and inappropriate government use of polygraphy, a committee under the chairmanship of John Moss was directed in 1963 to investigate the government use of the technique.[66] Its conclusions, two years later, were drawn from discussions with both researchers and examiners in the field, reviews of the literature, and evaluation of the usage of the polygraph by various governmental agencies. The committee also studied a report by Orlansky who evaluated lie detection procedures in 1962 and concluded that:

1. Objective data to demonstrate the degree of effectiveness of the polygraph as an instrument for the detection of deception has not been compiled by the agencies that use it in the Department of Defense. This is true despite the fact that about 200,000 such examinations have been performed over the last 10 years. Up to the present time, it has proved impossible to uncover statistically acceptable performance data to support the view held by polygraph examiners that lie detection is an effective procedure.

2. There can be no doubt that the measurement of physiological responses in the context of a structured interview provides a basis for the detection of deception by objective means. Extensive research by physiologists and psychiatrists shows that humans exhibit many physiological responses in stressful situations; however, such research was not performed to explore its relevance to lie detection. Thus, we do not know at present the increment in effectiveness which the polygraph brings over an interrogation without a polygraph.

3. There is a lack of professional standards for the regulation of lie detection activities throughout the Department of Defense.

4. Many aspects of the technology of lie detection are inadequately developed. Areas which require study are the reliability and validity of lie detection in laboratory and real life situations, the incremental value of new physiological indicators, improvement of the interview procedure, application of automatic data processing to polygraph records, and examination of the

possibility that individuals exhibit unique patterns of autonomic response. Recent developments in medical electronics provide more reliable and convenient sensors than those now used in lie detection. . . . The research problems in lie detection are straightforward and there is every reason to believe that a research program would achieve its objectives.

5. There is evidence that training, possibly supported by drugs and hypnosis, can be used to introduce spurious effects into test records. The extent to which such methods could succeed or an examiner could counteract them is unknown.

6. Improvements in the art of lie detection would be useful not only for its present applications to security and criminal interrogations, but for screening foreign personnel and as one means of inspection in an arms control agreement.[67]

In April of 1963, Moss's committee adopted a report in which it indicated that ". . . there is no 'lie detector' neither mechanical nor human."[68] They indicated further that this technique had not been proved to be valid in either laboratory research or actual criminal investigations. These conclusions were reached in spite of the fact that two of the committee's own witnesses, Drs. Orne and Kubis testified that they had attained an accuracy as high as 80 to 90 percent in their own research. A review of the literature by Abrams[69] is also in disagreement with the committee findings. At the recommendation of this committee, the federal government reduced its use of the polygraph.

Continued attempts were made to develop a firmer foundation for polygraphy. In addition to further research being carried out, as recommended by Orlansky, polygraphists moved to establish more professionalism within their group. In August of 1966, the American Polygraph Association was formed by a merger of three predecessor organizations. The 376 members in good standing of these groups were accepted as charter members, and by 1976 the membership consisted of over 1,000 individuals. The purpose of the American Polygraph Association was described as follows: ". . . Fortunate is he who, being accused or suspected of misconduct, is able to produce credible witnesses to attest to his innocence. Now therefore, and be it known hence forth, it shall be the primary responsibility of the American Polygraph Association to foster and to perpetuate an accurate, reliable and scientific means for the protection of the innocent. To verify the truth—fairly, impartially and objectively—shall be our purpose."[70] The organization functioned to promote research, foster training and professionalism, accredit the schools, and police the ethics of its membership. Active attempts were made to motivate the passage of legislation for licensing to assure that only trained and experienced examiners using adequate instrumentation could administer polygraph examinations. By 1976, nineteen states had laws requiring that examiners be licensed. These included Alaska, Arkansas, Florida, Georgia, Illinois, Kentucky, Michigan, Mississippi, Nevada, New Mexico, North Carolina, North Dakota, Oklahoma, Oregon, South Carolina, Texas, Utah, Vermont, and Virginia.[71] While there was some variance among the laws, the usual requirements consisted of the completion of two hundred supervised examinations, a baccalaureate degree, having passed an oral and written examination, and graduation from an accredited polygraph school. By 1976 there were fourteen accredited schools that taught a minimum of 240 hours of class work consisting of psychology, physiology, instrumentation, test construction, and chart interpretation.

While there were laws that favored polygraphy, there are also antipolygraph laws. As of June of 1975, fifteen states had legislated statutes prohibiting the use of the polygraph in the area of preemployment and periodic testing as a condition of employment.[72]

This legislation was obviously not directed at the use of polygraphy in criminal or civil cases or at police investigative work. The employment of the polygraph in these areas favors the rights of the individual so that neither the ACLU or the unions should oppose it. For example, a defense attorney can have a polygraph administered to his client, and as long as there is no stipulation that it will be admitted as evidence, the defense is free to dispose of it as he wishes. If the results are favorable for his client, prosecution may even drop the charges. Moreover, there appears to be a slowly growing trend in the direction of admitting the polygraph over the objection of prosecution.

Unions and the ACLU have attempted to thwart attempts at legislating licensure assumably to block any inroads into employee testing. This of course effects all polygraphists including those involved in criminal and civil matters only.

Researchers, however, have ignored the conflict between the opponents and proponents of polygraphy and have continued to study this technique and have expanded the accumulated knowledge. Horvath and Reid compared the accuracy of examiners with four to six months of experience with those with more than a year in interpreting forty verified charts.[73] The validity of the less-experienced group was at the 79 percent level in contrast to 92 percent for those with a greater degree of experience. In another study, the same investigators determined that a response was not necessary to be able to detect deception.[74] When subjects were instructed to answer to themselves, a response still occurred, but there was a lessened distortion in the tracing that had been due to a verbal response. Accuracy of the Galvanic skin response tended to increase and the silent answer test had a stimulating effect upon subsequent tests. In contrast to these findings, Gustafson and Orne, as well as Ellson, reported that a greater reaction was generated when a subject responded in the negative to a lie rather than not responding at all.[75] In another study, Gustafson and Orne demonstrated that being motivated to deceive resulted in a greater physiologic reaction during deception causing a lie to be more readily detected.[76] This finding explains why a lesser validity is attained in laboratory research as compared to investigations conducted on actual criminal suspects.[77]

One of the major theories that attempt to explain the physiologic changes that take place during a polygraph examination is associated with the arousal of the sympathetic nervous system by the fear of the lie's being discovered. Thackray and Orne examined subjects who were unaware of their being tested.[78] They found no evidence that the detection of deception was inferior during this state. Findings of this nature cast some doubt on a single-cause theory and suggests that conflict associated with lying, a conditioned response, or generalized excitement may be equally meaningful as an explanation.

An area of difficulty that has existed in polygraphy from its inception has been the excessive pressure upon the subject's arm and the prolonged period in which circulation is blocked by the blood pressure cuff. The procedure can result in a level of discomfort that could have a distracting influence, limit testing time, and preclude the attainment of a sphygmographic reading on hypertensive or excessively obese individuals. Marston had to use a discontinuous approach because of this resulting in valuable data being lost. While Larson's technique was continuous, only a relatively small number of questions could be asked before the blood pressure cuff had to be deflated. The advent of the Cardio Activity Monitor produced by Stoelting in 1972[79] and the Amplified Cardio manufactured by Lafayette Instrument Company in 1973 permitted a measure of cardiovascular changes with a greatly reduced pressure.

In 1973, Ash conducted the third survey of opinions related to polygraphy to determine whether the degree of acceptance had changed since Cureton's study in 1953.[80] In this investigation, he polled 5,679 behavioral scientists, attorneys, and polygraphists. Of that sample, 29.7 percent responded with the results shown in Tables 2-1, 2-2, and Table 2-3.

A comparison of the findings of the surveys by McCormick in 1926, Cureton in 1953, and Ash in 1973 reveals a clear trend toward the "general acceptance" rule set forth in *U.S.* v. *Frye*. In the first poll, 58 percent of the psychologists responding indicated that with qualifications, it was an accurate approach. In 1953, 63 percent of the psychologists viewed it as an highly valid measure of physiologic responses. Twenty years later, 20 percent of psychologists indicated that it was always or usually of great value in investigation work, while an additional 70 percent responded that it was sometimes of value. An even more obvious trend is seen when the Cureton and Ash studies are compared in the area of admissibility. In 1953, 51 percent pf psychologists indicated that it should be admitted into court, and twenty years later 70 percent of the psychologists responding believed it should be admitted under stipulation. An even greater increase was found among the polygraphists in this regard. In Cureton's investigation only 47 percent favored admitting polygraph findings as evidence, while in Ash's study, those favoring it increased to 92 percent.

By the 1970s, polygraph evidence was routinely being admitted into many courts under stipulation, and in California, Massachusetts, Ohio, and at least one federal court, it was admitted over the objection of prosecution.[81] Scientists, attorneys, and the courts were indicating a greater acceptance of the polygraph as a valid and reliable measure of truth and deception. In spite of this, its use by

Table 2-1

Summary of Attitudes of Behavioral Scientists and Attorneys toward Five Issues Relating to the Use of the Polygraph in Criminal Proceedings (Percent who "Strongly Agree" or "Agree")

	Behavioral Scientists			Attorneys		
	Psychologists	Sociologists	Other	Prosecutors	Defense	Other
Polygraph should be admissible on prior stipulation	69.3	59.6	68.3	82.1	71.9	77.1
Polygraph should be admissible in exceptional cases, even over objection	38.2	23.1	35.0	42.2	29.8	25.7
Polygraph should be generally admissible, even over objection	27.9	13.4	25.3	31.6	10.7	13.7
Polygraph should be used as investigative aid in criminal cases	76.4	58.7	84.2	95.6	75.1	88.5
Favor state licensing of polygraph examiners	82.7	75.9	81.0	90.8	88.0	85.7

Source: Ash, Philip, "Survey of Attitudes on the Polygraph," 2 *Polygraph* (September 1973), p. 215. Reprinted with permission.

the government was again questioned. On June 4 and 5 of 1974, a House committee again evaluated the polygraph.[82] The testimony of polygraphists, scientists, and representatives of the American Civil Liberties Union, various governmental agencies, and labor unions were heard. The committee was chaired by Moorehead, but oddly enough, after the testimony was heard, the member-

Table 2-2

Attitudes of 193 Polygraph Examiners to Polygraph Use

	Yes		No		Qualified		No Answer	
	No.	Pct.	No.	Pct.	No.	Pct.	No.	Pct.
Should the polygraph be admitted into evidence without reservation?	32	16.6	160	82.9	–	–	1	0.5
Should the polygraph be admitted by stipulation?	178	92.2	0	4.7	–	–	6	3.1
Should the polygraph be used only as an investigative aid?	8	4.1	90	46.6	92	47.7	3	1.6

Source: Ash, Philip, "Survey of Attitudes on the Polygraph," 2 *Polygraph* (September 1973), p. 215. Reprinted with permission.

Table 2-3

Attitudes of Attorneys and Behavioral Scientists to the Question: "Overall How Would You Rate the Polygraph as an Investigative Aid?"

| | Behavioral Scientists | | | | | | Attorneys | | | | | |
| | Psychologists | | Sociologists | | Other | | Prosecutors | | Defense | | Other | |
Rating	No.	Pct.	No.	Pct.	No.	Pct.	No.	Pct.	No.	Pct.	No.	Pct.
Almost always of great value	8	1.9	1	1.0	1	1.6	122	17.4	26	8.2	5	7.1
Usually of great value	77	17.9	16	15.4	12	19.0	297	42.2	94	29.7	28	40.0
Sometimes of value	301	70.2	68	65.4	45	71.4	266	37.8	157	49.5	32	45.7
Usually of little value	38	8.9	12	11.5	5	7.9	17	2.4	31	9.8	3	4.3
Never of any value	5	1.2	7	6.7	0	0	1	0.1	9	2.8	2	2.9
Total	429	100.0	104	100.0	63	100.0	703	100.0	317	100.0	70	100.0

Source: Ash, Philip, "Survey of Attitudes on the Polygraph," 2 *Polygraph* (September 1973), p. 215. Reprinted with permission.

ship of the committee was changed and Bella Abzug became the chairperson. "None of those who were involved in the preparation of this report were present at the 1974 hearings held by the Subcommittee. Yet the 1974 hearings are said to be the basis for this report."[83]

The committee made the following recommendation:

It is the recommendation of the committee that the use of polygraphs and similar devices be discontinued by all Government agencies for all purposes.

While recognizing that there has been substantial compliance with the committee recommendations of 1965 calling for increased uniformity of administration of the polygraph and comprehensive research into their validity and reliability, the clear import of the hearings upon which this report is based leads to the same conclusion as was reached in 1965. The conclusion at that time was that:

There is no "lie detector," neither machine nor human. People have been deceived by a myth that a metal box in the hands of an investigator can detect truth or falsehood.

The Department of Justice continues to maintain the position that the results of polygraph examinations would not be admitted as evidence in the federal courts. The committee adopts this position and further affirms that since such examinations are considered invalid for evidentiary purposes, there is absolutely no reason for continuing the use of such examinations for investigatory purposes.

Although there is indication that efforts are being made to upgrade the training and educational requirements of polygraph operators, the committee finds that unproven technical validity of the polygraph devices themselves makes such efforts a meaningless exercise.

Even if the committee adopted the positions of some agencies that the polygraph is useful solely as a secondary investigative technique and that the results of a polygraph examination alone are never considered conclusive, the committee finds that the inherent chilling affect upon individuals subjected to such examinations clearly outweighs any purported benefit to the investigative function of the agency.

The committee additionally recommends that the use and/or acquisition of other so-called "lie detectors" such as the PSE or the voice analyzer be discontinued. Evidence presented in the hearings upon which this report is based demonstrates that such devices have even less scientific validity than the polygraph. Although no agency of the federal government is using such other devices at this time as a substitute for polygraph examinations, the committee recommends that additional federally-funded research into such devices be discontinued.[84]

One must seriously question the feasibility of a committee composed of elected officials being able to objectively evaluate an approach of this nature. It is quite evident that the American Civil Liberties Union and the labor unions are quite actively antagonistic toward polygraphy, and both of these groups represent a very large block of votes. Therefore, the findings of this committee and their recommendations must be viewed in terms of their bias, and for an objective picture, one must turn to the sciences.

The direction that will be taken by polygraphy in the future seems to be readily predictable. If we can best foresee where we are going by where we have been, the course appears clear. There will be an increased usage of the polygraph by law enforcement agencies and attorneys; both defense and prosecution will rely on it more heavily. The polygraph findings will be admitted as evidence more routinely, and the courts will make many of these requests. It will be recognized that if a stipulated polygraph is a valid and reliable procedure then it should also be admitted over objection. It is expected that this trend will grow.

The licensing of examiners will expand to other states, but at the same time, other polygraph legislation is also expected to increase in an effort to protect employees from a possible loss of their livelihood. At the same time, however, an expansion of the use of polygraphy in business will occur simply because of the very real fact that it is a massively effective means of reducing employee theft.

Notes

1. Schneck, J.M., *Hypnosis in Modern Medicine* (Springfield, Ill.: Charles C. Thomas, 1959).

2. Neilson, G., *Trial by Combat* (London: Williams and Norgate, 1890).

3. Trovillo, P. V., "A History of Lie Detection," *J. Crim. Law and Criminol.* 29 (1939): 848-81.

4. Roberts, R.A., presentation before the Northwest Polygraph Association, Vancouver, B.C., Canada, April 1976 (available through Calgary City Police, Alberta, Canada).

5. Lifton, R.J., *Thought Reform and the Psychology of Totalism* (New York: W.W. Norton, 1963).

6. Beigel, H.G., "Prevarication under Hypnosis," *J. Cln. and Exp. Hypn.* 1 (1953): 32-40.

7. Bryan, W.J., "Jury Selection," National Workshop on Polygraph Procedures, Delta College, University City, Mich., May 9, 1974.

8. Arons, H., *Hypnosis in Criminal Investigation* (Springfield, Ill.: Charles C. Thomas, 1967).

9. Moll, A., *Hypnotism* (London: Walter Scott, 1890), and Kauffman, M., *Suggestion and Hypnose* (Berlin: Jules Springer, 1920).

10. Kubis, J.F., "Instrumental, Chemical, and Psychological Aids in the Interrogation of Witnesses," *J. Soc. Studies* 13 (1957): 40-49.

11. Orne, M., "The Potential Uses of Hypnosis in Interrogation," in A.D. Biderman and H. Zimmer (eds.), *The Manipulation of Human Behavior* (New York: Wiley, 1961), pp. 169-215.

12. House, R.E., "The Use of Scopolamine in Criminology," *Texas State J. Med.* 18 (1922): 256-263.

13. Inbau, F.E., "Methods of Detecting Deception," *J. Crim. L.* 24 (1934): 1140-47.

14. Wolfe, D., *Truth Serums* Report prepared for the Emergency Committee in Psychology of the National Research Council, Seattle, October 8, 1941.

15. Eliasberg, W., "Forensic Psychology," *S. Calif L. Rev.* 19 (1946): 349-409.

16. Kubis, "Instrumental, Chemical, and Psychological Aids."

17. Brengelmann, H., "Expressive Movements and Abnormal Behavior" in H.J. Eysenck, *Handbook of Abnormal Behavior* (New York: Basic Books, 1961), pp. 62-107, and Allport, G.W., and Vernon, P.E., *Studies in Expressive Movement* (New York: MacMillan, 1933).

18. Bryan, W.J., *The Chosen Ones* (New York: Vantage Press, 1971).

19. Wigmore, J.H., *Evidence* 2nd ed. (Boston: Little, Brown, 1923).

20. Reid, J.E., and Arthur, R.O., "Behavior Symptoms of Lie Detector Subjects," *J. Crim L.* 43 (1953): 104-08.

21. Eliasberg, "Forensic Psychology."

22. Munsterberg, H., *On the Witness Stand* (Verona, Va.: McClure Co., 1918). Reprinted with permission.

23. Jung, C.G., "The Association Method," *Amer. J. Psychol.* 221 (1910): 219-69.

24. Crosland, H.R., "The Relative Efficacy of Visual and Two Auditory Methods of Presenting the Word Stimuli in an Experiment which Combines the Association Reaction Time Technique with the Psychogavonic Technique," *Univ. Ore. Publ.* 1, no. 3 (1931): 133-202.

25. Marston, W.M., "Psychological Possibilities in the Deception Test," *J. Crim. Law* 2 (1921): 551-70.

26. Crane, H.W., "A Study in Association Reaction and Reaction Time," *Psych. Rev. Monog. Suppl.* 18 (1915).

27. Lombroso, C., *Crime Its Causes and Remedies*, Modern Criminal Science Series, (Boston: Little, Brown, 1905).

28. Larson, J.A., *Lying and Its Detection* (Chicago: University of Chicago Press, 1932).

29. Benussi, V., "Die Atmungssyptome der Lüge Arch Für, *"Die Gesante Psycholgic*, 31 (1914): 244-73.

30. Marston, W.M., "Systolic Blood Pressure Symptoms of Deception," *J.Exp. Psychol.* 2 (1917): 117-63.

31. Larson, *Lying and its Detection.*

32. Burtt, H.E., "The Inspiration-Expiration Ratio during Truth and False-hood," *J. Exp. Psychol.* 6 (1921): 1-23.

33. Marston, "Systolic Blood Pressure."

34. Marston, W.M., "Sex Characteristics of Systolic Blood Pressure Be-havior," *J. Exp. Psych.* 6 (1923): 387-419.

35. *U.S.* v. *Frye*, 293 F. 1013 (D.C. Cir. 1923).

36. McCormick, C.T., "Deception Test and the Law of Evidence," *Tenn. L. Rev.* 15 (1927): 108-33.

37. Larson, J.A., "Manipulation of the Marston Deception Test," *J. Crim. L.* 12 (1921): 390-99.

38. Highleyman, S.L., "The Deceptive Certainty of the Lie Detector," *Hastings L.J.* 10 (1958): 47-64.

39. Larson, J.A., "The Cardio-Pneumo-Psychogram in Deception," *J. Exp. Psychol.* 6 (1923): 420-54.

40. Larson, *Lying and its Detection.*

41. Ibid.

42. Barland, G.H., and Raskin, D.C., "Psychopathy and Detection of Deception in Criminal Suspects," presented at the Society for Psychophysiologic Research Salt Lake City, October 25, 1974, (available through Psychology Dept., University of Utah).

43. Raskin, D.C., *Psychopathy and Detection of Deception in a Prison Population*, Report No. 75-1, Contract 75 NI 99-0001, June, 1975, University of Utah, Salt Lake City.

44. Larson, *Lying and its Detection.*

45. Keeler, L., "Scientific Methods of Criminal Detection with the Poly-graph," *Kansas Bar Assoc.* 2 (1933): 22-31.

46. Gustafson, L.A., and Orne, M.T., "Effects of Perceived Role and Role Success on the Detection of Deception," *J. Appl. Psychol.* 49 (1965): 412-17; Barland, G.H., and Raskin, D.C., "An Experimental Study of Field Technique in Lie Detection," *Polygraph* 1 (1972): 22-26; and Ellson, D.G., David, R.G., Saltzman, I.J., and Burke, C.J., *A Report on Research on Detection of Deception*, Contract No. N6 onr 18011, Office of Naval Research, September 15, 1952 (available through University of Indiana, Bloomington).

47. Keeler, L., "Debunking the Lie Detector," *J. Crim. Law, Criminol. and Police Science* 25 (1934): 153-59.

48. Keeler, L., "A Method of Detecting Deception," *Amer. J. Police Science* 1 (1930): 38-51.

49. Trovillo, P.V., "A History of Lie Detection," *J. Crim. Law and Criminol.* 30 (1939): 104-19.

50. Barland, G.H., and Raskin, D.C., "The Use of Electrodermal Activity in the Detection of Deception," in W.F. Prokasy and D.C. Raskin (eds.) *Electrodermal Activity in Psychological Research* (New York: Academic Press, 1973).

51. Galvani, L., *Commentary on the Effect of Electricity on Muscular Motion*, Eng. translation of 1791 book. 1953.

52. Trovillo, "A History of Lie Detection."

53. Summers, W.G., "Science Can Get the Confession," *Fordham L. Rev.* 5 (1939): 334-54

54. *People* v. *Kenny Misc.* 51, 3, N.Y. (Supp) 2d 348 (1938).

55. Wolfle, D., "The Lie Detector: Methods for the Detection of Deception," prepared for the Emergency Committee in Psychology of the National Research Council, October 8, 1941, Appendix E.

56. Eliasberg, W., "Forensic Psychology." Reprinted with permission of the *Southern California Law Review*.

57. Reid, J.E., and Inbau, F.E., *Truth and Deception: The Polygraph Technique* (Baltimore: Waverly Press, 1969).

58. Reid, J.E., "Simulated Blood Pressure Responses in Lie Detection Tests and a Method for their Detection," *J. Crim L.* 36 (1945): 201-14.

59. Reid, J.E., "A Revised Questioning Technique in Lie Detection Tests," *J. Crim. Law, Criminol. and Police Science* 37 (1947): 542-47. Reprinted by special permission of John Reid and the *Journal of Criminal Law and Criminology*, Copyright 1947 by Northwestern University School of Law.

60. Reid and Inbau *Truth and Deception.*

61. Reid, "A Revised Questioning Technique." Reprinted by special permission of John Reid and the *Journal of Criminal Law and Criminology*, Copyright 1947 by Northwestern University School of Law.

62. Bailey, F.L., and Rothblatt, H.B., *Investigation and Preparation of Criminal Cases, Federal and State* (Rochester, N.Y.: Lawyers' Cooperative Publishing Co., 1970).

63. Backster, C., *Technique Fundamentals of the Tri-Zone Polygraph Test*, (available through 645 Ash St., San Diego, Calif. 92101).

64. Cureton, E.E., "A Consensus as to the Validity of the Polygraph Procedures," *Tenn. L. Rev.* 22 (1953): 728-42. Reprinted by permission of Dr. Cureton, Professor Emeritus, Psychology, University of Tenn., and the Tennessee Law Review Association, Inc., from 22 *Tennessee Law Review* 740 (February 1953).

65. Barefoot, J.K., *The Polygraph Story*, published by the American Polygraph Association, N.Y., 1974 (available through Cluett Peabody and Co., 510 5th Avenue, New York 10036).

66. U.S. Congress, House, Committee on Government Operations, *Use of Polygraph as Lie Detectors by the Federal Government*, 89th Cong., 1st. sess., 1965, H.R. 198.

67. Orlansky, J., *An Assessment of Lie Detection Capability* (declassified version) Technical Report 62-16, Contract SD-50, Task 8, July 1964. Institute for Defense Analysis, Arlington, Va. Reprinted with the permission of Jesse Orlansky, Institute for Defense Analyses, Arlington, Va. Publication of this material does not imply endorsement of its factual accuracy or opinion by the Department of Defense.

68. U.S. Congress, "Use of Polygraph as Lie Detectors."

69. Abrams, S., "Polygraph Validity and Reliability: A Review, *J. Forensic Sciences* 18 (1973): 313-26.

70. American Polygraph Association Membership Book, (available through Milton Berman, 315 Nolan Bldg. Louisville, Ky. 40205).

71. Romig, C.H.A., "State Laws and The Polygraph in 1975," *Polygraph* 5 (1975): 95-107.

72. Ibid.

73. Horvath, F.S., and Reid, J.E., "The Reliability of Polygraph Examiner Diagnosis of Truth and Deception," *J. Crim. Law, Criminol. and Police Science* 62 (1971): 276-81.

74. Horvath, F.S., and Reid, J.E., "The Polygraph Silent Answer Test," *J. Crim. L., Criminol. and Police Science* 63 (1972): 285-93.

75. Gustafson, L.A., and Orne, M.T., "The Effects of Verbal Responses on the Laboratory Detection of Deception," *Psychophysiology* 2 (1965): 10-13, and Ellson et al., *A Report on Research.*

76. Gustafson, L.A., and Orne, M.T., "Effects of Heightened Motivation on the Detection of Deception, *J. Appl. Psych.* 47 (1963): 408-11.

77. Abrams, S., "The Polygraph: Laboratory vs. Field Research," *Polygraph* 1 (1972): 145-50, and, Orne, M.T., "Implications of Laboratory Research for the Detection of Deception," *Polygraph* 2 (1973): 169-99.

78. Thackray, R.I., and Orne, M.T., "Effects of the Type of Stimulus Employed and the Level of Subject Awareness on the Detection of Deception," *J. Appl. Psych.* 52 (1968): 234-39.

79. Decker, R.E., Stein, A.E., and Ansley N., "A Cardio Activity Monitor," *Polygraph* 1 (1972): 108-24.

80. Ash, P., "A Survey of Attitudes on the Polygraph," *Polygraph* 2 (1973): 200-23.

81. *People* v. *Cutter*, 12 *CLR* 2133 (Calif. Super. Ct. 11/6/72); *Commonwealth* v. *A Juvenile* (No. 1), 15 *CLR* 2323 (Mass. 1974); *Ohio* v. *Sonnie Court of Common Pleas*, Lake County, Ohio (No. 23 CR 100 opinion, 6/20/74); and *U.S.* v. *Ridling* 350 F. Supp. 90 (Ed Mich 1972).

82. The Use of Polygraphs and Similar Devices by Federal Agencies. Hearings before a Subcommittee of the Committee on Government Operations, House of Representatives, Ninety-third Congress, 2nd Session.

83. Ansley, N., "An Editorial Report on the Abzug Report," *Polygraph* 5 (1976): 1.

84. The Use of Polygraphs and Similar Devices by Federal Agencies. Hearings before a Subcommittee of the Committee on Government Operations, House of Representatives 94th Congress, 2nd Session, House of Representatives Report No. 94-745 H. Report 89-118 1.

3 The Psychophysiologic Basis of Polygraphy

A person entering a polygraph testing situation brings with him all that he has experienced and everything that he has learned: his beliefs, biases, and values. These determine how he responds, his view of himself and others, and what he will expect from them in terms of rejection or acceptance, respect or derogation. These and many other concepts are inexorably intertwined with his physical makeup and thus result in a very stable and self-perpetrating personality structure that remains fairly consistent in all situations. No one environment is exactly the same for any two people, no matter how similar their backgrounds have been. Even siblings raised in the same home by the same parents can experience very different worlds and thus mature with very divergent personalities.

Because of these differences, what a person brings into each new experience colors it in a manner that makes it unique for him. What he believes reality to be, regardless of how much he has misperceived it, is real to him, and he responds accordingly. The more he has suffered rejection, for example, the more he expects it, and in anticipating it, he sees it, whether it is there or not. In expecting rejection, he may even act in a manner that provokes it, thus fulfilling his prophesy and reinforcing his beliefs even more thoroughly. In a similar fashion, the greater the person's self doubts, the greater the likelihood that he will presume that any of his endeavors will end in failure. Because of the feelings of inadequacy, he will depreciate each success and exaggerate every failure, so that the feeling of worthlessness will feed on itself and the cycle will be maintained with the feelings becoming more deeply engrained with each demonstration that his expectations are correct.

Inevitably, the very same stimulus can have a different connotation for different people. For one person, an authority figure can represent a parent-like figure on whom he can be dependent, while for another, the authority figure is someone with whom to compete. Where feelings of trust and respect may be engendered in some, fear and hostility predominate in others. In a polygraph testing situation, the subject's response to the examiner will vary in relation to all of these factors. All of his emotional, mental, and physical traits that combine to comprise his personality will determine both his perception of the situation and his response. His past experiences with parents, men, if the polygraphist is a male, authority figures, or police will effect his reaction to the examiner. Whether he feels anger, anxiety, guilt, fear, or indifference will influence both his reaction and degree of responsiveness to each question asked.

41

The guilty and innocent alike will utilize their characteristic defense patterns to ward off the stress associated with the test. Psychopaths, for example, will typically employ rationalization and projection as a means of dealing with their criminal activities. In the case of the former, they develop good reasons to justify their actions and to replace their actual motivations. They may explain their robbery of a business by claiming that it charges unfair prices and bilk the consumer, so that their getting even is appropriate. Thus, they completely deny that their goal was their own financial gain. When using projection, they place the blame on others for their antisocial actions by stating that "if treatment had been provided instead of imprisonment, I would not be involved in crime now."

Individual differences exist in people's overall degree of emotional responsiveness. Some people tend to be quite emotional and quick to express feelings of anger, love, or despondency, but others tend to be phlegmatic in their response. Variations occur also in the expression of specific affective status. Explosive temper outbursts can be quite common in a particular person, while another is more prone to experience anxiety. Physiologic functioning will vary from one individual to another as well, with some demonstrating their greatest reactions in heart rate and others in a blood pressure or a sweating response.[1] Over and above these inherent and acquired characteristics, the polygraph testing situation itself will influence the subject's response. It would seem likely that the more that the examinee had to lose if he were found to be deceptive, the greater the degree of tension, anxiety, and fear that would be experienced. All things being equal, larger reactions would be expected in cases involving a felony as compared to a misdemeanor. On another dimension, a juvenile offender, who might view a sentence to a juvenile detention home as a status symbol, would probably react very differently from a professional person who is risking the loss of so much more.

The degree and combinations of fear, guilt, conflict, anger, and generalized excitement that are present will determine the ease with which polygraph tracings can be analyzed. The extent to which they exist will be dependent on the individual and the stress associated with the situation. While the examination is a threat to both the guilty and innocent, the extent of the impact will be directly related to the manner in which the polygraphist manipulates the environment. If this is accomplished effectively, extremely accurate results will be attained. He must convince the subject that his answers will be accurately interpreted. If this is achieved, the innocent will be less fearful when responding to the crucial questions and demonstrate a correspondingly lesser amount of physiologic responsiveness. In direct contrast, the guilty will show an even greater fear of detection and be more motivated to deceive, thereby evidencing a higher degree of reactivity. Both the innocent and the guilty will respond in a similar manner, but in a reversed fashion to the control questions. The guilty subject, despite the fact that he is lying to both the control and relevant questions, will manifest large responses to the latter and only minimal reactions to the former. Obviously, fear that deception to the control questions will be detected produces only a minor threat in comparison to the fear associated with lying to the key questions. The innocent, on the other hand, will respond in just the opposite way. While the innocent subject will be threatened by the control questions and react accordingly, the controls will provoke the greater stress because the examinee has been informed that he must be honest in his answer to all of the questions. Since, in his mind, being discovered in a lie to the control question might cause the examiner to diagnose him as guilty, his fear is more intense in association with the control questions. Therefore, unlike the guilty subject, his largest physiologic responses will be demonstrated on the control questions rather than the relevant. Backster explained this phenomenon in terms of the principle of the psychological set.[2]

To understand this concept, we must conceive of the environment as constantly bombarding a person with a wide range of stimuli. Obviously, since attending to all of these cues is impossible, the person perceives selectively. In order to function, in fact in order to survive, he must focus on some stimuli and ignore others. What he attends to is dependent upon both his heredity and learning. His genetic constitution prepares him to respond to certain kinds of cues such as loud noises, bright colors, or movements that automatically dominate the perceptual field. Other areas of attention are learned and vary from person to person. Among a group walking down a street, a painter would be most aware of the houses; a gardener, the lawns; and a roofer, the roofs. For each of these persons, the remainder of the environment would be ignored and remain essentially unseen and unremembered.

A stimulus must compete with many others. What makes one stimulus stand out over the others may be novelty, complexity, suddenness, intensity (loudness, brightness, and so forth), or relevance to a person's needs. Drives or needs are capable of lowering sensory thresholds so that the person becomes selectively sensitive to particular stimuli. Objects related to satisfying a need or reducing a drive are focused upon, while others are relatively ignored. Therefore, a hungry person would be more apt to perceive food, while being relatively unaware of the other aspects of his environment.

In polygraph testing, factors of suddenness, intensity, complexity, and novelty are avoided, with each question being equivalent in all of these areas. The competition between stimuli should exist only between the control and relevant questions, with the irrelevant questions having little or no distracting effect. Distraction in this sense can be defined as the interference that is created by other stimuli that are not in harmony with a particular goal. In contrast, a set is a combination of the body's orientation and expectancy, both of which involve perception, attention, and motivation.

The subject in a polygraph examination is actively avoiding being caught in a lie. His attention, therefore, is riveted on those questions—whether they are relevant or controls—to which he intends to be deceptive. For the innocent, detection of a lie on a control question—for example, "Prior to June 1974 did you ever think of killing someone?"—is a threat because it might create an impression that could imply guilt. His set, regardless of his fear of being seen as deceptive on the relevant item, is on the control. For the guilty subject, his set is on the relevant question even though he is lying to both the control and the key question. Deception to the control question cannot compete with lying to the relevant item because of the implications of being detected in a lie to the latter.

It is expected that generalized anxiety will exist in almost every polygraph subject, and while it can be reduced, it cannot be eliminated. Although anxiety is related to fear, generally, we can distinguish between the two. Anxiety tends to be chronic and attenuated, with the cause not usually being discernible. The predominant feeling is apprehension and is often related to some vague future threat. In contrast, fear is acute; the precipitating causes are real and recognizable, and the physiological responses are immediate. The examinee's response to the test situation in general is anxiety, while to deception to a particular question, the reaction is fear. Thus, the anxiety would be present throughout the test, but fear would occur only in response to deception. In the pretest interview, the examiner must stimulate this emotion as a response to deception. What seems to be lacking in much of the literature is that fear must be created as a reaction to deception on the control questions as well as the relevant. Both the guilty and the innocent must be convinced of the polygraphist's ability to detect lying, and while the importance of deception on the relevant items is obvious, it should be made clear that truthfulness on the control questions is also of significance. If this is not accomplished, an honest subject might not demonstrate a sufficiently strong physiological reaction to deception on the control questions.

While fear is the emotion most likely to be elicited during deception and probably creates the largest physiologic reaction, conflict and guilt can also alter the physical state of the subject.

Fear and conflict are inherent responses, but what a person reacts to is learned. Guilt, on the other hand, is a learned response that had its beginnings in early childhood. Parents, church, and important people in a child's life teach a specific set of values, attitudes, and morals. These teachings are begun early and taught so thoroughly that they become very firmly ingrained within the person. Through the process of reward and punishment, these ideas are introjected to the extent that they seem almost inborn. When the values become part of the child, the parental figures no longer have to punish any infractions of their rules; the child does it himself. Every time he goes against their teachings, he punishes himself through guilt until he, like most people, functions within the bounds of his conscience. Thus, during a polygraph examination deceptive behavior generally results in some degree of guilt and thus causes physiologic change. It must be remembered, however, that the development of conscience in some individuals, notably the psychopath, is considerably limited, but the fear of detection exists and probably accounts for their reactivity.

Conflict causes tension or anxiety that, like guilt, activates the body processes. A conflict may take three different forms. The first is a situation in which a decision has to be made between two positive goals; for example, a choice between two equally good positions. The second type of conflict is associated with the necessity of selecting one of two negative goals. In this instance, it becomes a matter of choosing the lesser of the two evils. The final conflict, and the one relating to polygraphy, is the situation in which the person, to attain something of value, must also accept something detrimental. When the subject is deceptive in response to a relevant question, the positive aspect is related to an avoidance of implication in a criminal action and the resulting freedom from the ensuing penalty. The negative aspect refers back to guilt and the fear of being caught in a lie. The greater the significance of the conflict and the longer the delay in making the decision, the more intense the stress. Again, the result of this stress is a physiologic reaction.

In the case of fear, which is the major activator of a physical change in the polygraph situation and the emotion that is felt to be most directly related to the ability to detect deception, no conditioning process need be traced back to childhood. The penalty for being caught in a criminal activity is reasonably clear. The threat of imprisonment, financial loss, or personal embarrassment are sufficiently obvious to the suspect so that no life-long conditioning process is necessary to explain the fear response.

Just as the subject brings all of his background of experiences into the test situation, so too does the polygraphist. In addition to that, there is a tendency for all of the persons involved in the case to present their data in a manner that meets their own needs. The examiner must, therefore, guard against developing any bias based on the reports of attorneys, police, witnesses, or other polygraphists. This impartiality is particularly important because he can unconsciously make his opinion known to the examinee and affect him accordingly. Any added emphasis upon the relevant questions in the form of inflection or loudness could result in a greater reaction to those items because of those factors rather than deception and could be particularly important in a peak of tension test in which any emphasis on the critical item could cue the subject as to the correct stimulus.

The examiner who allows himself to become biased can be readily influenced, even in the scoring of the tracings themselves. If he believes that the subject is guilty, either because of his behavior or because of information that he has received, he is more likely to interpret the charts in this manner. Numerical scoring, since it enhances objectivity, should definitely be employed to reduce this risk.

Psychological factors influence every facet of the examination, and the subject's responses can be appropriately modified by a competent polygraphist. The impact of psychological interactions upon the subject's physiologic functioning is the cornerstone of the polygraph procedure. Stress associated with the fear of a lie's being detected activates a portion of the nervous system, which, in turn, causes a series of physiologic changes to take place. Some of these are measured and recorded in the form of tracings on a moving polygraph chart. From the variations in the responses related to truthfulness and lying, the examiner can deduce with a high degree of accuracy the veracity of each examinee. He is not, however, measuring lying per se, but changes in the person's body reactions related to the stress associated with deception.

This physiologic response of the organism to threat is a normal function of the body and occurs in any stress situation. It enables a person to cope more effectively with the threat through the utilization of the body's resources. What the particular danger is matters relatively little for the body reacts in much the same manner. The stimulus can be real or imagined; it can be something recalled from the past or anticipated in the future. The affective state involved can be fear, shock, anger, guilt, conflict, or generalized excitement. There are other states that are not emotional but can cause a similar response to be displayed. Pain, intellectual activity, or even physical exertion can result in comparable physical manifestations, and the examiner must be certain that these variables do not exist during the test procedures.

Fully understanding the basis for the polygraph approach requires some comprehension of physiology. The most logical beginning is with the most basic structure of the body: the cell. In higher animals it has become specialized to perform specific functions, so that nerve cells are capable of conducting electrical impulses, effector cells (muscles) are able to contract, and receptors (sense organs) demonstrate the characteristic of irritability. The receptors, stimulated by information from the environment, internal or external, transform this energy into nerve impulses. These electrochemical charges are transmitted through sensory (afferent) nerve fibers toward the spinal cord and brain. The role of the spinal cord is to provide a reflex function and to conduct impulses to the brain and back, thereby permitting an integration of nervous activity. The information that is provided by these impulses is decoded by the association area of the cerebral cortex, and nerve impulses are then transmitted through the brain, spinal cord, and efferent fibers (motor) to effectors (muscles).

Each neuron is separate and makes no physical contact with the other nerve cells. In order for an impulse to be transmitted from one neuron to another, there must be some means by which the impulse can jump the gap between nerve cells. This junction between the neurons is called the synapse, and it is here that the axon (terminal end) of one nerve must make functional contact with either the cell body or dendrite (forward end) of another neuron. While some disagreement persists, it is generally believed that the transmission of an impulse across the synapse is primarily due to chemical factors rather than electrical. These chemical substances are formed and stored in the nerve endings and released through the effect of the action potential of the nerve impulse. This chemical can act in an excitatory fashion facilitating the transmission of the impulse over the synapse or it can serve to inhibit it.

The nervous system itself is composed of two main branches: the central nervous system (CNS) consisting of the brain and spinal cord and the peripheral nervous system. The latter is made up of the afferent neurons that carry impulses from the receptors to the CNS, the efferent neurons that transmit impulses from the CNS to the effectors (skeletal muscles), and the autonomic nervous system (ANS) that activates the smooth muscles such as the intestines and blood vessels, the glands, and the heart. The ANS is of particular interest in the study of polygraphy.

The ANS has also been called the vegetative nervous system because it innervates the viscera and mediates most of the functions of the visceral organs. It is intimately related to the endocrine system and together they regulate most of the internal functions of the body and maintain homeostasis or internal equilibrium. The endocrine system is composed of glands that produce and secrete chemical substances, such as adrenalin, into the blood stream to effect other organs. It is unclear whether the endocrine system is subservient to the ANS or the reverse, but both are integrated and controlled by the hypothalmus. This is the portion of the brain that is considered to be the master controller of homeostasis and regulates the control of smooth muscles and hormonal (endocrine) secretions.

The ANS functions automatically and involuntarily so that for the most part it is beyond the control of the individual. There are two branches—the sympathetic nervous system (SNS) and the parasympathetic nervous system (PNS)—that operate in opposition to each other. Therefore, one activates a function while the other inhibits it. The term *PNS* originated from the fact that its fibers are derived from either end of the spinal cord, the brain stem, and sacral regions. This branch of the ANS is dominant most of the time and particularly during periods of rest and tranquility. It enhances visceral functions leading to growth, digestion, and repair and, as such, is essential for survival.

Metabolism can be defined as the life process of cells and organisms, and the PNS is involved in the anabolic stage, which has to do with the building up of the protoplasm, conservation of energy, and the restoration of the organism after activity or damage.

Unlike the SNS, PNS reactions are initiated by individual reflexes of a group of nerves that are chemically and anatomically similar. Under specific conditions, they respond at about the same time. One of the conditions that stimulates PNS arousal is SNS activity, and it reacts in order to return the state of the organism back to equilibrium or homeostasis.

All ANS nerve fibers liberate chemical substances at their terminal endings to facilitate or inhibit the transmission of an impulse across the synapse. The organs that these nerves stimulate are reactive to those substances, whether they originate from the nerve fiber or through the blood stream. In the PNS, acetylcholene (ACH) is released through the action of the nerve impulses. The vagus nerve is the primary nerve in the PNS, and it stimulates, among other organs, the islet cells of the pancreas. This stimulus causes the release of insulin, which acts to facilitate the PNS response through the reaction of the various organs. In addition, vagus nerve activity slows the heart, constricts the bronchia of the lungs, and increases peristalsis and secretion in the gastrointestinal tract.

During PNS dominance, the digestive processes are operative. Salivation and secretions in the gastronintestinal tract occur along with peristalsis and a relaxtion of the sphincter muscles (rings of smooth muscle at the outlets of the bladder and intestines) to allow for digestion and elimination. The eye adjusts for near vision accommodation, and the bronchia (passages in the lungs) constrict. Heart action decreases, and the blood vessels to the skeletal muscles are narrowed so that there is a lesser supply of blood to these areas in comparison to the blood supply to the gastrointestinal system and to the genitalia. Sexual activity, like digestion, takes place during parasympathetic dominance.

Sympathetic arousal is brought about through a threat situation of any kind. Unlike the PNS, the SNS operates largely as a unit with each organ functioning in sympathy with the others. They are interconnected by a number of fibers that form a chain on either side of the spinal cord, which provides for the mass action of the total system. The neurons originate in the central portion of the spinal cord at the thoracic and lumbar regions. In contrast to the PNS, which is involved in the buildup of the organism, the SNS is associated with the catabolic phase of metabolism (the expenditure of energy and the breakdown of the protoplasm), and it functions to prepare the body to cope with an emergency. It is what Cannon called the flight or fight reaction and serves to temporarily increase and mobilize organism's energy supply.[3] Like the PNS, it acts to maintain homeostasis by initiating reactions that are concerned with the protection of the individual through an increase in the firing of neural impulses of its nerve fibers and the activation of neurons that are at rest.

These neural impulses initiate the secretion of norepinephrine (substance similar to adrenalin) at its terminal nerve endings. As was the case with acetylcholine during PNS dominance, almost all of the organs stimulated by the sympathetic fibers are reactive to norepinephrine. In addition, this chemical substance stimulates the adrenal medulla (the centers of the adrenal glands) to secrete adrenalin (epinephrine) into the blood stream, which facilitates SNS activity. These substances, epinephrine and norepinephrine, function in both an excitatory and inhibitory fashion by stimulating some organs to respond while reducing the reactions of others such as in the gastrointestinal tract. Therefore, during sympathetic arousal the digestive processes stop, including salivation, which accounts for the dryness of the mouth during fear states. Peristalsis and the secretion of hydrochloric acid, pepsin, and mucous are discontinued, and the internal sphincter muscles contract. Vasoconstriction takes place in the peripheral blood vessels and causes an increased flow of blood to the skin, thereby allowing for a dissipation of the heat engendered by muscular effort and fostering a reduction of blood loss should injury occur.

Vasodilation occurs in the skeletal and cardiac muscles so that the increased blood supplied to these areas can provide more metabolic fuels to these regions. These include oxygenated blood, hormones, and nutriments for energy to allow for increased muscular activity and the removal of waste. The arterioles (smaller arteries) are constricted, which results in greater peripheral resistance and thereby raises the blood pressure. The adrenal medulla is activated and releases adrenalin into the blood stream, thereby causing, among other reactions, the liver to secrete glycogen, which increases the blood sugar level. In the lungs the bronchia dilate to allow for a greater intake of oxygen. There is an increase in both the heart rate and the strength of the contractions, thereby causing greater cardiac output and thus enhancing the oxygenation of the blood. The pupils of the eyes dilate and the eyes accommodate for distant vision. Perspiration in the "emotional sweating areas"—the palms of the hands and soles of the feet—increases probably to allow for more effective locomotion and grasping. Table 3-1 lists the various autonomic functions.

In addition to these changes, vasoconstriction occurs in the area of the genitalia as in the digestive tract so that the blood supply to those regions is reduced and transported to where it is needed: in the skeletal and cardiac muscles. The effects of the shift from PNS dominance to sympathetic control is perhaps best demonstrated in the genitalia. Since sexual activity is parasympathetic, the dilation of the blood vessels at the male genitalia allows for an

Table 3-1
Autonomic Nervous Functions

Organ	Sympathetic	Parasympathetic
Heart	Increase in contractility and heart rate	Decrease in contractility and heart rate
Lungs		
Bronchia	Dilate	Contract
Blood Vessels		
Skin	Constrict	Dilate
Skeletal	Dilate	Dilate
Stomach and Intestines		
Secretion	Inhibited	Stimulated
Sphincters	Contracted	Relaxed
Motility	Decreased	Increased
Salivary Glands	Decreased	Increased
Sweat Glands	Active	—
Liver	Secretes Glycogen	—
Adrenal Medula	Secretes epinephrine	—
Eyes		
Ciliary Muscle	Accommodate for far vision	Accommodate for near vision
Iris	Dilates	Constricts

increased blood supply, which is necessary for an erection to occur. Should a threat state occur during coitus, such as in the case of an impotent male's being concerned about his sexual performance, a change from parasympathetic to sympathetic dominance will result. Vasoconstriction would take place in the genitalia, while the blood vessels in the skeletal muscles would dilate. The ensuing reduction of blood to the genitalia would cause a loss of the erection, and the increased blood supply to the skeletal muscles would obviously not be of benefit to him at that time.

While there are occasional instances in which the arousal of one system or another does not foster the well-being of the organism, such as in impotency or peptic ulcers, most of the time the changes that take place serve to improve the functioning of the organs and the operation of the body in general. It is through the utilization of these resources that a person can accomplish feats that ordinarily would not be possible. Fear and anger stimulate the body to perform at levels that are not ordinarily available, and we often hear of remarkable acts of endurance and strength that could not generally be achieved. Sympathetic arousal clearly serves to assist the person in coping with stress. It is an immediate reaction to a threat of any kind, and when the stress has ended, the PNS takes over just as rapidly.

In a polygraph examination, the subject's generalized anxiety raises his level of sympathetic activity, but when his emotional state is aroused during the telling of a lie, a much greater physiologic response will be generated. The blood volume in the arm may increase along with the increased flow of blood to the skeletal muscles; the skin's resistance to electricity may be lessened because of the tendency of the palms of the hand to perspire; the respiratory rate and pattern may be altered; and the pulse may vary. Not all of these changes necessarily occur, but usually changes are seen in at least two of these functions. Once the threatening question has been answered, the PNS seeking to maintain homeostasis again becomes dominant, and a rather rapid return to the former level of functioning results.

There are a number of situations that appear to operate in opposition to the theory of SNS emergency arousal. During stress some persons faint in association with a drop in blood pressure, while others develop an asthmatic attack that is characterized by a congestion of the bronchia. Not infrequently there is a loss of continence in fear situations, which is indicative of a dilation rather than a constriction of the sphincter muscles. Ulcer conditions, typically associated with stress, are paradoxically tied in with an increased peristalsis and secretion of hydrochloric acid. All of these physiologic changes are usually indicative of PNS dominance, which would be in direct contrast to the sympathetic arousal that would be expected with stress. An explanation of this behavior has been presented in terms of parasympathetic overcompensation.[4] When the SNS is activated by stress, the PNS is aroused as well in an attempt to regain dominance and maintain homeostasis; however, there is an overreaction and excessive parasympathetic physiologic reactions result. In the case of peptic ulcers, it has been demonstrated that anger creates both sympathetic and parasympathetic reactions, with the latter causing the secretion of hydrochloric acid during stress rather than an inhibition of digestive processes.

While much of ANS functioning is carried out in a reflex fashion, the integration of ANS responses for homeostasis is effected at various levels of the CNS. Although the hypothalamus plays a major role in the coordination of visceral and somatic reactions, its activity is mediated by other regions of the brain. There are centers for vasomotor and respiratory control in the medulla oblongata. The limbic system, frontal lobes, and the cerebullum play a role in ANS functioning as well.

The psychophysiologic foundation of polygraphy is well accepted by the sciences, and the physiologic changes that occur with sympathetic arousal have been well documented. It has also been demonstrated, however, that persons do not react to stress in the same manner—neither emotionally nor physiologically. Moreover, different stimuli will evoke different patterns of physiologic response. It is quite conceivable that a subject participating in a study involving a mock crime will react in a very dissimilar fashion physically than if he were a suspect in an actual criminal investigation. It is also quite likely, due to varying techniques and degrees of expertise, that two polygraphists examining the same subject will obtain different degrees of responsiveness and dissimilar patterns of response. Because of variables of this nature, the polygraph test is by no means a simple evaluation of physical reactions associated with a series of questions that will evoke stress. Since the examination is a very complicated procedure, it requires a competent polygraphist to administer the test and interpret the findings. He does not have to be well versed in physiology, but he should be particularly capable in those areas that relate to manipulating the individual's emotional state.

Notes

1. White, J., *The Autonomic Nervous System* (New York: MacMillan, 1952).

2. Backster, C., *Technique Fundamentals of the Tri-Zone Polygraph Test*, (available through C. Backster, 645 Ash St., San Diego, Calif. 92101).

3. Cannon, W.B., *Bodily Changes in Pain, Horror, Fear and Rage* (New York: Appleton-Century-Crofts, 1929).

4. Wenger, M.A., Jones, F.N., and Jones, M.H., *Physiological Psychology* (New York: Henry Holt, 1956).

4 Precursor to the Polygraph Test

The purpose of this discussion on polygraph test administration is not to teach the approach, but rather to give the reader an understanding of the basic principles of polygraphy. Such understanding will enable the attorney, for example, to critique the polygraphists' procedures and ascertain whether any weaknesses exist that would invalidate the test findings. It will also prepare him to argue at a trial in favor of keeping the test results out if the test was not properly administered or in favor of admission of the results if they are favorable and the test was appropriately conducted.

The polygraph examination must be administered much like a controlled scientific experiment. All of the variables must be controlled with the exception of those being studied. Therefore, it is of great importance that the test be conducted in an environment that limits any external stimuli from impinging on the procedure. Any stimulus, internal or external, can cause emotional reactions that will result in physiologic changes that will show up on the chart. It is of importance that noise, distracting stimuli (such as pictures or unusual decor), or any aspect of the physical surroundings that creates discomfort (such as high temperature or humidity) be eliminated. Any internal factors that operate as a distracting influence must be ascertained and in some manner removed. Fatigue, hunger, the need to excrete, distrust, or pain all can serve to invalidate the test findings. In many instances, the examiner simply has no alternative but to have the subject return in several days rather than risk obtaining inaccurate results.

These conditions clearly emphasize that the polygraph test does not measure dishonesty or truthfulness, only physiologic changes from which the examiner deduces deception. While these factors clearly effect the test results, polygraph validity and reliability can be viewed as resting on a tripod in which each leg is a necessary foundation for the process. Of the three, the instrument, the examinee, and the examiner, the latter is by far the most important. If the instrument is operating according to the manufacturer's specifications and has been recently calibrated to verify that it does, no cause for inaccuracies should be expected. The polygraphist should keep a log indicating the dates on which he calibrated his instrument, and there should have been a recent check of his instrumentation prior to the examination. If these steps have been taken and the subject is in a reasonably good physical, mental, and emotional state, the validity of the findings rest almost completely with the polygraphist. Polygraphy is no different from any other profession that relies on electronic or mechanical devices in making diagnoses. The specialist must develop an examination, see that it is properly conducted, and then interpret the results. Thus, whether in radiology, cardiology, or polygraphy, the strength of the findings is dependent upon the competence of the examiner.

The Instrument

The polygraph is composed of receptors that measure respiration (pneumograph), the galvanic skin response (galvanometer), and blood volume and pulse rate (cardiosphymograph). The latter, however, is acutally an occlusion plethysmograph, and many polygraphists mistakingly describe it in terms of recording blood pressure. While these are the main sensors in use, there are several others that are available and used by a relatively small number of examiners. Figure 4-1 shows a polygraph and its usual components.

A measure of respiration is recorded through the use of one or two corrugated pneumatic tubes positioned about the chest or upper abdomen. While one tube is sufficient, more information is obtained when two are employed, because breathing takes place in two different manners. Thoracic breathing is influenced by the enlargement and constriction of the thoracic cavity, while abdominal (diaphragmatic) respiration is a result of the diaphragm being lowered and raised, forcing the abdominal wall out and in. Two separate respiratory patterns result and signs of deception or truthfulness may be evident on both or only on one. Figure 4-2 shows the distinctly different patterns obtained.

The corrugated tube is closed at one end, while the other is connected by a narrower tube to a tambour or bellows system within the instrument. When the thoracic cavity expands during inspiration or when the abdomen is forced outward, the size of the tube is increased, thereby causing a partial vacuum within the system. This vacuum reduces the internal pressure against the bellows which then moves backwards. This movement is transmitted to the pen causing an upward stroke and then a descending swing as the subject exhales and the process reverses itself. The graphic picture of the respiratory pattern that is obtained demonstrates both the pattern and the rate of breathing. An actual stoppage of breathing, for example, would be transcribed as a straight horizontal line, while deep breathing would be demonstrated in cycles of greater amplitude (greater distance between the base line and ceiling).

Cardiovascular activity is measured by placing a blood pressure cuff, similar to that employed in medicine, about the upper arm and over the brachial artery. In instances of discomfort or poor recording, the forearm or wrist can be used. The cuff is inflated to a point about midway between the subject's diastolic and systolic blood pressure. The contractions of the heart (systoles) force the blood through the arterial system, thereby causing an increase in blood volume that results in an actual expansion of the arm. When the heart is at rest (diastole), there is a reduction of blood volume. These variations in blood volume and,

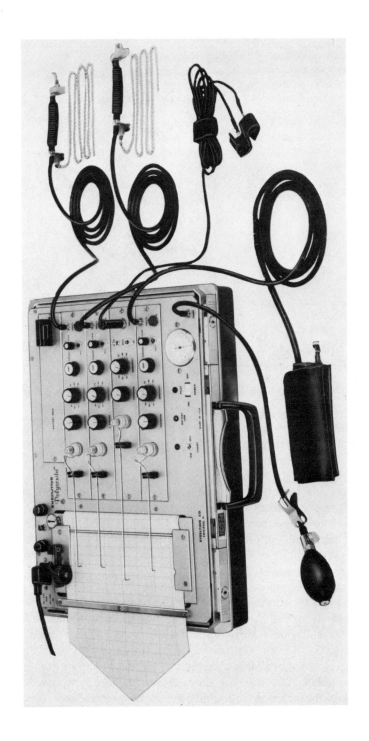

Figure 4-1. The Polygraph and Its Components.

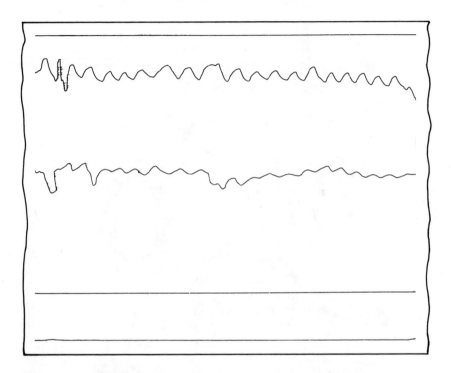

Figure 4-2. Difference between Thoracic and Abdominal Breathing Patterns.

therefore, arm size cause corresponding increases and decreases in the pressure against the bladder in the arm cuff. An increase in the pressure forces the air from the bladder through the tubing and, in a mechanical system similar to the pneumograph, pushes the bellows forward. This in turn causes the pen to move upward, while the reduction in blood volume occurring during the diastolic phase results in a downward swing of the pen. Since each contraction of the heart is represented through an upward stroke in the tracings, a measure of pulse rate can be calculated easily by totaling the number of times that this occurs between the vertical lines of the chart. These lines are generally situated at five or fifteen second intervals.

In addition to the pulse rate, the change in the position of the tracing (a rise or drop) is indicative of corresponding changes in blood volume and possibly some measure of relative blood pressure. The cardio sphygmographic (cardio) tracings shown in Figure 4-3 demonstrate a typical ascending and descending limb in each cycle. A portion of the way down the descending limb, there is a short upward stroke followed by a continuance of the downward swing. This is the dicrotic notch. The ascending limb of the tracings is produced at the contraction of the heart. At this time, the blood is forced out of the left

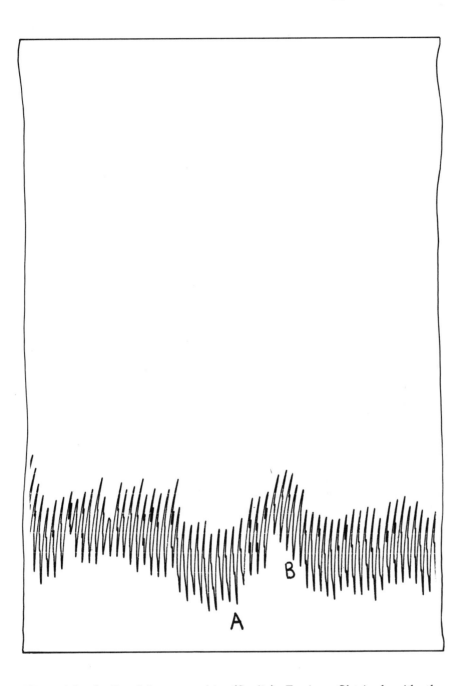

Figure 4-3. Cardio Sphygmographic (Cardio) Tracings Obtained with the Polygraph.

ventricle into the aorta, dilating it. As the heart relaxes, the tracing descends. With the relaxation of the heart, the distended aorta recoils, forcing most of the blood forward, but some spurts backward closing the aortic valve. As it rebounds, a similar situation is created as when the heart contracted, in that this blood, though certainly a lesser quantity, increases both the pressure and volume in the aorta as it moves forward in the artery. This produces a short rise in the tracing, the dicrotic notch, followed by a continued decline. Following the course of the blood flow to the arm, the ascending limb of the tracings is a result of the pulse wave that causes an expansion of the arterial wall, while the descending limb occurs when the pulse wave passes the bladder of the cuff. The dicrotic notch is produced by the minor secondary pulse wave passing under and then beyond the blood pressure cuff.[1]

At point A on the chart there is an upswing of the tracings typical of sympathetic arousal associated with deception. Point B shows the relief following the reaction. Vertical lines may be placed on the chart at five-second intervals so that the pulse rate is easily ascertained by totaling the number of cycles within twelve of these five-second spaces.

The usual test is composed of eight to twelve questions and lasts from two to five minutes. An interval of fifteen to twenty seconds must be maintained between the subject's answer and the start of the next question. If this period is too short, approaching ten seconds, enough significant data may be lost to cause that question to be diagnosed incorrectly. Throughout the questioning period, the pressure at which the bladder is inflated is dependent upon the subject. Typically, 80 to 90 mm Hg. of pressure are required to obtain an adequate set of tracings—approximately an inch in amplitude. In some subjects who are suffering from hypertension or excessive obesity, a higher level of pressure is required. Because of the pain and the numbing sensation in the hands and fingers due to the reduction in blood flow, testing time may have to be drastically shortened. In addition, since pain can cause SNS arousal, the discomfort in itself can cause artifacts in the tracings. It is also quite possible that an adequate set of tracings cannot be obtained in the cardio component because of this. An example of an inadequate tracing is shown in Figure 4-4.

In an attempt to reduce these negative features of the cardio, the electronically enhanced cardio (amplified cardio) and the Cardio Activity Monitor (CAM) were developed. In the former, clear tracings can be attained at as low a pressure as 45 mm Hg., which allows for longer testing with little or no discomfort. The CAM in present use is placed on the thumb and records capillary volume changes through an apparatus similar to a blood pressure cuff.

These approaches appear to be effective equivalents to the cardio without the negative aspects of discomfort and reduced testing time.[2]

Electrodermal activity is measured by the skin resistance response (SRR), which measures the skin's resistance to electricity. This measurement is obtained by placing two electrodes on the fingers or hand while an imperceptible amount

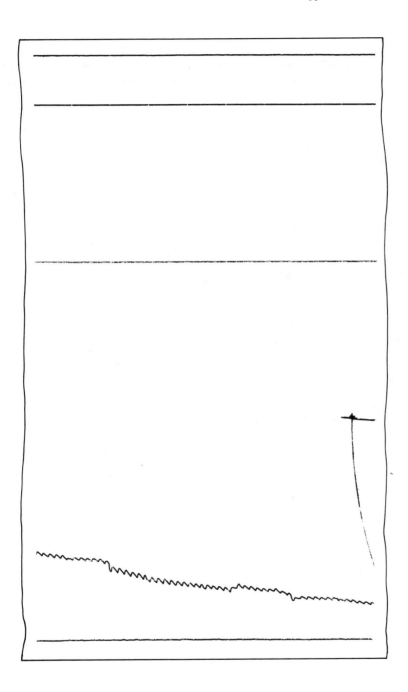

Figure 4-4. Inadequate Cardio Tracings Due to Hypertension.

of current is passed through electrodes on the hands or fingers. The variations in the conductance of the external current are recorded. The physiologic basis of electrodermal activity still remains at a theoretical level, but the sweat glands are evidently involved. Hydration (perspiring) assists the organism in defense, locomotion, and tactile discrimination,[3] and when there is a threat and sympathetic arousal, the palms of the hands perspire, thereby allowing for greater conductance of the electric current. As the resistance to electricity decreases, there is an upward swing of the pen that results in a very clear and measurable response. As the hydration is discontinued, the skin's resistance to electricity increases, and there is a downward drift of the pen.

Some instruments contain a photoelectric plethysmograph, which is also placed over the thumb and records a measure of blood volume. Unlike the CAM the plethysmograph is sensitive to the optical density of the tissue lying between the light and photoelectric cell. The change in optical sensitivity produced by each pulsation of the blood is converted to electrical energy and recorded. Many other tranducers have been studied,[4] but at this time, those in use appear to be the most effective.

All of these measures are recorded simultaneously on a moving chart (kymograph), which, in the majority of instruments, travels at six inches a minute.

The Subject

A person within his environment is constantly bombarded by a wide range of stimuli from both outside himself and internally. People, objects, sound, color, all impinge upon his senses from his external world, while his own thoughts, emotions, and physical sensations effect him from within. In the case of the polygraph subject, an effort must be made to eliminate as many of the distracting influences as possible, for as he reacts to them, physiologic changes occur that can create artifacts in the tracings.

Emotional states that cause sympathetic arousal include excitement, anxiety, anger, fear, and probably guilt and conflict as well. While not within the realm of emotion, both pain and intellectual activity can result in similar reactions. Of these responses, anxiety, anger, pain, and thought processes outside the area of questioning must be dealt with in some manner to avoid contaminating the test findings.

Anger is a natural résponse to a person's being placed in a threatening situation in which he feels he cannot extricate himself. While there may initially be resentment directed at the entire situation, it may well increase with each accusatory question and could easily produce a pattern that resembles deception. Therefore, the responsibility of the polygraphist is not only to recognize the anger, but to remove it. The examiner must be certain that the test is being taken voluntarily and that no resentment is growing out of any pressure placed on the subject to accept the examination. The subject must know that the examiner is going to interpret the findings in a complete objective manner. Regardless of whether the polygraphist is testing the subject for the prosecution or defense, the examinee must be convinced that the only identification that the examiner has is with polygraph—that is, with finding the truth. The subject must also believe that the only area of interest in the examination is related to the accusations made against him. Should he suspect that information related to other criminal activities is being solicited, inaccurate findings might result because of his fear related to the discovery of these activities.

Anxiety, in contrast to fear, can be defined as a diffuse apprehension not clearly referable to any specific threat. Fear, however, is an affective state that is directly related to a real threat. Since an excessive amount of anxiety will preclude obtaining an interpretable set of tracings, the polygraphist must be able to allay the apprehension of the subject. This goal can be accomplished through a thorough description of the test procedures, an explanation of the instrumentation, and an image created by the examiner of competence, objectivity, and trustworthiness. Attitudes of suspiciousness and distrust must be eliminated for accurate testing to take place. While assurances as to the accuracy of the technique serve to reduce the nervousness of the innocent, the very same approach enhances fear that a lie is likely to be detected in the case of the guilty.

A person in pain clearly should not be tested for with each painful sensation, sympathetic arousal will result. These reactions could just as readily produce a false positive response (diagnosing a nondeceptive subject as deceptive) as it could a false negative (labeling a deceptive individual as nondeceptive). If the pain occurs during the asking of a key question, a large physiologic reaction can be expected, regardless of whether the question is answered truthfully. The painful stimuli can also have a strong distracting effect so that the deceptive subject is too involved with the pain to react to his lying response. For this reason, purposeful attempts at creating pain or the use of mental activity as a distraction have been used as countermeasures against polygraph procedures. These will be discussed in detail in Chapter 6.

The physical state of the subject must also be evaluated in order to determine whether he is testable. Anyone who is excessively fatigued, intoxicated, acutely ill, or who has used drugs excessively on that day should not be tested. At times, a suspect is brought to a polygraphist after an interrogation, which, quite obviously, can have caused physical and emotional reactions that preclude polygraph examination at that time.

The attitude of the subject is also of prime importance. As has been discussed in Chapter 2, laboratory research probably yields a lesser degree of validity because the subject has little to fear if his lie is detected. With minimal fear, or none at all, physiologic reactions would not be expected to be extreme and errors in diagnosis and inconclusive findings would increase. A similar situation could occur in ex parte cases. The suspect, aware that the results would be discarded if the findings indicated that he was untruthful, has little to fear. It is conceivable that a false negative could result. Prosecution might then request that police examiners test the person in order to verify the results, with the second examination being conducted on a stipulated basis. The subject clearly has something to lose in the retest, and he could demonstrate a very deceptive chart. Thus, an examinee taking an ex parte test should be made to feel that the results will be employed in some manner. Since achieving an accurate result is advantageous to the examinee, the attorney and polygraphist might inform the subject that the results will be available to the court. If such misleading of the examinee is offensive, then it is most important that the subject be made aware that the charges may be dropped if he is found to be nondeceptive. This prospect should be sufficient to motivate the subject to become emotionally involved in the examination.

A person's culture can greatly determine many facets of his personality. What he has learned early in his life can be so thoroughly ingrained as to seem almost a genetically inherited part of his makeup. It effects all aspects of his functioning, beliefs, learnings, attitudes, expectations, and even his perceptions. His vocabulary is influenced to the extent that communication can be greatly impaired and concepts can develop very different meanings. The continuum of meaning that exists between the words *force* and *rape* is an excellent example of an area in which confusion can occur. Both the victim and the perpetrator could be answering truthfully in their minds when she states she was raped and he denies it. Truth and deception in a polygraph test has no objective reality, but exists only in the minds of the examinees. If they believe they did not commit an act, even if they did, when they deny it they will be found truthful. If, on the other hand, they are uncertain, their response could be indicative of deception, in spite of their actually being innocent. It is, therefore, highly important for the polygraphist to stress to the subject that he must be completely certain that there is no doubt in his mind that he can answer each question with an unequivocal "yes" or "no."

Identical words can have different meanings for different people. To be "bad," for example, can mean to be "cool." In one case a suspect denied having stolen several pairs of shoes from a house in his neighborhood. This offense did not relate to the crime under investigation, but the subject was later shown that it was on his police report, to which he replied, "Man, that's not stealin', that's takin'." It would seem that in his view a theft carried out in his own neighborhood was different than stealing, and he might well not have demonstrated a deceptive response when asked whether he had participated in this theft. This example emphasizes the need to understand the suspect, his ideas, and even his vocabulary to be certain that realistic and understandable communication is taking place.

There are actually few medical problems that preclude polygraph testing. It is possible that one measure might be uninterpretable, but the others are generally left unaffected. Conceivably, a heart condition could distort the cardio tracings, but the pneumograph and galvanometer would still act as effective measures. Persons with certain psychological conditions—psychotics,[5] mental retardates,[6] and those with various forms of severe brain damage—cannot be accurately examined. Fortunately, errors are rarely made in testing such people because their disorganized behavior is either so obvious that they are not examined, or if they are, their tracings are too erratic to interpret. It has also been found that a higher risk of error occurs when evaluating children under the age of twelve.[7] In those instances in which the subject has a severe medical problem that might be exacerbated by the examination, the testing should first be cleared in writing through his physician. A polygraphic evaluation can be stressful, and conceivably, it could precipitate a convulsion in an epileptic, cause an infarction in a heart patient, or even induce labor in a pregnant subject.

In a society that relies very heavily upon drugs, legal and illegal, it is almost rare to meet a person—including one who is imprisoned—who has not used some drug in the last twenty-four hours. Since a polygraph situation is anxiety provoking, the innocent as well as the guilty are likely to deal with the threat by taking a drug. Unless excessive amounts are utilized, generally drug use does not preclude testing. Some drugs, of course, have a greater effect than others, and a real tendency exists in these to flatten out the physiologic responses. Sympatholytic acting medications, for example, are frequently prescribed for patients with heart problems since they operate to inhibit the sympathetic nervous system, and undoubtedly little physiologic reaction to threat will be observable in subjects using such drugs. But whatever the drug or the dosage, no chemical can selectively inhibit a response to an accusatory question while allowing reactions to other questions to occur normally. Therefore, the very most that a drug can accomplish is to produce inconclusive findings.

For those persons who are chronically tense and anxious, discontinuing their medication for the examination could easily result in a chart that is too erratic to evaluate. A decision should be made prior to the testing as to whether regularly used drugs should be discontinued for the test. If that is felt to be appropriate, then usage should obviously be discontinued by the subject's physician, not the examiner or the attorney.

Many subjects deny having used drugs prior to the examination. Analysis of a urine sample can readily clarify their truthfulness on this issue; in fact, most examinees are quick to recall that they had recently employed drugs when they learn of the planned urinalysis.

Since it is generally accepted that any variable present in the testing situation can effect the tracings, it has always been emphasized that no one other than the examiner and the examinee should be present in the testing room. Reid and Inbau indicated that it was advisable to utilize an observation room with a one-way mirror so that the test could be seen and heard without any distracting influence on the testee.[8] In this manner, attorneys who feel their observing the test is necessary could be accommodated, and also, witnesses would be available if the subject later claimed that misconduct had occurred during the testing.

This approach is felt to be quite appropriate as long as the examinee is made aware that he is being observed. The entire test procedure should be taped and kept on file to demonstrate that nothing inappropriate was said or that improper inflection was used to cause the subject to respond. In one case in which a subject was being tested to determine whether he had been involved in a rape, he disclaimed any knowledge of where it had taken place. A peak of tension test was employed in which six parks were listed, one of which was the site of the rape. After the subject consistently reacted to the correct location and was informed of this, he stated that the examiner had told him the name of the park prior to the testing. Reminding the examinee that the test was being taped eliminated his complaints.

When a male is examining children or members of the opposite sex, it is often advisable to have a woman present. An assistant has frequently been used to read the questions, and this person has been simply accepted as being part of the examination with no untoward effects. The presence of an assistant seems to be reassuring to children and female subjects and at the same time affords the examiner a degree of protection against unfounded accusations motivated by attempts to counter conclusions indicative of deception.

While various conditions of the subject and the instrument can invalidate the test findings, these almost always can be eliminated so that testing can be carried out. Whether the conditions described above and other potential weaknesses in the test procedure are recognized and corrected is solely dependent on the examiner.

The Examiner

The value of polygraphy and its validity and reliability are almost completely dependent upon the competence of the examiner. Obviously, then, much care must be taken in selecting a polygraphist. The need for selectivity is equally true for the defense attorney who is choosing an examiner for an ex parte examination as it is for a law enforcement agency in determining who of its people should receive specialized training in this field. Since the polygraphist must play so many different roles, each requiring a different set of talents, there is no single aptitude that would be indicative of a good examiner. Horavath and Reid demonstrated the importance of experience in the accurate scoring of polygraph charts.[9] A competent examiner should also be bright, trained in an accredited polygraph school, and a member of, or possibly an officer in, the local and national polygraph societies. If there is a licensure law in the state, the examiner, of course, should be licensed. Ideally, he should have a college degree in which he has had a substantial number of psychology and physiology courses. In addition, he should regularly attend seminars and other training programs to keep up with the changes in the procedures as they are developed. The examiner should also be an excellent interviewer who functions in a very objective manner and has a strong enough character and the integrity to make a decision in spite of the influences from others who might attempt to bias him. His image should indicate to others that he is an expert capable of developing a test strictly in accordance with polygraph principles rather than bowing to the pressures of superiors or attorneys who employ him. The examiner should also be able to present a professional appearance and to speak well and with self-assuredness so that he can garner the trust of the subject, attorneys, and the court. He should be a good expert witness who has testified well on other occasions. In court he should be able to demonstrate a knowledge of the literature and ideally have done research and have published and presented papers of his own.

It is often asked how an attorney or the courts can find an examiner who meets these qualifications. This question can be answered in the same manner as how one finds a good dentist or physician, for any professional person's reputation in the community, good or bad, rapidly spreads. Other attorneys, the district attorney's office, or court officers can provide information on which examiners in their experience are more expert than others. The American Polygraph Association at 315 Nolan Bldg., Louisville, Ky. 40205 can also be contacted for its recommendations as well as any of the accredited polygraph schools listed in the appendix to this chapter.

As has been indicated in the sections on the instrument and the subject, the polygraphist's responsibility is to ascertain the working condition of his instrument and eliminate any subjects who are not testable. Moreover, he must dispel any attitudes or reduce any affective states that would interfere with an accurate test finding. All variables must be controlled with the exception of the fear of a lie's being detected. He must also gather and to some extent verify the data on the accusation, in recognition of the fact that police reports and lawyers' presentations of the facts could be in error. It is not unusual for law enforcement officers to present data related to other similar crimes in which the subject has been involved so that the examiner will have the whole picture. At the same time, attorneys sometime leave out some details so as not to bias the examiner. If, however, the polygraphist is relying on his charts and his numerical scoring only, he should not be prejudiced by anyone's input. Nor should he be influenced by the examinee's demeanor, intelligence, position, or any of the expressive movements previously discussed. If the examiner were to do that, then he would be relying on factors that have much less accuracy than polygraphy and also on data that he would be hard put to defend in court. A diagnosis on every examination should be made strictly from an interpretation of the charts, and the findings should be sufficiently clear so that other examiners can reach the same conclusion through their own surveys of the charts.

The polygraphist, in general, must engender enough of a feeling of confidence in the subject to relieve the anxiety of the innocent and at the same time increase the fear of the guilty. He must be able to weed out from the examinee's background any pertinent facts—ranging from a recent death in the family to the examinee's concern about another crime being detected—that might interfere with the testing. The instrument must be explained in clear terms so that the testee can accept its accuracy and has some understanding of how it operates to detect deception. The questions must be developed in a manner that is unambiguous and understandable and must be presented in a fashion that does not in itself cause a reaction. The polygraphist must be knowledgeable enough to be able to vary the test technique to obtain clear deceptive or nondeceptive reactions. Finally, he must be able to interpret the tracings objectively by using a numerical scoring system and reach a diagnosis that would be in agreement with other competent examiners.

Bailey and Rothblatt emphasized the importance of selecting a capable polygraphist in order to protect the results of the findings from attack by the prosecution and reducing the likelihood of the prosecution's obtaining contradictory results with their own examiner.[10] It should be quite evident that the value of this approach depends on the examiner. Since competent examiners should obtain exactly the same results, battles of the experts in the courtroom should not be expected. Hopefully, polygraphy will never deteriorate to that state.

Notes

1. *Keeler Polygraph Institute Training Guide, The Keeler Technique*, Chicago 1964 (available through Keeler Institute, 160 East Grand Avenue, Chicago, Ill. 60611).

2. Decker, R.Z., Stein, A.E., and Ansley, N., "A Cardio Activity Monitor," Polygraph 1 (1972): 108-23.

3. Lacey, J.I., "Psychophysiology of the Autonomic Nervous System: Master Lectures on the Physiological Psychology" (tape), American Psychological Association (1200 17th Street, N.W.), Washington, D.C. 20036, August 1974.

4. Ellson, D.G., David, R.C., Saltzman, I.J., and Burke, C.J., *A Report of Research on Detection of Deception*, Contract No. N60NR-18011, Office of Naval Research, September 15, 1952, (available through the University of Indiana, Bloomington).

5. Abrams, S., "The Validity of the Polygraph with Schizophrenics," *Polygraph* 3, (1974): 328-37.

6. Abrams, S., and Weinstein, E., "The Validity of the Polygraph with Retardates," *J. of Police Science and Admin.* 2 (1974): 11-14.

7. Abrams, S., "The Validity of the Polygraph Technique with Children," *J. Police Science and Admin.* 3 (1975): 310-11.

8. Reid, J.E., and Inbau, F.E., *Truth and Deception: The Polygraph ("lie detector") Technique* (Baltimore: Williams and Wilkins, 1966).

9. Horvath, F.S., and Reid, J.E., "The Reliability of Polygraph Examiner Diagnosis of Truth and Deception," *J. Crim. Law, Criminol. and Police Science* 62 (1971): 276-81.

10. Bailey, F.L., and Rothblatt, H.B., *Investigation and Preparation of Criminal Cases, Federal and State* (San Francisco: Bancroff-Whitney Co., 1970).

Appendix 4A:
Accredited Polygraph Schools

American Institute of Polygraph
   Technology and Applied
   Psychology
Parklane Towers West—Suite 1213
Dearborn, Michigan 48128

Backster School of Lie Detection
645 Ash Street—Suite A
San Diego, California 92101

Chicago Professional Polygraph
   Center, Inc.
407 South Dearborn—Suite 1175
Chicago, Illinois 60605

Gormac Polygraph School
501 South First Avenue
P.O. Box 424
Arcadia, California 91006

Keeler Polygraph Institute
5906 North Milwaukee Avenue
Chicago, Illinois 60646

Mumford Institute of Polygraph
69 Brookwood Drive N.E.
P.O. Box 77-1, Station C
Atlanta, Georgia 30309

National Training Center of Lie
   Detection
57 West 57th Street—Suite 1109
New York, New York 10019

Polygraph Personnel Research
   Laboratory and School for Lie
   Detection
Lafayette Building
5th and Chestnut Streets
Philadelphia, Pennsylvania 19106

Reid College of Detection of Deception
600 South Michigan Avenue
Chicago, Illinois 60605

Texas A. & M. College
F.E. Drawer K
College Station, Texas 77843

Virginia School of Polygraphy
7909 Brookfield Road
Norfolk, Virginia 23518

Zonn Institute of Polygraphy, Inc.
100 Colony Square, 1175 Peachtree
   Street N.E.
Atlanta, Georgia 30309

University of Baltimore
North Charles and Mt. Royal Streets
Baltimore, Maryland 21201

Military-Federal (only)

U.S. Army Polygraph School
Building 3165
Ft. McClellan, Alabama 36201

5 Polygraph Test Procedure

The polygraph examination consists of four separate phases: data collection, pretest interview, test administration, and the posttest interview. Prior to even meeting the subject, the examiner must accumulate all of the necessary information that will give him a complete and exact picture of the area under investigation. If the subject is accused of armed robbery, the place, date, time, witnesses' statements, and the police report are all necessary. It is just as important to have an accurate account of the suspect's activities of the time in question along with any statements of his witnesses that might be available. Quite obviously, a polygraph examination of the people who have corroborating stories can be as important as that of the suspect.

Any factors that might influence the subject's reactions during the test must be determined so that any history of medical, psychiatric, or educational problems can be evaluated through other sources. Contact with physicians or hospitals might be appropriate in some instances.

A conference with the attorney should delineate exactly what information is required. It is perfectly acceptable for him to draw up a series of suggested questions as long as he recognizes that the final decision as to which ones are asked and how they are phrased rests with the polygraphist. The lawyer does decide, however, whether he wants the examiner to attempt to obtain an admission from his client, should his charts be in the direction of deception. While it is not necessary for the attorney to be in the testing area, it is advisable for him to be available at the time of the examination should problems arise.

The importance of the pretest interview can not be overestimated. Rapport is established, inappropriate feelings are allayed, the procedure is explained, and background information is attained, all of which serve to insure valid testing. A complete and detailed report of the subject's knowledge of the crime is established, regardless of whether the data is ascertained through actual criminal involvement, through the subject's attorney, the arresting officers, or the news media. When this report is complete, a decision can be made as to whether a peak of tension test or a controlled question technique will be employed. The questions are then developed and discussed with the examinee since the vocabulary must be understandable and the meaning of the questions unambiguous. Just as the examination itself must be completely voluntary, the subject should be agreeable to the use of each question.

For those people who indicate that they have no recall of participating in an activity, because of alcohol or some other factor, the questions must be worded in a different manner. To query him in terms of "Did you ... " becomes meaningless. If he performed the act, but has no memory of it, his response will probably be nondeceptive. There is some evidence, however, that unconscious processes are available to polygraph testing,[1] so that conceivably a deceptive pattern might be shown. The results, however, become meaningless since a truthful reaction would not necessarily indicate that he did not commit the act and a lying response does not have to indicate that he both participated in it and recalls it. For those who claim amnesia, accuracy is likely to be greater if the question is prefaced with "Do you actually remember. ..." A subject's stating that he is not certain whether he were involved in a particular act is comparable to part of him saying "yes," while the other part denies that he was. To deny participation in the act during the test can be conceptualized as part of the person lying and the remainder responding truthfully. Added to this is the emotional reaction associated with the doubt in his mind and the pattern, regardless of whether he is actually guilty, will be deceptive. In many instances, the question simply cannot be asked.

A case in point is a woman who was involved in a knife fight. When tested and asked whether she had cut the other woman, a clearly deceptive response was shown. Later she told her counsel that in the heat of the battle, she was not certain whether she in fact knifed the woman or that someone else had. Everyone had said she did it and the knife was hers so she assumed that she had. Whether she was making an excuse for failing the polygraph examination or whether she committed the act was not clarified by the polygraph test and will probably never be known. A careful pretest interview and question formulation should have eliminated this problem.

When the list of questions is completed, the subject is aware of every item that will be used. No surprise questions are used because the subject would show a reaction to any question that was not expected, and differentiating between a deceptive response and the reaction associated with surprise would be most difficult.

In those rare instances when the suspect is not given all of the details of the crime of which he has been accused, a *peak of tension test* (POT) can be utilized. An example of this approach is a case in which a murder was committed and the type of weapon used was not made available to the news media, and neither the investigating officers nor the attorney made this information known to the suspects. Therefore, the following test could be administered:

1. Do you know whether Eugene Samuels was killed with a 243?
2. Do you know whether Eugene Samuels was killed with a 257?
3. Do you know whether Eugene Samuels was killed with a 270?
4. Do you know whether Eugene Samuels was killed with a 30-30?
5. Do you know whether Eugene Samuels was killed with a 30-06?

This test is administered a number of times with the subject knowing all of the questions. He is unaware of their placement during the first administration, but after that, he knows the order of presentation as well. The question containing the correct answer is never in the first or last position because there is a tendency for the subject to react to those items simply because they are at the beginning and end of the test.

The innocent subject, having no idea as to which weapon was employed, is likely to respond to each question with the same magnitude of physiologic reactivity. This test is quite different from the situation in which he is asked: "Did you shoot John Smith with the 270 rifle?" In this type of question, even though he is responding truthfully, inevitably some degree of anxiety will be engendered and physiologic changes will be produced. In the POT test, the examinee simply does not know which question that he should be anxious about and therefore the lack of reaction to the critical item is quite apparent. In direct contrast to the innocent, the person with guilty knowledge not only knows which question is critical but where in the series it will be presented. Two different reactions may occur. If the weapon used was the 270 listed in question 3, the subject's anxiety will increase with each question until the 270 item and then it will peak; after that, with the key question passed and the stress over, the fear diminishes. This results in a peak-like effect, with the cardio and GSR tracings showing a consistent rise until question 3 and then dropping. An example of this response pattern is shown in Figure 5-1.

A second type of reaction that can occur without the peak effect is that the

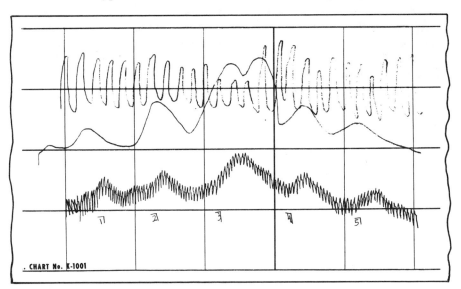

Figure 5-1. Response Pattern in the Polygraph Peak of Tension Test.

physiologic changes in response to the critical question are much greater than the reactions to the other questions. Since the test is repeated three or more times and the examiner is comparing the subject's reaction on all three components, a very definite and consistent difference would be expected between the key question and the others. Moreover, if tests could be administered related to a number of factors, such as point of entry, scene of the death, and time of death, an extremely valid notion of guilty knowledge could be obtained. Lykken in dealing with this technique on a statistical basis indicated that with this approach the likelihood of determining guilty knowledge is extremely high.[2]

It should be recognized that this technique is not necessarily detecting reactions to lies, but rather a generalized excitation associated with the subject's recognition of the correct item.

The POT test must be administered in a manner in which the subject does not receive the slightest clue as to the critical word or phrase. Therefore, the questions must be presented in a monotone with no change in the examiner's inflection. In fact, it would be desirable if someone else who did not know the key word were to read the questions. The wording of each question must be developed in a similar manner so that each question is composed of words of the same relative significance and in the same general category. In the example previously presented, the questions were exactly the same with the exception of the caliber of rifle employed. Moreover, one caliber does not stand out any more than another, and any one could have been used as the murder weapon.

If the critical phrase is composed of two words—*white shirt*—then the other questions should contain phrases of similar composition—*yellow sweater* or *black shoes*. If the peak is used to investigate something stolen, there should be no great difference in the value of the items or anything else that would set them apart. Care must be taken when dealing with losses of money or merchandise since it is quite possible that the victim exaggerated the loss for insurance purposes or the thief's partner took more than his share. In those instances, the subject could respond to the wrong amount and could appear to be truthful when he is actually guilty.

The areas under questioning must be sufficiently significant for the examinee to have been aware of them. Recognizing that witnesses are notoriously poor in recalling specifics or identifying suspects because of their loss of attention and recall due to stress, we should not expect more from the criminal who also would forget many of the details of his crime. He would no doubt remember his means of entry, but it is unlikely that he would recall the color of the house or even the clothing worn by the victim.

It is just as important to eliminate any of the noncritical items that the subject indicates are significant to him. Otherwise, he will react to them, possibly more than to the critical item. This situation occurred in the polygraph examination of Patty Hearst. In order to evaluate her responsiveness and to stimulate her reactivity, a "stim" test was administered. She was asked to select a number between six and ten and then instructed to respond "no" each time she was asked whether she had chosen each particular number, including the one she actually had selected. Obviously, she would have been lying to that number, and the examiner assumedly should have been able to detect the lie. Miss Hearst, however, responded to two numbers: the one she had selected and lied about—ten—but even more to the number nine. In the Hibernia Bank robbery for which she was tried and found guilty, she had been assigned the number nine by the leader of the SLA. Quite naturally, that number had a considerable emotional impact on her, and she had reacted accordingly on the "stim" test.

A second type of POT test can sometimes be used. In the approach already described, the examiner knows the correct key, but none of the suspects except the guilty person is aware of it. In the *searching peak test*, the guilty person alone knows the answer. The test most often relates to finding the location of something that is missing: a weapon, stolen property, or a body. The assumption is made that the suspect knows where the object is in spite of his continued denial. Since he is still protesting his innocence, he is hesitant to refuse the examination.

The examination begins with an investigation into broad areas and when the subject reacts to one of these, the areas are narrowed down until the exact location is discovered. An excellent example of this approach was provided by Corporal Bruce Lattin, a polygraphist with the Oregon State Police.

In 1971 a woman disappeared from her residence under rather suspicious circumstances, and an investigation by the police did not reveal enough to warrant further action. Her husband reported that she had left him and returned to Mexico to care for her mother. Reportedly, she had written him a month later and stated that she was going to remain there. Three years later, when the husband was being examined by Corporal Lattin on a larceny charge, he agreed to answer questions related to his missing wife. The first test administered indicated that he was deceptive in denying that he had killed his wife and that he did not know where the body was. Two searching peaks were administered with the subject being asked in the first:

1. Is your wife's body in the river?
2. Is your wife's body by the railroad tracks?
3. Is your wife's body in the potato field?
4. Is your wife's body by the farm buildings?
5. Is your wife's body by the house?

After the subject responded to the questions relating to the body being near the buildings, a second test was administered to determine at exactly which building the body might be found. The following questions were asked:

1. Is your wife buried by the house?
2. Is your wife buried by the barn?
3. Is your wife buried by the shed?
4. Is your wife buried by the machine shop?
5. Is your wife buried by the silo?

A larger reaction was obtained at question 3, and a search of the farm in the vicinity of the shed revealed that the body was buried three feet ten inches from the corner of the shed.

The technique applied in the vast majority of cases is the *control question approach*. Exactly how it is employed varies with the different schools of thought, but all use essentially the same types of questions.

1. *The irrelevant or neutral question*: This question is typically used at the beginning and end of the test, and in some approaches, it is placed among the other questions as well. The neutral questions are related to neutral subjects like date of birth, age, name, and so forth. Their purpose is to bring the subject down to his essentially "normal" physiologic base line after responding to a question that created stress. They are also positioned at either end of the test because subjects generally respond at these points regardless of the question. Therefore, any pertinent item placed there would be wasted because it could not be accurately interpreted.

2. *The relevant question*: This question is the critical one. A typically phrased example is: "On June 5th at 8th and Vine did you rob the Safeway Store?" The relevant questions should be brief but clear enough so that they refer only to that specific occurrence. Emotion-laden words like *murder* and *rape* should be replaced with *kill* and *force sex on* to reduce the likelihood of a reaction to the word rather than a deceptive response. Only one issue should be raised at a time and phrases such as "Did you rob and shoot . . . " should not be used for the obvious reason that the subject might have committed the theft but not the murder.

3. *The control question*: The importance of this question, as discussed in Chapter 2 cannot be overestimated. It is undoubtedly every bit as important as the relevant question in determining truth and deception. Its entire purpose is to serve as a basis of comparison with the relevant question, and without it, the relevant question is of little or no value. If the control question were not employed, a large reaction to a relevant question could be indicative of deception or simply demonstrate that the subject tends to be highly responsive. A subject who shows little response to the critical item may be truthful or maybe someone who displays little physiologic reactivity. The control question, therefore, is a necessity.[3]

The control question is a known or assumed lie. In the case of the former, information is used that the subject is unaware that the polygraphist possesses, and in the test the subject is untruthful about it. The information might relate to some criminal activity in the past or some other background information obtained from a family member or the attorney. The assumed lie relates to an activity discussed with and denied by the subject and about which his being truthful in the denial seems highly unlikely. Probably, in an attempt to impress the examiner, through creating a good impression, both guilty and innocent examinees avoid admitting to antisocial activities. Questions such as the following, are rather typical of such denials:

Did you ever take anything of value from an employer?

Did you ever take advantage of a friend?

Did you ever want to see anyone seriously hurt?

Did you ever use any force in getting a female to do something sexual?

Should the individual admit to these, the question might be prefaced with—"Other than that one time, did you ever . . . ?"

The questions that are denied are then employed as controls. They are always chosen from a similar category as the accusation against the suspect. Therefore, if the case involves a theft, the control question relates to stealing, and if an assault, the controls involve some form of violence. Obviously, the controls selected should not be more powerful than the relevant questions. If the charge were assault and battery, a control dealing with murder would not be used.

One of the most important aspects of the control question that will determine its effectiveness is the need to avoid any overlap with the relevant question. The control must be limited in a manner that completely excludes it from being part of the accusation. If for example, the crime under investigation is a murder, the control can not be stated: "Did you ever in your life think of seriously hurting someone?" If the suspect is guilty of the charge against him, then he, in fact, did think of hurting the victim. The control then is of no value, for the guilty will respond to it as if it were a relevant question. The question: "Did you lie to your attorney about his matter?" is equally poor since the innocent suspect too may conceal information from his lawyer and will respond deceptively even though the matter he lied about does not directly relate to the case.

For a control question to be meaningful and serve its purpose, it must be limited in a manner that completely excludes the crime questions. This can be accomplished by phrasing these questions in terms of:

"Prior to this year . . . "

"Between the ages of 15 and 30 . . . "

"Before 1975 . . . "

Of the entire test, the concept of the control question is the most difficult for the lay population to understand and evidently the most difficult aspect of the examination for polygraphists to explain. The troublesomeness lies in the fact that accusatory questions, such as "Did you kill John Smith?" seem to be so much more of a threat, even to the innocent, than a control question like "Prior to this year, did you ever want to seriously hurt anyone?" The control question for the innocent is the greater threat because, knowing that he is responding deceptively, he is fearful that the examiner will recognize this deception and assume he is lying on the relevant question as well. For the guilty person, however, while he is being deceptive to the control and relevant items, the real threat obviously lies in his reaction to the critical question. Until recently, the threat to the innocent was assumed since the control question was never presented to him as a threat. Nevertheless, judging by the high validity achieved in polygraphy, the control question technique has been effective. This author has altered this approach and made the threat to the innocent real by informing each subject that his truthfulness to the control questions is every bit as important as his honest response to the crime questions.[4] Any decision made relating to his honesty in the matter under investigation is based on his truthfulness to both the critical and the control questions. This explanation serves to spell out what had only been assumed in the past—that is, the control questions are real threats to the innocent. When the controls are utilized in this manner, the innocent subject's attention is diverted from the relevant questions to the controls because he believes that detection of his deception to these items will result in his being labeled *guilty*.

When the control questions are applied in this manner, the polygraph examination discriminates truth from deception more readily. Nondeceptive subjects react to the control questions to a greater degree, and the procedure does not negatively influence the deceptive examinee's response to the relevant questions. Moreover, the concept of psychological set described in Chapter 2 becomes much more meaningful. The greatest threat to the guilty person's well-being is in the relevant question, but for the innocent, the threat lies clearly in the controls.

4. *The outside issue question*: This concept was developed by Backster in an attempt to determine whether some other factors might be impinging on the test, thereby distorting the results.[5] One such issue might be the examinee's fear that another crime, might be discovered. The usual question applied to deal with this is—"Are you afraid I'll ask a question that we didn't discuss?" If the subject demonstrates a larger reaction to this, the test is discontinued until this matter can be resolved in some manner. Once the individual is reassured that the polygraphist is only interested in the present charge, the examination can be continued. This is corroborated by his lack of response to the outside issue questions.

5. *The guilt complex question*: This question, which was discussed in

Chapter 2, is in actuality misnamed, for it probably does not relate to guilt, but serves to detect a person who is so anxious and fearful that he will respond to any accusatory question. As previously indicated, a fictitious crime is developed and presented to the subject in a highly realistic manner so that he believes that he is a suspect. If, in the testing, a large deceptive reaction occurs when he denies his involvement in this crime, it can be assumed that he will react to any accusatory question. The only conclusion that can be drawn from these findings is that the person is not a suitable subject for polygraph testing.

There are several basic criticisms of this technique. The first is that should the fictitious crime resemble one that the examinee actually committed, a large reaction will occur because he is being deceptive in denying it. A response would also occur if the subject became aware that the situation was not real or because he felt another charge was being placed against him. Due to these possibilities, there is now a very mixed reaction to the use of this approach. In a survey by this author, twenty-five polygraphists who were viewed as having accomplished something noteworthy in the field were polled as to their view of the guilt complex technique. Of the twenty-two who responded, eleven indicated that they do not use it because they see it as being of little worth. In contrast, the remaining eleven have found it of value and reported cases of innocent subjects who would have been diagnosed as deceptive if the examiner had not employed the approach. This author has found it to be a mixed blessing in that in the four instances in which large reactions occurred in response to the use of a guilt complex test, two were later verified as truthful and two as deceptive.

The only published study on the guilt complex test was carried out by Podlesny et al.[6] Their purpose, however, was to determine whether the guilt complex question was effective as a substitute for the control question as suggested by Lykken.[7] Podlesney et al. employed a mock crime paradigm, and their findings indicated that the use of the control question as a basis of comparison with the relevant question was more effective in differentiating truth from deception than the guilt complex approach used in the same manner.

As in any other field of study, there are a number of different schools of thought. With the exception of the relevant-irrelevant technique taught at the Keeler School, all of the approaches are essentially the same. They vary mainly in their question placement and in the number of control and relevant questions utilized. The following are the usual question series employed by the various schools.

Reid School:	Arther School:	Backster School:
1. Irrelevant	1. Irrelevant	1. Irrelevant
2. Irrelevant	2. Control	2. Sacrifice Relevant
3. Relevant	3. Relevant	3. Outside issue
4. Irrelevant	4. Relevant	4. Control

Reid School:	Arther School:	Backster School:
5. Relevant	5. Control	5. Relevant
6. Control	6. Guilt complex	6. Control
7. Irrelevant	(if appropriate)	7. Relevant
8. Relevant	7. Relevant	8. Outside issue
9. Relevant	8. Control	
10. Control		

In the Reid and Arther techniques, the relevant questions consist of queries relating to different aspects of the crime under investigation. For example, the relevant questions in the test might be:

Do you know who robbed the Safeway Store at 4th and Main?

Did you rob the Safeway Store at 4th and Main?

Do you know where the money taken from the Safeway Store is?

In contrast, the Backster approach uses two relevant questions that are basically the same with the only variation being in their wording. The questions related to the robbery would be phrased:

Regarding the robbery at the Main Street Safeway Store, did you participate in it?

Did you participate in the robbery at the Safeway Store on Main Street?

The purpose of directing the questions to only one narrow aspect of the crime under investigation is to avoid a competitive or distracting effect among the relevant questions. Should one of the questions present a greater threat to the suspect, he may react only to that question even though he had responded deceptively to all of the critical items. Backster labeled this phenomenom the anticlimax dampening effect.[8] The principle is essentially the same as that governing a reaction to a control versus a relevant question. The subject reacts to that question that generates the greatest threat. In a case involving an armed robbery, the following three relevant questions were asked in the sequence indicated:

4. On June 5th did you participate in the Oak Street State Market Robbery?
6. Did you hold the gun in the robbery of the State Market Store on June 5th?
8. Regarding the get away car used in the June 5th robbery of the State Market, did you drive it?

Each relevant question was paired with a control question, and the subject reacted to question 6 but none of the others. While he lied to all three items, a large response occurred only to 6 because it was clearly the most threatening to him. Results of this nature can be quite confusing because the subject obviously could not be truthful in his responses to questions 4 and 8 and lying on 6. Such results can also be rather difficult to explain in a courtoom, and thus there is a clear advantage in taking up only one issue in each test.

Backster also developed the concept of the super-dampening effect.[9] In this situation, the examinee's responses are blunted out of fear that the examiner might discover something else unrelated to the present investigation and probably of greater threat. For example, the test may be for the purpose of determining involvement in a burglary, but the subject may be much more concerned about a murder he committed two years before. This fear can cause a sufficient distortion of the tracings to result in a misdiagnosis. The outside-issue questions in the Backster system are an attempt at determining whether the examinee has concerns of this nature.

While differences do exist among the various approaches, there are definitely enough similarities for one examiner to be able to interpret the charts of another polygraphist with a high degree of agreement. The three schools discussed employ basically the same types of questions and utilize the comparison between control and relevant questions to determine their findings. The one exception is the Keeler School, which teaches the relevant-irrelevant technique.[10] In the past this approach has not employed a control question on the basis that predicting the impact of that question upon the subject was not possible and the comparison between it and relevant questions could be misleading. More recently, Harrelson indicated that control questions are being used.[11] The question format that had been previously described and is probably still in use by many former students of the Keeler School is as follows:

1. Irrelevant
2. Irrelevant
3. Relevant
4. Relevant
5. Relevant
6. Relevant
7. Relevant
8. Irrelevant
9. Relevant
10. Relevant

The Keeler technique utilizes what is termed a control stimulus question. The questions are specifically designed to elicit sympathetic arousal by their being phrased in an ambiguous or accusatory manner. The purpose is to determine whether the subject has the capability to react. When this capability is demonstrated in his response to other questions, employing the control stimulus is not necessary.

Within the several schools of thought, a number of techniques are utilized to serve specific functions. When a subject is unresponsive, overly reactive, or demonstrates an erratic performance, certain measures are employed to avert what could result in an inconclusive finding. The "stim," mixed question, and silent answer tests serve this function.

The purpose of the "stim" test is to demonstrate the ease by which the polygraphist can determine a lying response. Thus, it reduces the anxiety of the innocent while it increases the fears of detection in the guilty. As indicated earlier in this chapter, the subject is instructed to choose or write a number or name that he selects from a series, which is done without the polygraphist being aware of the number or name chosen. The subject is then told to respond "no" each time he is asked whether he chose each specific number or name listed in the series. Generally, the examiner is easily able to ascertain which response is a lie. Typically, this determination is made by evaluating the GSR tracings, which are much more sensitive to the procedure than the other components of the polygraph. The pattern is then interpreted like a POT test in that the deceptive response is usually either at the peak or at the point of highest reactivity. Figure 5-2 shows typical GSR tracings in a "stim" test. Note the flattening out of the reactions once the lie has been passed—like a sigh of relief. It should be noted again that neither Gustafson and Orne nor Barland and Raskin found increased accuracy in their research when their subjects were shown the effectiveness of the polygraph procedure.[1,2] In spite of this finding, most examiners strongly feel that the "stim" test accomplishes this very thing.

A second approach is the mixed question test. In this procedure, the questions are presented in a different order. No new questions are added, but some may be excluded, while others may be repeated several times within the test. The subject must be told prior to the test of the procedural change or else the reaction will be due to surprise rather than deception.

Reid and Inbau have indicated that the application of this approach increases responsivity, which makes for greater ease of differentiating truthful from deceptive responses.[13] In addition it allows the examiner to change the control-relevant comparison pair so that the relevant questions can be paired with different control questions. It also makes the polygraphist aware of any tendency of the subject to react to a question because of its placement, for example, early in the test, or because he is anticipating the question once he has learned the order.

In the silent answer test (SAT) the examinee is instructed not to respond verbally to the questions, but rather to think the correct answer.[14] This approach has been found to enhance the examinee's responsivity in both the SAT test and the subsequent test. It has the additional advantage of eliminating any changes in the tracings, generally in the pneumograph, that are due to the actual physical aspects of responding.

In a different category, the "yes test" promotes an opportunity for the

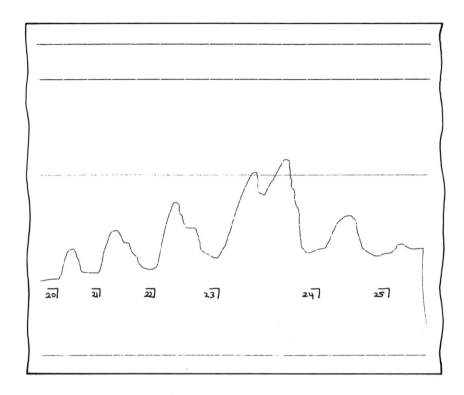

Figure 5-2. Typical GSR Tracings in a Polygraph "Stim" Test.

deceptive subject to attempt some countermeasures. The subject is instructed to respond "yes" to every question. In the case of the relevant questions, which should be developed so that the examinee is responding in the negative, saying yes is an admission. Many guilty persons tend to attempt some maneuvers to distort the test findings so as to appear truthful, especially in responses to this particular test. They expend considerable effort making their "yes" answer to the relevant question appear like a lie. Often, this attempt becomes blatantly obvious and can then be employed as a wedge in attaining an admission.

Regardless of the test that is used or the school that is followed, the polygraphist should adhere to a standardized approach that is acceptable to a large number of experts in the field. The questions should be formulated in a manner that is acceptable polygraph procedure, and the charts should be developed so that they can be readily interpreted by other examiners and can be clearly explained in court. To accomplish these goals, the chart markings must thus be understandable and universally accepted.

The chart should contain the name of the subject, date of the examination, and the name of the examiner. When the chart is in segments, the information, along with the subject's signature, should be placed on each portion. Which test in the series and the type of examination should be indicated immediately before the test begins. For example, the second chart in the first peak of tension test should be shown as POT 1 C2, and the first run of the second zone of comparison test would be labeled as ZOC II C1. The pressure at which the cardio was adjusted should be listed at both the beginning and end of each test as well as the level of sensitivity employed. Whether the galvanometer is placed on manual or self-balancing must be noted along with the setting used. The galvanometer, if it is set on automatic or self-balancing, results in the pen returning to the same base line after each reaction and is much easier to operate since it generally does not require an adjustment once it is set at the beginning of the test. Some polygraphists feel that valuable data is lost when it is operated in the automatic or self-balancing system. In the manual position, the pen operates in a free floating manner often requiring adjustments when it rises too high or drops too low.

The tracings of all the components can raise or lower to the extent that the pen is touching the pen stops and valuable data is lost as the upper and lower portions of the tracings are cut off. Changes in the position of the tracings must be made to avoid such losses, and these adjustments must be indicated on the chart with arrows to show the direction of change. Without these symbols, a possibility exists that these adjustments might be misinterpreted as the subject's physiologic reactions. A series of symbols are available to the polygraphists that are used every time an artifact occurs that could be reflected in the tracings. An "N" is utilized to indicate some noise that occurred at that point, while "CT" shows the subject cleared his throat. Employing these signs in this manner allows other examiners to differentiate between reactions related to deception and disturbances caused by some other factor.

Several different methods are used to indicate where a question was asked, but the most common is a horizontal line starting at exactly the point at which the question began and terminating with the end of the question. The number of the question is placed over or under the line, and a + or − is used to represent the subject's "yes" or "no" reply at exactly the point at which he responded. The value of the accuracy of these markings can not be overestimated since the subject's reactions as seen in the tracings must be exactly correlated with the asking of the question and his answer. Some instruments have marking pens that are activated by pressure on a button just as the question is asked and discontinued as the question is ended. This device allows for greater accuracy and enables the polygraphist, since he does not have to mark the chart, to be more aware of the examinee's behavior.

The use of accurately placed chart markings results in greater test validity and permits other polygraphists to score the charts with a high degree of reliability.[a] A clear set of rules is followed with almost universal agreement as to what changes in the tracings constitute a deceptive response. Each person, however, has his own characteristic pattern of sympathetic arousal, with some subjects tending to respond more in one area of measurement than another. Reactions should be registered consistently in all three components throughout each test, but this ideal pattern does not occur regularly. In one test there may be an extreme reaction, while in the next series of questions, the reaction may be minimal. Large changes may be demonstrated in the cardio section, but absolutely none in the GSR or pneumo pattern. Nevertheless, a consistent pattern will generally develop and a clear indication of truthfulness or deception will be obtained in all but about 10 to 15 percent of the charts.

A numerical scoring system should always be applied to the tracings for it unquestionably enhances objectivity, validity, and reliability. Moreover, the courts are beginning to expect this approach and recognize its value. There are several different systems, but Backster's approach will be described here since he was the first to develop the concept.[15] This description, however, will be a very simplified version of a long and detailed procedure.

The reaction to each relevant question is compared to its control question for each of the three components. In the zone of comparison technique, two relevant questions are compared with their two controls so that there are six comparisons made in the one test. If the test is administered three times, a total of eighteen comparisons are available. For each comparison, a seven-point scale is employed with numerical values on a continuum from +3 to −3.

The positive end of the scale is indicative of truthfulness, 0 denotes no decision, and the negative side indicates deception. Of the tracings of the three sensors, the GSR is the most easily scored. If the reaction to the control question is twice as large as that of the relevant question, a score of +1 is given. Reactions that are three and four times as great are scored +2 and +3, respectively. If the reactions were of the same magnitude but with the greater response occuring on the relevant questions, the scores would be the same but in the negative or deceptive direction. If the difference in reaction is not twice as large, regardless of the direction, no score is given.

In the cardio and pueumo components, the scoring criteria are less objective and are based on the comparative magnitude of the reaction between the control and relevant questions. If the reaction to the control question is clearly larger than the response to the relevant a score of +1 is given. A larger difference would be counted as a +2 and an extreme difference as a +3. (Again, note that this description is a simplified version and completely disregards the long and rather intricate set of rules devised by Backster.)

---

[a]The term *reliability* is used in the statistical sense and refers to the degree to which a number of examiners can score the same chart and achieve identical results or how often the same results are attained with repeated testings of the same subject.

A final decision is made by totaling the scores on two or more tests. A sum falling between +9 and −9 is considered inconclusive while a score that is greater than +9 is indicative of truthfulness and greater than −9 denotes deception.

Figures 5-3 through 5-14 will demonstrate characteristic patterns of sympathetic arousal typically indicative of deception. In the first series of charts, the tracings from each component will be shown individually, with question 1 being irrelevant; question 2, a control; and question 3, a relevant item. Some reaction can be expected to occur in response to every question, but whether the reaction will be greater to the control or relevant question is dependent upon the subject's truthfulness to the latter. Once again, it can be assumed that all subjects are responding deceptively to the controls, therefore, they all will react to that question. However, if they are lying to the relevant question, their fear of detection of that lie will be great enough to flatten out their reaction to the lie on the control question. The person who is deceptive to the relevant item will show a reaction to it, whereas, the person who is truthful to the relevant question will demonstrate a greater response to the control question.

Vertical lines may be positioned on the charts at five-second intervals. They can be utilized to measure the duration of the examinee's reaction as well as his rate of respiration and heart beat.

Figure 5-3 shows a typical GSR pattern with little reaction to irrelevant question one, but a large response to control question two. Since it is greater in both height and duration than relevant question three, the individual can be assumed to be nondeceptive in his response to the relevant question.

Figures 5-4 to 5-8 demonstrate deceptive patterns found in the respiratory tracings. In Figure 5-4 the breathing is quite rhythmic at question 1 in contrast to the suppression that is seen at question 2. This reduced intake of air is indicative of sympathetic arousal and evidence of deception. The increased amplitude of the respirations that follow it are necessary to make up for the reduced oxygen intake and is mistakenly judged to be a deceptive reaction because it can occur during the following question. In this case, by question 3 the subject's breathing has become more regular and indicates truthfulness to the relevant question.

A more extreme example of the suppressed breathing is shown in Figure 5-5, where respiration has actually stopped (apnea) for about five seconds at question 2. Another indication of a deceptive response is a change in the base line of the respirations as seen at question 2 in Figures 5-6 and 5-7. In Figure 5-8 a change in the breathing pattern in control question 2 is also suggestive of truthfulness to the relevant question.

Figures 5-9 and 5-10 demonstrate a deceptive pattern usually seen in the cardio component. In Figure 5-9 a large increase in the blood volume of the arm is reflected in the rise of the cardio tracings at question 2. Clearly, there is much greater sympathetic arousal in response to the control question than to the relevant item. In Figure 5-10, while a large reaction is shown in response to

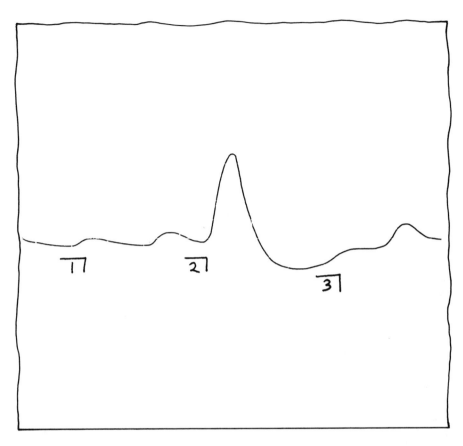

Figure 5-3. GSR Tracings Showing Greater Response to Control Question 2 than to Relevant Question 3.

relevant question 3, a comparison cannot be made between it and the control question 2 because of the movement made by the subject at point A. The difference in the tracings caused by a movement in contrast to changes due to sympathetic arousal is quite evident. It can be readily seen why attempts at distorting the tracings by purposeful movements in order to mislead the examiner are not effective.

The charts in Figures 5-11 through 5-14 are portions of tests that have been administered to criminal suspects. The upper two sets of tracings are the measures of thoracic and abdominal respiration, and beneath these are the GSR and then the cardio tracings. In order to avoid contact among the pens, the GSR pen is somewhat longer, which results in its appearing to record seven seconds earlier than the others. To avoid confusion to the reader, this measure has been

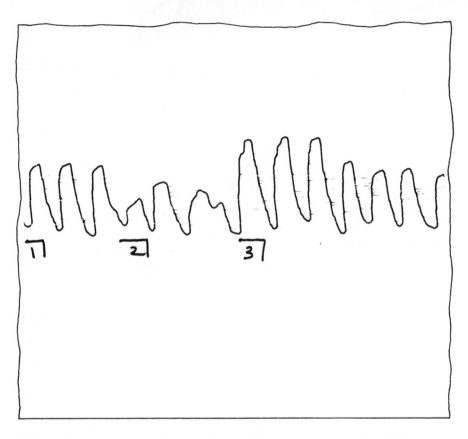

Figure 5-4. Respiratory Tracings Showing Deception at Question 2 (Suppression).

marked separately. The chart markings at the very top of the figure show where the question was asked, where the subject responded, and the numbers of the questions that appear in the lower portion for pneumograph and cardiograph recordings.

Figure 5-11 shows the tracings from a "stim" test, in which the numbers available to the subject ranged from 20 to 25. The numbers 19 and 26 were used as buffers at the beginning and end of the test. The examinee responded, as instructed, in the negative each time he was asked whether he had chosen each number and thus lied when asked the number he had actually selected. The test was administered twice, with the numbers being presented in reverse order the second time. On the first test, a base line change is seen in the upper pneumo and a suppression at the lower pneumo at the number 24. The very large rise in the GSR that occurs at 23 is followed by a lessor reaction at 24. After that, there is a sudden drop associated with the relief of having passed the critical

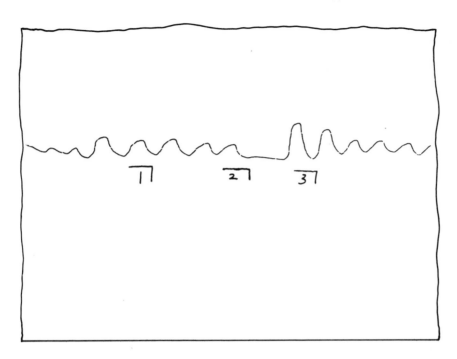

Figure 5-5. Respiratory Tracings Showing Deception at Question 2 (Apnea).

question. This drop suggests that 24 is the number on which he lied and that the reaction of the GSR to 23 relates to an anticipatory response. When this anticipatory pattern was tested by reversing the order, the anticipatory reaction on the GSR occurs at 25, while a large reaction continues to occur at 24 followed again by a downward trend. The very obvious suppression almost approaching an apnea (stoppage of breathing) at the lower pneumo at 24 corroborates the GSR findings.

The sign X̊ at the end of the test is where the subject was informed that the particular test would end. The arrow at the GSR at the first 23 indicates that the GSR was lowered at that point so that the next number could be asked.

In Figure 5-12 a portion of a zone of comparison test is shown. The order of the presentation has been changed but questions 6 and 4 are controls while 5 and 7 are relevant questions. In a comparison of 6 with 5 and 4 with 7, the GSR reactions to the relevant questions are considerably larger than the response to the controls in both amplitude and duration of response. On the cardio, the tracings have drifted down on 5 so that no comparison can be made between the first pair of questions. On the second set, however, a reaction to 7 results immediately after the subject recognizes the first few words of the question, while there is only a slight response to question 4. The lower pneumo on 5 demonstrates a suppression, which is also seen at 7 but for only one breath.

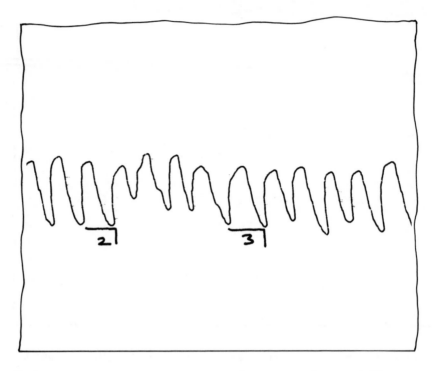

Figure 5-6. Respiratory Tracings Showing Deception at Question 2 (Change in Baseline).

A numerical scoring approach for control question 6 and relevant question 5 provides the following results:

pneumo	−2
GSR	−1
cardio	0 (unscorable)

A comparison of control question 4 with relevant question 7 provides these results:

pneumo	−1
GSR	−3
cardio	−1

It is not completely unusual to be unable to obtain a GSR on a subject, as was the case of the subject whose chart is shown in Figure 5-13. Nevertheless, by

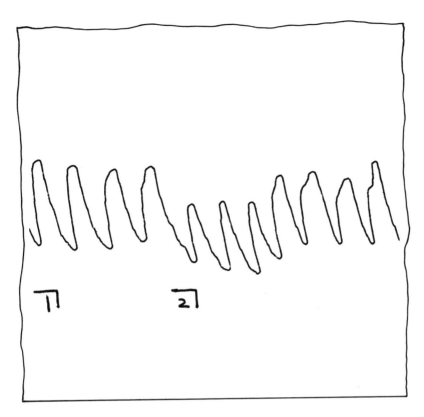

Figure 5-7. Respiratory Tracings Showing Deception of Question 2 (Change in Baseline).

comparing questions 6 and 9, a determination of deception can still be made. Note the large reaction seen in the cardio to relevant question 9 and the short apnea in both the upper and lower pneumo.

In Figure 5-14 a base line arousal is seen on question 8 at the upper pneumo and the large GSR, with a saddle-like effect, corroborates the indication of deception in the respiratory response. In contrast, however, a greater reaction is seen in question 5 on the cardio. Should these inconsistencies persist, a decision of inconclusive must inevitably result.

The charts presented show only some of the more obvious signs of deception. At times clear and consistent findings are attained from all three sensors, while at other times they disagree. On some occasions, no changes of any nature can be detected on one particular component. In the vast majority of cases, however, with the aid of some of the stimulating techniques, a diagnosis of deceptiveness or truthfulness can be made. Once the diagnosis has been made, the final stage of the examination—the posttest interview—can be initiated.

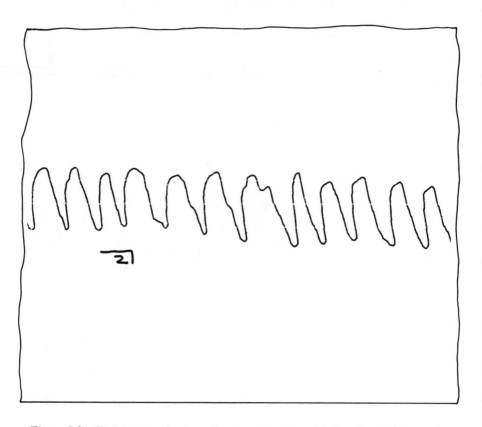

Figure 5-8. Respiratory Tracings Showing Deception at Question 2 (Change in Breathing Pattern).

The results of the polygraph test are discussed with the subject and if the findings indicate deception, an attempt is made to determine whether this result could have been due to any factor other than the fact that the subject had lied. If he can present a logical explanation, the questions can be reworded and the test readministered. In one such instance, a service station employee was tested to determine whether he had participated in the robbery of the station where he worked. The polygraph findings indicated that he was deceptive in denying involvement in the robbery. When the finding of deception was discussed with him, he admitted to having always hidden fifty dollars of the day's receipts on the possibility of being robbed. When a robbery had finally occurred, he had pocketed the money. When he was reexamined and the questions were phrased to exclude the fifty dollars, the findings were clearly indicative of nondeceptive responses.

In law enforcement settings, obtaining deceptive findings is generally

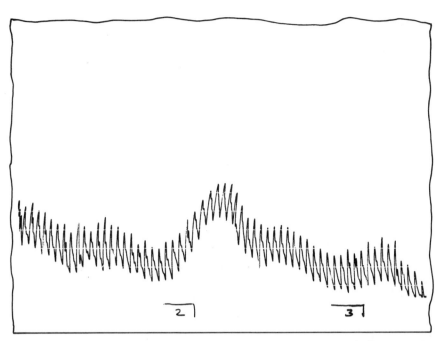

Figure 5-9. Cardio Tracings Showing Deception at Question 2 (Increase in Blood Volume and Relative Blood Pressure).

followed by interrogation. The polygraph results are then employed as a very effective wedge in obtaining an admission of guilt. The subject is shown his reaction to lying to a number on the "stim" test and then shown the same response on the questions related to the crime under investigation. This demonstration paves the way for his confession.

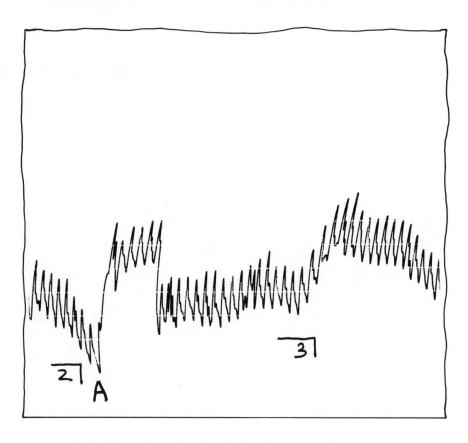

Figure 5-10. Cardio Tracings Showing Movement Response at A.

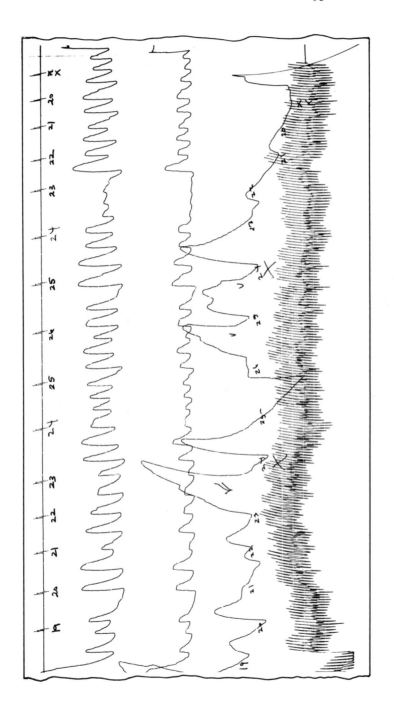

Figure 5-11. Stim Test Showing Deception at 24.

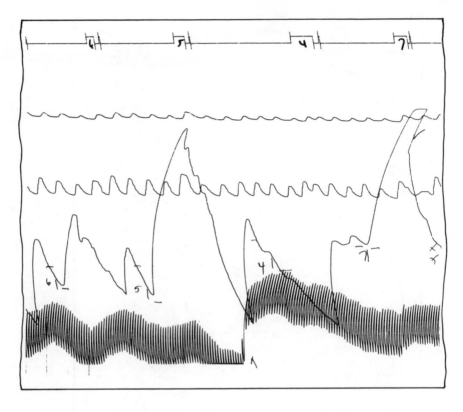

Figure 5-12. Zone of Comparison Test with 5 and 7 Relevant Questions.

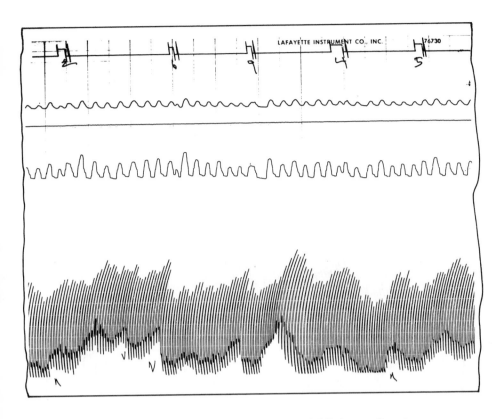

Figure 5-13. Mixed Question Test with 9 and 5 Relevant Questions.

96

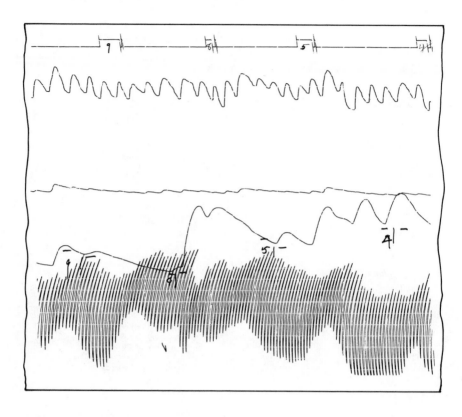

Figure 5-14. Inconsistent Findings in Mixed Question Test with 8 and 4 Questions Relevant.

Notes

1. Weinstein, E., Abrams, S., and Gibbons, D., "The Validity of the Polygraph with Hypnotically Induced Repression and Guilt," *Amer. J. Psychiatr.* 126 (1970): 143-46, and Bitterman, M.E., and Marcuse, F.L., "Autonomic Response in Post Hypnotic Amnesia," *J. Exper. Psychology* 35 (1954): 248-52.

2. Lykken, D.T., "Psychology and the Lie Detector Industry," *Amer. Psychologist* 29 (1974): 725-38.

3. Reid, J.E., "A Revised Questioning Technique in Lie Detection Tests," *J. Crim. Law, Criminol. and Amer. Police Science* 37 (1947): 542-47.

4. Abrams, S., "The Control Question Revisited: A Technique for Effective Introduction," *Polygraph* 5 (1976): 290-92.

5. Backster, C., "Outside Issue Factor," unpublished manuscript available through Backster School of Lie Detection, 645 Ash St., San Diego, Calif. 92101.

6. Podlesny, J.A., Raskin, D.C., and Barland, G.H., *Effectiveness of Techniques and Physiological Measures in the Detection of Deception*, Report No. 76-5, Contract 75-N1-99-001 LEAA, 1976 (available through Department of Psychology, University of Utah, Salt Lake City).

7. Lykken, "Psychology and the Lie Detector."

8. Backster, C., "Anticlimax Dampening Concept," *Polygraph* 3 (1974): 48-50.

9. Ibid.

10. *Keeler Polygraph Institute Training Guide, The Keeler Technique*, Chicago 1964 (available through Keeler Polygraph Institute, 160 East Grand Avenue, Chicago, Ill. 60611).

11. Marcy, L., Backster, C., Harrelson, L.H., and Reid, J.E., "Technique Panel" in N. Ansley (ed.), *Legal Admissibility of the Polygraph* (Springfield, Ill.: Charles C. Thomas, 1972), pp. 220-54.

12. Gustafson, L.A., and Orne, M.T., "Effects of Perceived Role and Role Success on the Detection of Deception," *J. Appl. Psychol.* 49 (1965): 412-17, and Barland, G.H., and Raskin, D.C., "An Experimental Study of Field Detection Techniques in Lie Detection," *Polygraph* 1 (1972): 22-26.

13. Reid, J.E., and Inbau, F.E., *Truth and Deception: The Polygraph ("lie detector") Technique* (Baltimore: Williams and Wilkins, 1966).

14. Horvath, F.S., and Reid, J.E., "The Polygraph Silent Answer Test," *J. Crim. Law, Criminol. and Police Science* 63 (1972): 285-93.

15. Backster, C., "Rules of Interpretation," (available through Backster School of Lie Detection, 645 Ash Street, San Diego, Calif. 92101).

6   Validity and Reliability

While the first scientific attempts to differentiate truth from deception began with Lombroso in 1895,[1] relatively little experimentation has been conducted in the more than eighty years that have followed. In part, this lack may relate to the considerable difficulty inherent in any attempt to ascertain the exact degree of validity of the polygraph approach or it simply may be due to the scientists' loss of interest in polygraphy as used in lie detection.

Efforts to determine polygraph accuracy have been carried out in actual criminal investigations (field studies) and in laboratory situations. In the latter, volunteer subjects have endeavored to deceive researchers in such varied situations as denying that they participated in a simulated crime to lying when questioned as to which number of a series they had selected. One very real difficulty associated with the use of varied paradigms is that different stimuli arouse varying emotional states, which in turn, cause dissimilar patterns of autonomic nervous system response.[2] Moreover, as demonstrated by Gustafson and Orne, different degrees of motivation affect people's reactions.[3] Those who were more motivated, were found to be more readily detected when they responded deceptively. Berrien indicated that the laboratory subject has little at stake in the research situation and thus is little concerned about his deceit being discovered.[4] In direct contrast, the criminal suspect literally bets his life, his freedom, and his reputation on his being able to "beat the test." These and many other factors make generalizing from laboratory research to the use of the polygraph in the investigation of criminal suspects rather risky.[5] Kugelmass and Lieblich have also emphasized that laboratory experimentation may have only limited generality for lie detection procedures in the field.[6]

Besides the relative lack of fear among laboratory subjects, there are additional factors that affect the experimental findings and inevitably diminish the accuracy of the laboratory research. Perhaps because of cost or time factors, most researchers have limited the number of polygrams obtained from each subject and employ only one procedure. In actual criminal investigations, the tests are repeated and the techniques varied until a clear picture of truth or deception is determined. Moreover, few experimentalists have utilized trained and experienced examiners for their research, which serves to further reduce the likelihood of their achieving a high degree of correct judgments. Laboratory studies also have been weakened by their use of instrumentation that is not only different from that employed in the field, but frequently equipped with fewer sensors.

99

While there are very basic limitations inherent in laboratory research, studies conducted in the field also have definite weaknesses. Because the subjects vary in their age, intelligence, education, and the crime of which they have been accused, the experimentation cannot be well controlled. More importantly, however, verification of the results through an external objective criterion is lacking in approximately 35 percent of the cases.[7] Confirmation of the findings is generally obtained through the confessions of the subjects themselves or others. There are some critics who argue that this source of validation is unreliable since an innocent, but suggestible person might confess or a person, though not guilty but fearing the court will find him guilty, confesses in order to plead guilty to a lessor charge. Other possible sources of verification, such as judicial decision, are probably even more subject to error than the admissions of suspects.

The research dilemma is all too obvious. Laboratory studies are unable to simulate the emotional and physiologic reactions of a criminal suspect, while field research cannot be well controlled nor the findings completely confirmed. There were, however, five investigations reported with large numbers of suspects and complete verification achieved. In 1921, Larson sought to determine which of one hundred women living together in a large hall was responsible for a series of thefts totaling about six hundred dollars.[8] After examining thirty-five of the women, all, with one exception, demonstrated a marked uniformity of response. This person was confronted with the findings and admitted to being involved in the thefts. In a second, rather similar case, Larson tested thirty-eight college women in an attempt to determine which of them had shoplifted a large amount of merchandise.[9] Once again, only one of the women had a polygraph record that was indicative of deception, and she confessed. She admitted that she had sold over five hundred dollars worth of books and other articles that she had stolen from stores and from her classmates.

While Larson employed a combination of measures of blood volume and respiration, Summers utilized a galvanometer.[10] He reported 100 percent accuracy in the examinations of forty-three criminal suspects. Confirmation was obtained through confessions, subsequent investigations, and judicial decision where additional evidence affirmed the results. Bitterman and Marcuse reported a case in which one hundred dollars was stolen from the room of one of eighty-one men living in a campus dormitory.[11] At a meeting, they all unanimously agreed that each of them would submit to a polygraph examination. The majority of the subjects evidenced a considerable degree of anxiety, but only seven of them demonstrated charts that were suggestive of deception. After a number of reexaminations, the investigators concluded that none of the eighty-one subjects was deceptive. These conclusions were later verified when someone outside of the dormitory was found to have been involved in the theft. In the final study, Winter investigated a series of thefts in a women's dormitory.[12] Polygraph examinations were conducted on the twenty-five residents, and the one chart showing signs of deception was identified. As in the other cases, she admitted her guilt.

In each of these instances, the guilty person was accurately diagnosed, while those not involved were determined to be nondeceptive. Complete accuracy was obtained in these cases. All of the other field investigations reported have only been able to confirm a portion of the cases that they have studied. In 1917, Marston using a discontinuous measure of systolic blood pressure, administered twenty examinations to criminal suspects for the Psychological Committee of the National Research Council.[13] Of the eleven cases in which confirmation was available, all of the judgments were found to be correct. He reported that he was able to distinguish not only truth from deception in the subjects' overall statements, but in various portions of their comments as well.

Utilizing only a galvanometer, MacNitt obtained 99 percent accuracy in 266 subjects, of which 59 had been accused of embezzlement and the remainder were laboratory subjects.[14] Inbau and Reid indicated that in the 4,093 subjects that they had examined, only three verified errors were found.[15] In addition, in their 1966 text, they reported that their known rate of error in over 35,000 examinations was less than 1 percent.[16] Of all examinees who had been found deceptive and whose diagnoses were confirmed, 97 percent were accurate.

Trovillo, in surveying nine law enforcement agencies, found that only two of them had compiled any data to indicate inaccurate findings.[17] In both these, a 2 percent error rate was reported. The statistics reported by Trovillo for the Chicago Scientific Crime Laboratory were that of 1,127 subjects who were tested, 40 percent were diagnosed as deceptive and 40 percent as nondeceptive, with the remainder of the diagnosed being inconclusive.[18] In those instances in which verification of the results was available, only 2 percent were shown to be invalid. Trovillo also reported that of the 2,171 individuals examined between 1935 and 1938 at the Crime Laboratory at Northwestern University, only twelve incorrect decisions were discovered.[19]

In a similar survey of statistics accumulated, McLaughlin indicated that the Polygraph Laboratory of the Texas Department of Public Safety had made correct judgments in 99 percent of the cases in which verification had been possible.[20] Forty percent of the subjects had been found deceptive and 45 percent truthful, while 15 percent of the tests were inconclusive. Of those subjects on whom deceptive findings were reported, admissions were obtained in 65 percent of the cases. Arthur stated that between the years 1948 and 1965 the known error rate was less than 1 percent.[21]

Unfortunately, these reports are of relatively little value insofar as they do not provide scientific evidence of the polygraph's validity. Information relating to how the data was gathered, what examination procedures were employed, and what criteria were utilized to verify the findings are lacking. Anecdotal descriptions provide little for the scientific community to evaluate or attempt to replicate in order to make a judgment of the validity of polygraph. Therefore, with the possible exception of the studies of Larson, Bitterman and Marcuse, and Winter described in the preceding paragraphs, no field examiner had demonstrated any clear evidence of the effectiveness of the polygraph procedure with criminal subjects.

At the time of the beginning of the Second World War, Wolfle reviewed the polygraph literature and communicated with those who had extensive experience in the field in order to determine whether the approach were feasible for use by the government.[22] His findings indicated that 90 percent accuracy could be achieved if the tests were conducted by competent and experienced examiners. In 1962 Orlansky also reviewed the literature and evaluated the statistics of governmental agencies.[23] In contrast to Wolfle's earlier findings, Orlansky indicated that because of the failure of the polygraph departments to collect objective data, the validity of the polygraph approach was not known and that considerable more research was needed. To clarify this issue, this author had also surveyed the literature of about the same time period as covered by Orlansky and found 81 percent accuracy for laboratory research and a reported validity of greater than 90 percent for verified cases in actual criminal investigations.[24]

There are field investigations that while they have some weaknesses, do provide evidence for the efficacy of the polygraph approach. In 1936, Lyon studied validity by randomly selecting and then evaluating one hundred juvenile cases.[25] While affirmation of the results was only available on forty of these subjects, everyone of these was found to be accurate. Holmes drew one hundred verified polygraph charts from the files of the Miami Police Department.[26] Of these, twenty-five were randomly selected and then evaluated by six polygraphists in law enforcement. Each rater was given only the numbers of the questions, which would allow him to determine which were the relevant, control, and guilt complex questions. An average accuracy at the 75 percent level was attained. After the initial rating, each examiner was then presented with additional data consisting of such information as the police report, statements of witnesses, and descriptions of the subjects' demeanor and behavior during the examination. With the availability of this additional material, the polygraphists' correct judgments increased to 83 percent. Holmes, indicating that 98 percent accuracy is achieved in examinations conducted by competent examiners, assumed from his findings that 75 percent was determined by an objective analysis of the tracings, while the remaining 23 percent was derived from an assessment of both the available information and the subject's behavior.

In an attempt to develop a criterion to verify polygraph findings other than through a confession, Bersh compared the polygraph results with the opinion of a panel of four army judge advocate general attorneys.[27] Each lawyer based his decision of guilt or innocence on a study of the case files of persons who had been the subject of criminal investigations by the military service. These cases had been drawn at random from a pool of criminal investigations in which polygraph tests had been conducted. The polygraph material, however, had been deleted from the files. With a total of 157 subjects, the extent of agreement between the polygraphist and a majority of the panel was 75 percent. When the panel's decision was unanimous in their verdict, the accord with the polygraphist was 92 percent.

Horvath and Reid also tried to eliminate the research problems associated with incomplete confirmation of results.[28] Their procedure like Holmes' was to choose a series of verified charts, but unfortunately, they were not randomly selected. In fact, some were rejected because they reportedly were too easily interpreted. Twenty verified truthful charts and twenty verified deceptive charts were evaluated by ten polygraphists. Seven of the polygraphists had been engaged in polygraph testing for over a year while three had been involved in the field for only a period between four and six months. None of the polygraphists were familiar with the charts, and the only information that was available to them was knowing the numbers of the control and relevant questions. The experienced polygraphists made correct judgments in an average of 91 percent of the cases in contrast to the 79 percent accuracy achieved by those with less experience. The average accuracy for the group as a whole was 88 percent. Considering that these blind interpretations were made without the benefit of any information or observation of the examinees, these statistics are rather impressive. Horvath and Reid indicated that if the polygraphists had been given the opportunity of reading the records, comparing the charts of subjects in related cases, or had observed the actual testing, the validity ratings would have been even higher. They also pointed out that the errors that were made tended to favor the guilty so that they were more likely to be diagnosed as truthful than the innocent labeled as deceptive.

In a similar investigation, Hunter and Ash selected ten verified truthful charts and ten verified deceptive charts for seven polygraphists to evaluate.[29] Six of the polygraphists had been in practice for more than a year and the seventh one for only four and a half months. They were each given a brief explanation of the type of case and informed as to which were the relevant and control items. The average accuracy found was 86 percent with a range from 83 to 90 percent. No difference was found in the ability of the inexperienced polygraphist in interpreting the charts as compared to those with greater experience. A difference was found between the results of the polygraphists who scored the charts blindly and the original examiner who attained complete accuracy. It was assumed that this higher success level was due to his having access to the background data and his being able to observe the subject's behavior during the testing. Unlike the Horvath and Reid study, the errors did not favor either the guilty or innocent.

Barland, following the design of the Bersch experiment, evaluated the polygraph results of seventy-seven criminal suspects through a comparison of these findings with the decision of a panel composed of five attorneys and judges.[30] With the exception of the polygraph data, the panel had access to all of the available information on each individual. The polygraph decisions agreed with the direction of the panel in 79 percent of the cases, but when unanimity of the panel existed, concordance increased to 83 percent. When a comparison of the polygraph decisions was made with judicial outcome, in those instances in which the court did not have access to this data, agreement was present in 90 percent of the cases. In contrast to both the Horvath and Reid and Hunter and Ash studies, the trend of the "errors" was in the direction of labeling as deceptive those subjects who the panel viewed as innocent. In view of the disparity of findings, the assumption is that the advantage to either the deceptive or nondeceptive subjects will vary with different examiners under different conditions, is in spite of the fact that it seems to this author that a guilty subject will react more strongly to a relevant question than an innocent individual will to a lie on a control question.

All of the field studies reported thus far have demonstrated a high degree of validity for the polygraph procedure. A recent investigation by Horvath, however, reported a lessor degree of accuracy.[31] A random sample of 112 polygraph charts, both verified and unverified, was drawn from the files of a law enforcement agency. These were evaluated by ten polygraphists, half of whom had less than three years of experience while the remainder had been in practice for more than three years. The average accuracy was 63 percent with no statistically significant difference between the two groups of polygraphists.

Horvath attempted to account for the low level of validity findings in a number of ways. The most logical would seem to relate to weaknesses in the polygraph technique of the original examiners. The polygraph procedure is primarily a psychologic approach and only secondarily does the subject's physiology play a role. The degree to which a person is physiologically responsive may be an inherent aspect of his makeup, but how much this response is demonstrated is dependent on the expertise of the examiner. Through various psychologic techniques, the examiner can generate a degree of responsiveness that can result in a set of tracings that are much more readily interpreted. Without the benefit of a well executed original test, even the most competent polygraphists will have difficulty in making an accurate judgment. Regardless of the reason, Horvath's findings are important in that they clearly demonstrate that high validity is not always obtained and that the approach is only as accurate as the examiner is competent.

While much of the early field research was not adequately designed or reported, some assumptions regarding validity can be made from some of the better investigations. Table 6-1 lists the studies described above and the percentage of accuracy reported. Although averaging all of the findings is a weak statistic, the mean accuracy of 91 percent presents a reasonable estimate of polygraph validity. Thus, a generalized assumption can be made that competent examiners can be expected to achieve accuracy at this level and higher. Those

Table 6-1
Accuracy of Polygraph Field Research

Investigator	Percent of Accuracy
Larson (1921 study)	100
Larson (1932 study)	100
Bitterman and Marcuse	100
Winter	100
Marston	100
Lyon	100
Holmes	83
Bersch	92
Horvath and Reid	88
Hunter and Ash	86
Barland	83
Horvath	63
Average Accuracy	91

operators who are less than competent may well score as low as in the 63 percent area as reported by Horvath.

Validity is a measure of accuracy showing to what degree the test measures what it purports to. Reliability, on the other hand, is described as an indication of consistency, or the degree to which the same results will be obtained on repeated testings of the same person or the frequency of which different polygraphists will achieve identical results on examining the same subject. These statistics are much more readily determined than validity since confirmed results are not necessary.

In the study by Bitterman and Marcuse, of the eighty-one theft suspects, two examiners were used to test and interpret the findings.[32] A third person was shown how the records were classified, and he too was to place them in one of four categories. Since the concept of the control question had not been developed at that time, a relevant-irrelevant technique was employed. In the first classification were placed those records in which there was no significant response to any question. The second category included those in which a significant response was seen to all or nearly all of the questions, but no major difference was found between the relevant and irrelevant items. This group was then divided into those with moderate and those with extensive nondifferential responses. The final group consisted of those subjects in whom a more pronounced reaction to the critical items was found in comparison to the critical questions. The two investigators placed each of the subjects in one of the four categories, and a week later, they independently reclassified them. A third judge was instructed in categorizing the examinees, and he too made an independent judgment of the eighty-one charts. The contingency coefficients of .96, .92, and .87 for each judge were statistically significant and indicative of a high degree of agreement.

Rouke, employing only a galvanometer, reported that two examiners were in agreement in 88 percent and 91 percent of their evaluations of two separate groups of subjects.[33] The twenty polygraph charts in Hunter and Ash's experiment were examined by seven polygraphists on two occasions spaced three months apart.[34] The records were presented to them in a different random order so that they were unaware that they were evaluating the same charts. Agreement on the two separate ratings was 85 percent and ranged from a low of 75 percent to a high of 90 percent. Barland had the seventy-seven polygraph charts in his experiment rescored six months after the original evaluation.[35] While there was a trend toward more inconclusive findings, a decision was never reversed. Eighty-four percent of the decisions remained the same. Horvath and Reid's study demonstrated considerable evidence of agreement, but unfortunately, no statistical study of reliability was reported.[36] In Horvath's investigation, the concordance among the ten evaluators regarding truthfulness or deception was high.[37] Reliability coefficients of .89 for the verified charts and .85 for the unverified records were found.

Considering the ease with which research on polygraph reliability can be conducted, the paucity of reported studies seems strange. Examiners would only have to draw a random sample from their files of criminal cases and have other operators evaluate them. Since the degree of accuracy would not necessarily be pertinent, there would be no need to select only verified charts, and thus the sample would be easily obtainable. Perhaps, an examiner feels an underlying threat exists in comparing his results with another examiner's, and this threat has acted to reduce the research.

Table 6-2 shows the reliability findings translated into percentages for the studies presented. The average rate of agreement for the field studies is at the 84 percent level, which is indicative of a fairly high level of reliability and is essentially the same whether examiners reevaluate their own records or the

Table 6-2
Reliability of Polygraph Field Research

Investigator	Percent of Consistency
Bitterman and Marcuse	84
Rouke	89
Hunter and Ash	85
Barland	84
Horvath	77
Average Agreement	84

charts are scored by other polygraphists. The usual qualifying phrase must preface any statement about either reliability or validity: The examinations must be administered by competent and experienced polygraphists; otherwise, lower levels of accuracy and consistency will result.

Although the experimentation in the field has been minimal, it has been bolstered by the findings in the laboratory. In studying reliability, Van Buskirk and Marcuse, employing fifty volunteer subjects, requested that each draw a playing card from among four cards on two separate occasions.[38] When they were tested on a Keeler polygraph, they were to lie regarding which card they had selected on the first set and to be truthful on the second series. Two examiners made a judgment as to where the deception occurred, and one month later they reevaluated the charts. The results indicated an 84 percent agreement between the two decisions. In a second phase of this investigation, 91 percent consistency was reported.

Utilizing a mock crime paradigm, Kubis had five examiners score the charts of 336 subjects that had been divided into groups of three consisting of a thief, lookout, and innocent suspect.[39] The percentage of agreement among the five examiners on all of the cases ranged from 72 to 87 percent, with an average of 79 percent.

Barland and Raskin also used the mock crime design with seventy-two subjects.[40] In an attempt to increase the motivation of the examinees to avoid their lies being detected, thirty-six examinees "stole" ten dollars and were instructed that they could keep the money if they were able to "beat the test." The researchers hoped that this approach would enhance the subject's motivation so that their responses would more closely resemble a population of criminal suspects. The test was administered to each subject three times, and the charts then were evaluated by six polygraphists who were not present during the examination. Considerable agreement was found between the findings of the actual examiner and those who blindly scored the tests. Ninety-six percent agreement was achieved by the six polygraphists.

The mean level of consistency for the three laboratory studies reported was 88 percent, which was somewhat higher than the findings in the field research.

The laboratory studies of polygraph validity vary greatly in design, instrumentation, and results. In some experiments, attempts have been made to simulate a crime situation, and as in Barland's research, or to motivate the examinee by rewarding him with money or punishing him with electric shocks. The majority, however, are rather straightforward experiments in which the role of the subject is to attempt to deceive the investigator with little or no loss if he fails. The interaction becomes very complicated, and discerning which motivations and affective states are involved is difficult. Conceivably, the volunteer subject is interested in aiding the experimenter by having his lie discovered or he may be quite indifferent to the whole process. These and many other factors, which include the subject's perception of the purpose for the experiment, can influence the results.[41]

Obviously, there are many psychological influences operating in actual criminal investigations as well. The examinee's expectations of the whole process of the polygraph examination have an important bearing upon his perceptions of the test situation. They in turn effect his emotional state and his physiologic responses. While the competent examiner can generally deal with these variables, he must be constantly on guard that his own prejudices or expectations are not communicated to the subject. Any undue emphasis on either the control or relevant question could easily cause a reaction that is completely unrelated to the truthfulness or deceitfulness of the subject. While a great deal of emphasis has been placed upon the physiologic aspects of polygraphy, it should be clear that these are quite secondary to the psychologic factors operating.

The laboratory research on polygraph validity must be considered in this vein also. The results of the investigations must be evaluated in line with the psychological impact upon the subject as well as the variation in design, instrumentation, and the expertise of the examiners. Marston's research, for example, was not conducted with contemporary instrumentation, but only with a single discontinuous measure of systolic blood pressure.[42] In his study 107 records were made on volunteer subjects who were either honest or deceptive in several story-telling situations. The experimenter was correct in his judgments on 103 charts and erred in 4, for an accuracy rate of 97 percent. Marston concluded that his technique was ". . . a practically infallible test of the consciousness of an attitude of deception." Langfield compared Marston's blood pressure procedure with the word-association technique.[43] He reported that the latter was not that effective, but Marston's approach easily detected the "guilty" in a mock crime situation. In an experiment in which Marston's approach was compared with Benussi's respiration ratio, Burt applied three different procedures.[44] The subjects were instructed either to respond truthfully or to lie in regard to which letter or digit they had chosen, in relating stories and in their role in a mock crime. In addition, observers were present who attempted to determine whether the subjects were honest on the basis of their behavior. Deception was determined far less effectively in the first two conditions and by the observational approach than in the simulated crime paradigm. Ninety-one percent accuracy was obtained in this condition through the blood pressure technique as in contrast to the 73 percent correct judgments made through an interpretation of the respiratory ratio. Landis and Gillette, however, reported only 55 percent accuracy employing the same mock crime design.[45]

Ruckmick had his subjects respond deceptively to three-letter monosyllabic words of low affective value and achieved 78 percent correct judgments.[46] This rate was increased to 83 percent when one judge was eliminated. His findings indicated that certain persons have a greater aptitude than others for making interpretations of this nature. In addition, he found that the speed and accuracy of the interpretations increased with practice. The former was affirmed by Marston.[47] In his investigation he had thirty-five subjects enter a room and, if they chose, take one or more of the fifty articles placed there. They were to attempt to convince the examiner that they took nothing, and if they accomplished this, they were permitted to keep whatever they took. Utilizing the blood pressure measure alone, fourteen examiners, none of whom had ever administered the test before, obtained an accuracy rate of 74 percent. One group of examiners, however, achieved perfect accuracy. To retest their evaluating ability, this group was given an additional ten subjects to rate, and again, they were completely successful in their diagnoses. Marston himself scored the records of the thirty-five examinees and was correct in thirty-four of the cases for an accuracy level of 97 percent.

The difference in aptitude among people for interpreting the tracings is certainly true for contemporary polygraphists as well, but there are other talents that are even more significant. Considering the complex interactions that take place between the examiner and the subject, the most important area of competence for the examiner lies in his ability to direct the fears of the innocent to the control items and the concerns of the guilty toward the critical questions. This aspect of testing is the art of polygraphy, while the interpretation of the tracings through a numerical scoring system is the science. An ability to score the charts is meaningless if the examinee does not respond appropriately, which, to a very large extent, is dependent upon the expertise of the examiner.

In a series of studies in which only the galvanometer was used, Summers reported that in six thousand laboratory cases and fifty criminal cases, 98 to 100 percent accuracy was achieved.[48] Unfortunately, there was little information presented that would indicate his procedures. MacNitt reported that in one-hundred and ninety-four experimental cases, seventeen laboratory subjects involved in simulated crimes, and fifty-nine criminal investigations, ninety-nine percent successful judgments were made with the galvanometer.[49] Like Summers' work, these statistics were presented in an anecdotal fashion so that the findings cannot be validated. Lykken, using the simulated crime paradigm with forty-nine subjects, reported accuracy in 94 percent of his cases, in which he employed only a measure of the galvanic skin response.[50] To enhance the examinee's motivation to avoid detection of their lies, he had applied an electric shock each time he successfully discovered their deception. In a second study, twenty subjects were trained and given practice in inhibiting their GSR responses, and in addition, they were offered ten dollars if they could "beat the test."[51] With this procedure, no errors were made in detecting deception despite the training and practice that the subjects had undergone.

Kugelmass et al. further tested the effectiveness of the GSR by having the subjects respond with a "yes" to all conditions, and then with a "no."[52] With twenty-seven subjects, the degree of validity obtained under both conditions was statistically significant at the less than 0.001 level. The percentage of accuracy, however, was only at the 70 and 60 percent levels, respectively. No statistically significant difference was found between the two conditions when the subject either responded truthfully or lied. Knowledge of the critical item is enough in itself to result in a physiologic reaction in spite of the fact that the subject is responding truthfully or not at all. Whether the reaction is caused by generalized excitement, fear of detection, conflict, or fear of the consequences in each situation is not known, but probably is a result of a combination of these, with the degree of each varying with each person and the situation.

In another investigation of the GSR, Davidson divided forty-eight subjects into twelve separate simulated crime groups.[53] Each of these was composed of four persons, three of whom were motivated by a reward to commit the act, but only one was successful. Of those who actually took part in the "crime," half were given a reward ranging from twenty-five to fifty dollars and the remainder were given less than one dollar. Of the other two who attempted the criminal act, one failed and one did not try. The fourth subject was an innocent suspect. The findings indicated that 92 percent of the "guilty" and 100 percent of the "innocent" were correctly classified. In contrast to Gustafson and Orne's research findings,[54] no significant differences were found between the two motivation groups.

Employing field polygraph instrumentation, Baesen et al. attempted to differentiate who of fifty pairs of college students had guilty knowledge and who had actually participated in a mock crime.[55] Correct judgments were made in 86 percent of the cases. Van Buskirk and Marcuse used a Keeler Polygraph to determine which of four cards was chosen by each of fifty subjects.[56] When two charts were administered, accuracy was at the 72 percent level, but with four charts, successful interpretations increased to 84 percent. When the indefinite charts were eliminated, accuracy reached the 92 percent level. In a comparison of the various sensors, Ellson et al. achieved 80 percent success with the GSR alone.[57] They also reported that changes in pulse rate, systolic blood pressure, and breathing amplitude occurred with deception, while little difference was found in diastolic blood pressure and rate of respiration. Accuracy was increased with the number of charts administered with 50 percent success after the first testing, 62 percent following the second examination, and 79 percent accuracy at the completion of the third test.

In Kubis' 1963 study, which was discussed earlier under reliability, he also carried out a series of well-organized validity studies in which mixed results were obtained.[58] He employed a mock crime situation in which the subjects were assigned the roles of thief, lookout, and innocent suspect. Five examiners with three months of training but no experience rated the charts. Their average accuracy was 78 percent, but there was a considerable difference in the competency of the various evaluators. The operator with the lowest level of success was correct in 73 percent of his judgments, while those with a greater aptitude for this task achieved 92 percent accuracy. Since the examination time was only twenty minutes and the test was only administered twice by completely inexperienced examiners without the use of control questions, the results are fairly impressive. Their success level did improve as they became more experienced.

In the second phase of the Kubis investigation, a group of criminal offenders on parole acted as subjects. They were informed that the purpose of the examination was to ascertain how various groups reacted to being asked embarassing questions. The examinees had already been told to respond in the negative to any queries related to their criminal backgrounds since the experimenters had no right to such information. The twenty-three parolees were asked two questions about the criminal offenses that they had committed and two questions about criminal acts in which they were assumedly not involved. The five examiners who interpreted the charts fared quite poorly in detecting the two questions to which the examinees actually lied. In the first test, the five judges were able to detect both lies in an average of seven subjects, one lie in thirteen of the subjects, and missed both lies in three of them. In the second examination, five examiners were correct on both lies in a mean of five examinees, detected one lie in fifteen subjects, and were incorrect on both lies in three of the subjects. These findings, however, are complicated by the fact that the parolees were given permission to lie to those questions and therefore had little fear of the consequences if the deception were discovered. Some questions must also be raised as to the possibility of the subjects' actually having been involved in criminal activities similar to those that were used in the control questions and were assumedly not to have been committed by the subjects. Both of these factors could considerably reduce the validity findings of this investigation.

In the third and final procedure of the Kubis study, twenty-six government workers, prior to the research, were given what they were told was classified information. Two questions related to this information were asked in the examination. The examiners did even more poorly in this phase of the investigation: They detected both lies in an average of five subjects, one lie in nineteen, and none in two. The results were essentially the same for the second test.

In another study, Blum and Osterloh studied the effectiveness of the polygraph procedure from the perspective of its use by law enforcement agencies to differentiate true from false items of information presented by actual informants.[59] A total of twenty informants were instructed as to which of two stories to tell. Some of these had been verified as being completely truthful, others were simply made up, and the third category was composed of both truthful and fabricated elements. Using a Stoelting polygraph, the examiners were able to determine which stories were either completely or partially deceptive, and also when the stories were completely truthful. While the polygraphists were not able to detect every deceptive statement, they were able to determine one or more false statements in every story which contained deception. The researchers were satisfied with these results and indicated that the use of the polygraph was a practical approach to determining the veracity of informants since a law enforcement agency will investigate an informant's statement if they find that he has not been completely truthful.

In Barland and Raskin's study, a mock crime design was employed with seventy-two subjects, thirty-six of whom were "guilty" of "stealing" ten dollars and an equal number of whom were "innocent."[60] In order to increase the motivation of the "guilty" subjects to attempt to deceive the examiners, they were informed that they could keep the money if they were successful in doing so. Eighty-one percent of the cases examined, excluding those with inconclusive ratings, were correctly classified. An additional six polygraphists evaluated the charts without having seen the actual examinations and were successful in judging 79 percent of the cases. The "guilty" subjects were detected with fewer errors than the "innocent" ones.

The findings of the laboratory research are generally indicative of high validity, but not at the same level as has been reported for field investigations. Because of the great variety of research designs that have been used, it would be most difficult to present any statement of the general level of accuracy obtained in the laboratory studies. The accuracy does range from a chance level of detection to a level approaching complete success. It is unlikely that a research design will ever be developed that will result in the same affective state that exists in a criminal investigation, and because of that, the same level of validity will not be achieved.

The many claims that people with certain medical, psychiatric, or physical conditions are untestable have generally not been found to be true. Psychopaths, for example, were typically described as unfit subjects, although the logic beghind this statement is not quite clear.[61] People within this diagnostic category may be devoid of conscience and guilt, but there is no reason to assume that other emotional states, such as fear, conflict, or generalized excitement, are lacking. It is even conceivable that with their strong needs for immediate gratification and excitement, imprisonment might be an even greater threat to them than to other people. In an attempt to clarify this issue, Barland and Raskin studied seventy-seven criminal suspects on which polygraph tests were conducted and who had taken portions of the Minnesota Multiphasic Personality Inventory (MMPI).[62] A comparison was made of those fifteen subjects who had the highest score on the scale for psychopathy with those fifteen who scored at the lowest level. No difference in detectability between the two groups was found. The overall accuracy reached was 85 percent—excluding the inconclusive tests.

These findings were corroborated by a study by Raskin, who administered polygraph examinations to forty-eight inmates of a prison facility.[63] The subjects were diagnosed as psychopathic and nonpsychopathic according to the presence or absence of certain personality traits. Those subjects who were to "steal" twenty dollars were informed that they could keep the money if they were able to mislead the examiner. The "innocent" subjects were to be given twenty dollars if they could demonstrate their innocence through the polygraph procedure. Ninety-six percent of the subjects, excluding those with inconclusive tests, were correctly categorized. The two errors made involved "innocent" subjects who were misdiagnosed as deceptive. One of these was in the psychopath group and the other was in the nonpsychopath classification. The four inconclusive examinations all were obtained from the nonpsychopathic population. These results rather emphatically demonstrate that psychopaths are as easily and accurately examined as other subjects.

Several experiments have been conducted on psychotics in an attempt to determine whether they can be accurately evaluated with the polygraph technique. This author examined twenty hospitalized schizophrenics, half of whom were randomly placed in a control group.[64] The other ten subjects were each instructed to take five quarters and informed that they could keep the money if they denied receiving it and were successful in deceiving the polygraphist. While this amount of money seems like a small reward, it had considerable meaning for them since they had no money at all.

Three peak of tension tests were administered—twice to each subject. The following is typical of the tests:

1. Regarding the money that was taken, do you know whether it totaled $ .50?
2. Regarding the money that was taken, do you know whether it totaled $ .75?
3. Regarding the money that was taken, do you know whether it totaled $1.00?
4. Regarding the money that was taken, do you know whether it totaled $1.25?
5. Regarding the money that was taken, do you know whether it totaled $1.50?
6. Regarding the money that was taken, do you know whether it totaled $1.75?

While tests of this nature should be relatively easy to interpret, particularly since three were administered, this was not the case. Inconclusive charts were not eliminated from the study because there would have been only a few charts that could have been scored. Three polygraphists rated the records and obtained a mean accuracy of 67 percent. The average degree of agreement among the three examiners was 71 percent.

In a second investigation of psychotics, Heckel et al. examined five normal persons and compared the accuracy found with five psychotic and five neurotic subjects.[65] Four polygraphists accurately diagnosed all of the normal subjects, 75 percent of the neurotics, and 45 percent of the psychotics. No inconclusive charts were reported for the normal subjects but 20 percent of the neurotic group's charts and 35 percent of the psychotics' were inconclusive. Excluding these inconclusive cases, the authors report 87 percent of the neurotics were accurately diagnosed and 69 percent of the psychotics. Perfect agreement existed among the polygraphists in their evaluation of the normal subjects but the reliability decreased as the degree of emotional disturbance increased. These findings indicate the need to avoid the testing of the psychotic population in order to maintain a high level of validity and reliability. The validity of the neurotic population, however, was not reduced to the extent that testing of these persons is precluded.

Abrams and Weinstein reported on the only experimentation carried out on polygraph validity with retardates.[66] The subjects ranged in IQ from 12 to 75. Of the sixteen subjects, nine fell below the intellectual level of IQ 64, and they were completely untestable. While the two polygraphists were in complete agreement as to their findings of the remaining subjects, their accuracy was only at the 71 percent level. As is the case with psychotics, polygraph testing of retardates should be avoided. Further discussion of those persons who are considered unfit subjects for polygraph examination will be presented in Chapter 8.

Another measure of validity, but one that would not meet the stringent requirements of science, is the "general use principle." While this principle does not deal with accuracy in any meaningful statistical terms, it does present an indirect estimate of polygraph effectiveness. There is considerable usage of this technique by governmental agencies to uncover security leaks and to detect criminal activities. Bailey reported that Robert Brisentine had conducted over 50,000 examinations for the armed services and none of those who had been found to be nondeceptive were ever prosecuted in a military court.[67] Polygraphy is also utilized to a very great extent by law enforcement agencies as an investigative tool. Police departments often use it, in addition, as a means of screening their applicants so as to be certain that they have no criminal backgrounds.[68]

Another rather unusual employment of the polygraph is in the area of probation and parole.[69] These offenders can remain outside of prison, if they are willing to take periodic polygraph examinations that inquire into any areas of possible illegal activities. If they respond deceptively to their denials of activities in theft, drugs, and so forth, they must then complete the sentence that had been given them.

A final area in which there is considerable use of the polygraph technique is in business and industry. Estimates are that theft losses to business approach four billion dollars annually, with 60 to 75 percent of this loss being attributed to employee theft. Although most of these losses are passed on to the consumer in the form of increased prices, it has been estimated that employee theft is the principle cause of business failure.[70] Polygraphy has been so effective in reducing employee thefts through the periodic testing of employees that the demand for this service is constantly growing. The degree of accuracy of the procedure as used in business is not known, but what very definitely does occur is that when employees know that they will be examined periodically, they stop stealing.

In summary, the research findings indicate that both the accuracy and consistency of polygraph results can be quite high if the examinations are conducted by competent examiners. The exact degree of accuracy will probably never be known because of the limitations inherent in both laboratory and field experimentation. If, however, the accuracy of those unverified criminal cases can be assumed to be close to the findings for the confirmed cases, the polygraph technique can be considered to be one of the most accurate of all of the psychologic procedures.

Notes

1. Lombroso, C., *Crime, Its Causes and Remedies,* Modern Criminal Science Series (Boston: Little, Brown, 1905).

2. Lacey, J.I., "Psychophysiology of the Autonomic Nervous System: Master Lecture on Physiological Psychology" (tape), American Psychological Association (1200 17th Street, N.W.), Washington, D.C. 20036, August 1974.

3. Gustafson, L.A., and Orne, M.T., "Effects of Heightened Motivation on the Detection of Deception," *J. Appl. Psych.* 47 (1963): 405-11.

4. Berrien, F.K., "A Note on Laboratory Studies of Deception," *J. Exp. Psych.* 24 (1939): 542-46.

5. Abrams, S., "The Polygraph: Laboratory Vs. Field Research," *Polygraph* 1 (1972): 145-50; Orne, M.T., "Implications of Laboratory Research for the Detection of Deception," *Polygraph* 2 (1973): 169-99; and Barland, G.H., and Raskin, D.C., "The Use of Electrodermal Activity in Psychological Research," in W.F. Prokasy and D.C. Raskin (eds.), *Electrodermal Activity in Psychological Research* (New York: Acadamy Press, 1973).

6. Kugelmass, S., and Lieblich, I., "Effects of Realistic Stress and Procedural Interference in Experimental Lie Detection," *J. Appl. Psych.* 50 (1966): 211-16.

7. Abrams, S., "Polygraph Validity and Reliability: A Review," *J. Forensic Sciences* 18 (1973): 313-26.

8. Larson, J.A., "Modification of the Marston Deception Test," *J. Crim. Law and Criminol.* 12 (1921): 390-99.

9. Larson, J.A., *Lying and its Detection* (Chicago: University of Chicago Press, 1932).

10. Summers, W.G., "Science Can Get the Confession," *Fordham L. Review* 5 (1939): 334-54.

11. Bitterman, M.E., and Marcuse, F.L., "Cardiovascular Responses of Innocent Persons to Criminal Interrogation," *Amer. J. Psych.* 60 (1947): 407-12.

12. Winter, J.E., "A Comparison of the Cardio-Pneumo-Psychograph and Association Methods in the Detection of Lying in Cases of Theft among College Students," *J. Appl. Psych.* 20 (1936): 243-48.

13. Marston, W.M., "Psychological Possibilities in the Deception Tests," *J. Crim. Law and Criminol.* 11 (1921): 551-70.

14. MacNitt, R.D., "In Defense of the Electrodermal Response and Cardiac Amplitude as Measures of Deception," *J. Crim. Law and Criminol.* 33 (1942): 266-75.

15. Inbau, F.E., and Reid, J.E., *Lie Detection and Criminal Interrogation* (Baltimore: Williams and Wilkins, 1942).

16. Reid, J.E., and Inbau, F.E., *Truth and Deception: The Polygraph ("lie detector") Technique* (Baltimore: Williams and Wilkins, 1966).

17. Trovillo, P.V., "Scientific Proof of Credibility," *Tenn. L. Rev.* 22 (1953): 743-66.

18. Trovillo, P.V., "Deception Test Criteria: How One Can Determine Truth and Falsehood from Polygraphic Records," *J. Crim. Law and Criminol.* 33 (1942-43): 338-58.

19. Trovillo, P.V., "A History of Lie Detection," *J. Crim. Law, Criminol., and Police Science* 29 (1939): 848-81.

20. McLaughlin, G.H., "The Lie Detector as an Aid in Arson and Criminal Investigation," *J. Crim. Law and Criminol.* 43 (1953): 693-94.

21. Arthur, R.D., *The Scientific Investigator* (Springfield, Ill.: Charles C. Thomas, 1965).

22. Wolfle, D., *The Lie Detector: Methods for the Detection of Deception*, Confidential Report to the Emergency Committee in Psychology, October 8, 1941 (available through the University of Washington, Seattle).

23. Orlansky, J., *An Assessment of Lie Detection Capability*, (declassified version), Technical Report, 62-16, Contract SD-50, Task 8, July 1964. Institute for Defense Analysis, Arlington, Va.

24. Abrams, "Polygraph Validity."

25. Lyon, V.W., "New Deception Tests," *J. Genetic Psych.* 48 (1936): 494-97.

26. Holmes, W.D., "The Degree of Objectivity in Chart Interpretation," in V.A. Leonard (ed.) *Academy Lectures on Lie Detection* (Springfield, Ill.: Charles C. Thomas, 1965).

27. Bersh, P.J., "A Validation Study of Polygraph Examiner Judgments," *J. Appl. Psych.* 53 (1969): 399-403.

28. Horvath, F.S., and Reid, J.E., "The Reliability of Polygraph Examiner Diagnosis of Truth and Deception," *J. Crim. Law, Criminol. and Police Science* 62 (1971): 276-81.

29. Hunter, F.L., and Ash, P., "The Accuracy and Consistency of Polygraph Examiners' Diagnoses," *J. Police Sciences and Admin.* 1 (1973): 370-75.

30. Barland, G.C., "Detection of Deception in Criminal Suspects: A Field Validation Study," unpublished doctoral dissertation, University of Utah, Salt Lake City, 1975.

31. Horvath, F.S., "The Accuracy and Reliability of Police Polygraphic (Lie Detector) Examiners' Judgments of Truth and Deception: The Effect of Selected Variables," unpublished doctoral dissertation, Michigan State University, School of Criminal Justice, East Lansing, 1974.

32. Bitterman and Marcuse, "Cardiovascular Responses."

33. Rouke, F.L., "Evaluation of the Indices of Deception in the Psychogalvanic Technique," unpublished doctoral dissertation, Fordham University, New York, 1941.

34. Hunter and Ash, "The Accuracy and Consistency."

35. Barland, "Detection of Deception."

36. Horvath and Reid, "The Reliability."

37. Horvath, "The Accuracy."

38. VanBuskirk, D., and Marcuse, F.L., "The Nature of Errors in Experimental Lie Detection," *J. Exp. Psych.* 47 (1954): 187-90.

39. Kubis, J.F., *Studies in Lie Detection Computer Feasibility Considerations*, RADC-TR, 62-205, Fordham University, New York, June 1962.

40. Barland, G.H., and Raskin, D.C., "An Experimental Study of Field Techniques in 'Lie Detection'," *Polygraph* 1 (1972): 22-26.

41. Orne, M.T., "On the Social Psychology of the Psychological Experiment, With Particular Reference to Demand Characteristics and Their Implications," *Amer. Psych.* 17 (1962): 776-83.

42. Marston, W.M., "Systolic Blood Pressure Symptoms of Deception," *J. Exp. Psych.* 2 (1917): 117-63.

43. Langfield, H.S., "Psychophysical Symptoms of Deception," *J. Abnormal Social Psych.* 15 (1920-21): 319-28.

44. Burtt, H.E., "The Inspiration-Expiration Ratio During Truth and Falsehood," *J. Exp. Psych.* 4 (1921): 1-23.

45. Landis, C., and Gullette, R., "Studies of Emotional Reactions: III Systolic Blood Pressure and Inspiration-Expiration Ratios," *J. Comparative Psych.* 5 (1925): 221-53.

46. Ruckmick, C.A., "The Truth About the Lie Detector," *J. Appl. Psych.* 22 (1938): 50-58.

47. Marston, "Psychological Possibilities."

48. Summers, "Science Can Get the Confession."

49. MacNitt, "In Defense of the Electrodermal Response."

50. Lykken, D.T., "The GSR in the Detection of Guilt," *J. Appl. Psych.* 43 (1959): 385-88.

51. Lykken, D.T., "The Validity of the Guilty Knowledge Technique: The Effects of Faking," *J. Appl. Psych.* 44 (1960): 258-62.

52. Kugelmass, S., Lieblich, I., and Bergman, Z., "The Role of Lying in Psychophysiological Detection," *Psychophysiology* 3 (1967): 312-15.

53. Davidson, P.O., "Validity of the Guilty Knowledge Technique," *J. Appl. Psych.* 52 (1968): 62-65.

54. Gustafson and Orne, "Effects of Heightened Motivation."

55. Baesen, H.V., Chung, C.M., and Yang, C.Y., "A Lie Detector Experiment," *J. Crim. Law and Criminol.* 39 (1948): 532-37.

56. VanBuskirk and Marcuse, "The Nature of Errors."

57. Ellson, D.G., David, R.G., Saltzman, J.A., Burke, C.J., *A Report of Research on Detection of Deception*, Contract No. N6 ONR-18011, Office of Naval Research, September 15, 1952 (available through University of Indiana, Bloomington).

58. Kubis, "Studies in Lie Detection."

59. Blum, R.H., and Osterloh, W., "The Polygraph Examination as a Means for Detecting Truth and Falsehood in Stories Presented by Police Informants," *J. Crim. Law Criminol., and Police Science* 59 (1968): 133-37.

60. Barland and Raskin, "An Experimental Study."

61. Levitt, E.E., "Scientific Evaluation of the 'Lie Detector'," *Iowa L. Rev.* 40 (1955): 440-58. Floch, M., "Limitations of the Lie Detector," *J. Crim. Law and Criminol.* 40 (1950): 651-52.

62. Barland, G.H., and Raskin, D.C., "Psychopathy and Detection of Deception in Criminal Suspects," presented at the Society for Psychophysiological Research, Salt Lake City, Utah, October 25, 1974 (available through the Department of Psychology, University of Utah, Salt Lake City).

63. Raskin, D.C., *Psychopathy and Detection of Deception in a Prison Population*, Report, No. 75-1, Contract 75 NI, 99-0001, Department of Psychology, University of Utah, Salt Lake City, Utah, June 1975.

64. Abrams, S., "The Validity of the Polygraph with Schizophrenics," *Polygraph* 3 (1974): 328-37.

65. Heckel, R.V., Brokaw, H.C., Salzberg, H.D., and Wiggins, S.L., "Polygraphic Variations in Reactivity between Delusional, Nondelusional, and Control

Groups in a 'Crime Situation'," *J. Crim. Law and Criminol.* 53 (1962): 380-83.

66. Abrams, S., and Weinstein, E., "The Validity of the Polygraph with Retardates," *J. Police Sciences and Admin.* 2 (1974): 11-14.

67. Bailey, F.L., *For the Defense* (Chicago: Signet, 1975).

68. Arthur, R.O., "Screening of Law Enforcement Personnel," *J. Polygraph Studies* 6 (1971): 1-4.

69. Riegel, L., "Court Use of Polygraph in Probation Programs," *Polygraph* 3 (1974): 256-68. Partee, C.E., "Probation and the Polygraph," in N. Ansley (ed.), *Legal Admissibility of the Polygraph* (Springfield, Ill.: Charles C. Thomas, 1975), pp. 31-39.

70. Barefoot, J.K., *The Polygraph* Story, published by The American Polygraph Association, New York, 1974 (available through Cluett Peabody Co., 510 5th Avenue, New York 10036).

7

The Legal Status of the Polygraph

The pathway to the admissibility of polygraph testimony in the courtroom has taken an arduous and circuitous route that has been considerably longer than for other forms of scientific evidence. Breath intoxication devices, radar, ballistics, and even psychiatric testimony have been more readily accepted. They, however, have been admitted under a different set of standards than polygraphy.

In 1923, the Frye decision set the precedent for rejecting lie detection testimony on the basis of its lack of acceptance in the scientific community.[1] For years the courts declined to accept polygraph evidence for this reason. McCormick indicated that while general scientific acceptance is a proper condition for courts taking judicial notice of scientific facts, such acceptance is not a criterion for the admissibility of scientific evidence.[2] Judicial recognition is given a particular approach when it has demonstrated a reasonable measure of precision and is accepted in its particular profession. If these standards are met, testimony may be received without establishing a foundation because the court sees the approach as sufficiently reliable to dispense with requiring proof. The evidence concerning its reliability must be generally known to the trial judge, although he does not actually have to know the facts. It should be possible to determine through the literature that it is accepted by the profession to which it belongs. A more modern concept of judicial recognition accords approval upon the acceptance of those in the field who are utilizing or studying a given approach, in spite of the fact that the group as a whole is unfamiliar with it.[3]

In direct contrast to the lack of acceptance of polygraphy, most new scientific techniques are not held to the general acceptance standard. The only requirement of the majority of scientific evidence considered by the courts has been that its scientific principles be supported by expert testimony demonstrating that it is sufficiently valid to insure probative value. Had admissibility of polygraph evidence been based on its value as an aid to the jury, instead of demanding judicial notice, as has been the case with other scientific techniques, polygraph testimony would have gained admission years ago. Facts having rational probative value are admitted if the testimony assists in establishing a particular issue, unless the evidence acts in some manner to mislead or prejudice the jury, impair the right of cross-examination, or preempt the fact-finding province of the jury.

Polygraphy should be subject to the same rules of admissibility as any other scientific evidence. If it does not pass the test of judicial recognition, the facts then must be decided by a jury with the help of expert testimony. Any pertinent data that is supported by qualified experts should be received into evidence.

With scientific evidence of a more exact nature, in which there is less likelihood of error, the courts have been more lenient in their requirements.[4] While they were at first unwilling to accept radar findings without foundation testimony from an expert witness, some states rather rapidly passed statutes recognizing radar technology as sufficiently accurate to be received without foundation. The instrument, however, has to be shown to be in proper working order, and the operator must be qualified as having adequate training and experience. He does not have to be skilled in electronics or possess highly specialized knowledge.

In contrast to radar, a greater chance of error was seen as existing for breath intoxication devices. More was required of the operator than the mere operation of the instrument which could result in an increased opportunity of human error. In addition, such variables as the presence of physical illness and how long ago the alcohol had been ingested could alter the results. Because of these factors, evidence based on this procedure was not admitted quite so readily as was the case with radar devices, and acceptance by the courts has not been uniform in all jurisdictions. In general, however, the same pattern of acceptance did develop over time.

With the exception of *People* v. *Kenny* in 1938,[5] the courts have generally ruled lie detection testimony inadmissible. In the Kenny case, a trial court admitted lie detector evidence on behalf of the accused. Reverend Walter Summers, chairman of the Department of Psychology Graduate School of Fordham University, employed a galvanometer to examine the defendant. His findings were that he was truthful in his denial of participating in the robbery with which he was charged. Summers testified that his approach was 100 percent accurate when used with persons accused of committing a criminal act. The court permitted the jury to consider the findings over the objection of prosecution, and Kenny was acquitted. Since there was no appeal, the appelate court did not rule on the lower court's decision. In the same year, the defendant in *People* v. *Forte* requested an examination by Reverend Summers in an attempt to prove that the defendant was not involved in the murder of which he was accused.[6] The request was denied by the trial court, which indicated that the validity was not sufficiently established to warrant judicial acceptance. This decision was later affirmed by the New York Court of Appeals.

Developing a sound argument for the admission of polygraph testimony, however, was hampered by the difficulty in determining on what basis the technique was being rejected in the courts. Sell stated that the failure to be accepted by the sciences had an important bearing on the decision of the courts against admitting polygraph evidence.[7] In addition, he indicated that the instrument, techniques, and theory were not standardized. The procedure also was seen as only dealing with deliberate deception, which afforded little protection in those instances in which the subject was reacting because of suggestion or imagination or not responding because of memory loss.

Langley, on the other hand, believed that the two major reasons for exclusion were lack of scientific recognition and the paucity of qualified examiners.[8] In contrast, Silving implied that there was a more philosophical explanation for the rejection of this approach.[9] She saw the real issue as lying in the conflict between truth and dignity. The body, she indicated, could be subject to examination under appropriate conditions, but the freedom of the mind and will must be preserved. Richardson, however, stated that the real reason for the inadmissibility of polygraph evidence was that the technique directly attacked or affirmed the credibility of the witness, thereby usurping the jury's function.[10]

The courts have also varied in their motives for refusing to admit polygraph results. *Bowen* v. *Egman*[11] and *Rawlings* v. *State*[12] relied on the lack of acceptance in the scientific community that had been presented in the Frye decision. In *U.S.* v. *Urquidez*, polygraph evidence was ruled inadmissible because too many variables were involved that would produce a burden on the court because of the endless argument and cross-examination.[13] The lack of preparedness of the examiner was cited in *U.S.* v. *Lanza*;[14] the lack of experience of the polygraphist was cited in *State* v. *Tavernier*;[15] and the failure of the defendant to establish foundation evidence through the testimony of experts and scientists was the justification given for the ruling in *U.S.* v. *Wainwright*[16] and *U.S.* v. *Chaslian*.[17] In *U.S.* v. *Wilson*, polygraph evidence was ruled inadmissible because of the probability of error due to a lack of professional standards, particularly since the examination was administered by a friendly examiner.[18] It was believed that the findings would be less reliable since the subject knows the results will be kept in confidence if he is found deceptive. In somewhat the same vein, polygraph evidence was rejected in *U.S.* v. *Stromberg* on the basis of the testimony's being self-serving hearsay: Since the instrument cannot be cross-examined, its testimony was viewed by the examiner as being the " . . . most glaring and blatant hearsay."[19]

Lack of reliability was a frequent reason stated for refusal to admit polygraph evidence, as was cited in *Skinner* v. *Commonwealth*,[20] *Boeche* v. *State*,[21] and *People* v. *Becker*.[22] In *People* v. *Leone*, the court stated that there was no firm proof that lying produced physical reactions, and if it did, these responses would not be sufficiently universal to allow for standard measurement.[23] The court also emphasized that there are gradations of truth that are influenced by memory, perception, physical condition, and state of mind and are measured by an instrument that deals only with a "yes" or "no" response.

The soundness of the underlying theory of polygraphy was also questioned in *State* v. *Bohmer*,[24] while in *People* v. *Davis*[25] and *People* v. *Sinclair*,[26] the polygraph evidence was seen as an undue influence upon the jury. In fact, it was felt to have so much impact on the jurors that it was ruled inadmissible in

Henderson v. *State* because the court believed that the question would rest on the credibility of the examiner rather than on the major witness.[27]

A Committee on Polygraphy of the New Jersey Supreme Court concluded that the jurors would consider polygraph evidence as being infallible and, if it were offered in evidence, would draw unfavorable conclusions.[28] There was also concern that a battery of experts would be called and would cause confusion and consumption of time with their conflicting opinions. Another frequently expressed opinion is that the admission of polygraph testimony would constitute a violation of the Fourth and Fifth Amendments. Other criticisms relate to the lack of technical improvements;[29] the risks of "beating the test"; the inappropriateness of authorizing admission on behalf of the defendant but not the state;[30] and the possibility of unethical examiners. From the Frye decision until the 1940s, the courts continued rejecting polygraph evidence for a wide variety of reasons.

In 1943 in *Lefevre* v. *State*, a stipulation was established between the district attorney and the defendant to admit the polygraph findings.[31] Nevertheless, the trial court excluded this evidence. On appeal, it was held that the court had properly ruled against admissibility. While the court held that the exclusion was proper, it reversed the conviction on the grounds that there was not sufficient evidence to prove the defendant guilty beyond a reasonable doubt. Of interest is the fact that the court cited the polygraph findings as one of the reasons for reversing the decision. Polygraph findings were also excluded in *Pulaski* v. *State*,[32] *People* v. *Zazetta*,[33] and *Colbert* v. *Commonwealth*[34] in spite of stipulations by both parties to admit the results. In 1974, the Supreme Court of Nebraska held that an agreement with prosecution that a defendant will not be prosecuted if he passes a polygraph test is not enforceable absent the trial court's approval.[35] It was also indicated in *State* v. *Davis*[36] and *Butler* v. *State*[37] that court approval may be needed for agreements of this nature with prosecution to be binding.

In contrast to these decisions, other courts have ruled that the argument is binding on prosecution when truthful findings are attained[38] and when the government has agreed not to prosecute if the tests are favorable. It is a pledge of public faith that cannot be disregarded.[39]

In a kidnapping and assault case in 1947, *State* v. *Lowry*, prosecution was permitted to introduce polygraph testimony relating to both the complaining witness and the defendant, over the objection of the defendant.[40] While the defendant was found guilty, the Supreme Court of Kansas reversed the trial court's decision by holding that the polygraph had not gained scientific recognition. It was indicated, however, that its value as an investigative tool was amply demonstrated. A year later, in *People* v. *Houser*, the first appellate decision was made to admit polygraph test results in evidence.[41] The accused was charged with committing a sexual offense against a child, and an agreement was made between the opposing sides to obtain a polygraph examination on the defendant and admit the results regardless of the outcome. The findings were indicative of deception regarding his denial of the accusation, but after conviction, the guilty verdict was appealed on the basis that the polygraphist was not an expert in his field. The California District Court of Appeals affirmed the trial court's decision.

In 1949, in *Boeche* v. *State*, an agreement was made by the prosecution with the defendant that if he were found truthful on a polygraph examination the charges against him would be dropped.[42] The trial court found that this agreement was not binding on the state, and the case was appealed. The Nebraska Supreme Court, in agreement with the trial court's decision, stated that admitting the polygraph testimony would impair cross-examination. Admission was also denied on the grounds that the test was not infallible, had not received general scientific recognition, and would be too difficult for an untrained jury to evaluate. Nevertheless, Justice Chappell, the dissenting member of the Nebraska Supreme Court, stated that it was time for judicial acceptance of polygraph testimony based on a demonstration of the examiner's qualifications and scientific acceptance of this approach.

In *People* v. *Wochnick*, the defendant was charged with murder.[43] The trial court permitted the polygraphist to testify to both the conversation held with the accused and his test results, but the judge instructed the jury to disregard the latter. The California Court of Appeals reversed the conviction and indicated that the trial court had erred in allowing the examiner to testify.

Stone v. *Earp*, a nonjury trial in 1951, related to both the defendant's and plaintiff's claiming they owned a particular vehicle.[44] The trial judge refused to make a decision until a polygraph examination was administered to both parties. The findings indicated that the plaintiff was deceptive, and the court found in favor of the defendant. On appeal, the Michigan Supreme Court indicated that the court had erred because the polygraph findings were not competent evidence regardless who requested them. The higher court, nevertheless, did not reverse the trial court's decision because the polygraph testimony was not found prejudicial due to the preponderance of evidence supporting the trial court's decision.

At about this same time period, 1953, Inbau and Reid stated, in their text on polygraphy, that the procedure was not ready for judicial acceptance.[45] Their reasons were related to insufficient standardization of instrumentation, test technique, and examiners' qualifications. Some polygraphists were viewed as being incompetent and a few as actually dishonest. In 1966 their view changed, and they indicated that competently conducted examinations should be admitted into evidence.[46] They did emphasize that the court should require that the examiner possess certain requisites. These included a college degree, six months of internship, five years of experience, and his testimony be based on polygraph charts that are presented in court for the purpose of cross-examination. Reid and Inbau also recommended that the court instruct the jury that the examiner's findings are not to be viewed as conclusive, but should be considered along with the other evidence.

In 1960 in *State* v. *McNamara*, the Iowa Supreme Court upheld the stipulation to admit polygraph results.[47] The defendant had been charged with murder, and an agreement had been made prior to the trial among the defense and prosecution attorneys and the defendant to admit the polygraph findings. The test results indicated deception, and the defendant objected to the admission of the testimony on the grounds that the polygraph was not reliable. The trial court permitted the testimony, and its admission was affirmed by the higher court. In the case of *People* v. *Valdez*, the defendant was accused of possession of narcotics. Prior to the trial, the opposing attorneys and the defendant entered into a stipulation for a polygraph examination to be administered and for the admission of the results into evidence. The polygraph findings showed the accused to be deceptive, and although the defense objected to the testimony, it was admitted by the trial court and later upheld by the Arizona Supreme Court, which indicated that polygraph results were sufficiently probative to admit under stipulation. The Arizona Court also developed a series of procedures for the admission of polygraph findings under stipulation that have been used as an example for the cases that followed:

1. The county attorney, defendant, and his counsel all sign a written stipulation providing for defendant's submission to the test and for the subsequent admission at trial of the graphs and the examiner's opinion thereon on behalf of either defendant or the state.
2. Notwithstanding the stipulation, the admissibility of the test results is subject to the discretion of the trial judge, i.e., if the trial judge is not convinced that the examiner is qualified or that the test was conducted under proper conditions he may refuse to accept such evidence.
3. If the graphs and examiner's opinion are offered in evidence the opposing party shall have a right to cross-examine, with the examiner respecting: (a) the examiner's qualifications and training; (b) the conditions under which the test was administered; (c) the limitations of and possibilities for error in the technique of polygraphic interrogation; and (d) at the discretion of the trial judge, any other matter deemed pertinent to the inquiry.
4. If such evidence is admitted, the trial judge should instruct the jury that the examiner's testimony does not tend to prove or disprove any element of the crime with which a defendant is charged but at most tends only to indicate that at the time of the examination the defendant was not telling the truth. Further, the jury members should be instructed that it is for them to determine what corroborative weight and effect such testimony should be given.[48]

In 1963 the Illinois Supreme Court in *People* v. *Zazzetta* refused to accept a stipulation to a polygraph examination because the polygraphist did not testify and was not available for cross-examination.[49] Prosecution did not offer any evidence of his qualifications, which the court recognized as being intimately related to the validity of the approach.

While the cases described above illustrate the beginning of a trend to admit polygraph testimony on a stipulated basis, there are nevertheless many instances in which polygraph results have been ruled inadmissible. In *State* v. *Chavez* in 1969, the rule in New Mexico at that time was not to admit polygraph findings even if a stipulation had been developed was upheld.[50] In the appeal before the New Mexico Court of Appeals in December 1970, the court found that since the defendant had stipulated to the test and its admissibility and the results had been presented before the jury without objection, its admission constituted a waiver and did not provide grounds for reversible error. Polygraph testimony was admitted on stipulation in *State* v. *McDavitt*.[51] On appeal, the higher court affirmed the trial court's decision to admit the testimony because the defendant failed to attempt to exclude the results and because polygraphy had reached the point of reliability that a stipulation should be given effect.

Polygraph evidence was admitted over objection in *U.S.* v. *Oliver*.[52] The lower court allowed the admission of polygraph testimony which resulted in a conviction of rape. The U.S. Court of Appeals concurred and concluded that the polygraph testimony fell within the category of relevant evidence, which was defined as any evidence having a tendency to make the existence of any fact that is of consequence to the determination of the action more probable. Admission of the evidence was not seen as a violation of the defendant's civil rights, as he had contended, because the examination cannot be administered without the full cooperation of the examinee. The taking of the test was viewed as tantamount to a waiver of constitutional rights if adequate warnings are given. In *State* v. *Stanislawski*[53] in 1974, the State of Wisconsin reversed the rule against admissibility laid down in *State* v. *Bohner*[54] in 1933, forty-one years before. The court indicated that polygraphy has attained the standing and scientific recognition to preclude unconditional rejection of this testimony.

While polygraph testimony was ruled inadmissible in *U.S.* v. *Wainwright*, the court reported that there was evidence that the technique and instrumentation had considerably improved and markedly so in the last ten years.[55] There was a question related to the minimal standards that exist for examiners, but it was felt that a court-appointed polygraphist could be a solution to this problem. Polygraph testimony was not received in *U.S.* v. *Lanza*, but the court indicated that it could be admitted with proper foundation and at the discretion of the judge.[56] Since 1972 there has been a tendency to recognize polygraph evidence on a case-by-case basis if a proper foundation has been established. The Wainwright case is considered the turning point that resulted in automatic exclusion of testimony because of the defendant's failure to have an expert testify to its acceptance within the profession and to its validity. Numerous courts have routinely admitted polygraph evidence after a foundation had been established. Kaplan has indicated that there is widespread acceptance of polygraphy at the trial level, but since these cases are not appealed, they have not been reported.[57]

Tarlow has pointed up the fact that the polygraph approach is now admitted on stipulation because it has been demonstrated to have high validity.[58] He questioned, however, why a stipulation made polygraphy more acceptable since it did not enhance the test's accuracy nor effect it in any manner except to be certain that both parties will accept the examiner. In consideration of these factors he recommended that polygraph evidence should be admitted over objection as well.

In the 1970s, both federal and state courts have admitted polygraph testimony over objection. In *U.S.* v. *Zeiger*, it was admitted, but later rejected with no opinion given.[59] The defendant had been charged with armed assault and attempted to introduce the results of a polygraph examination administered by a District of Columbia police officer prior to his arrest. On the advice of his counsel, before the test he had signed a written stipulation indicating that the results would be introduced as evidence. The court held an extensive evidentiary hearing and then ruled the results admissible. Judge Parker, in making this ruling, indicated that the approach is now accepted by authorities in the field. He also noted that scientific study has been carried out and continues at this time, and the device has been confirmed to be effective in detecting deception. He saw its extensive use by law enforcement agencies, governmental security organizations, and private industry as corroborating its efficacy. Polygraphy was seen as being a profession in that it had a national professional organization, schools, publications, standards for qualifications, and yearly seminars. The accuracy of the approach was viewed as high, and because of these factors, Judge Parker believed it produced highly probative evidence in a court of law when the test had been properly conducted by a competent, experienced examiner. Any danger of having too great an impact on the jury, he felt, could be dealt with by the trial judge. By preparing the jury prior to the polygraph testimony, Judge Parker believed that they would be able to evaluate the polygraph testimony properly.

In *U.S.* v. *DeBetham*, the defendant was apprehended at the Mexican-American border in a car in which five grams of heroin were found.[60] He denied any knowledge of the presence of narcotics in the vehicle and submitted the results of a polygraph test as evidence. The prosecution opposed the admission of such evidence. After extensive evidentiary hearings, Judge Thompson indicated that the standard set for the admission of polygraph evidence is artificially high and that the judicial process would be sufficiently protected if the normal standard for the admission of scientific evidence were employed. It was recognized that many advances had been made since the Frye decision, and polygraphy had achieved the status of a department of systematized knowledge. Research was being conducted and polygraphy had something to add to the administration of justice. The court concluded that when a polygraphist qualifies before the court as an expert, he should be permitted to present foundational evidence to demonstrate its reliability and probative value.

In the DeBetham case, Judge Thompson found the polygraph approach to be sufficiently valid to warrant a finding of probative worth. Potential error lay within the province of the examiner, the condition of the subject, and the test conditions, but a competent examiner could eliminate problems in these realms. It was concluded that the probative value of the polygraph had been established. The court did not feel that there was a danger of the polygraph displacing the jury nor that the right to privacy would be violated. In spite of these findings, Judge Thompson relied on the rulings in other federal court decisions and elected to exclude the polygraph testimony. He admitted that there was no precise standard applied by the court of appeals in upholding the exclusion of polygraph evidence, but he ruled against admission on the basis of the defendant's not demonstrating that the polygraph had complied with the test of general acceptance.

In the *U.S.* v. *Ridling*, a perjury case, the defendant offered polygraph testimony as evidence of the truthfulness of his statements.[61] Judge Joiner concluded from the evidentiary hearing that the psychological basis for the polygraph was well established and that there was considerable usage of this approach by governmental agencies, law enforcement, and industry. Reliability was reported to be higher than that of ballistics experts and as high as the opinions of fingerprint experts. Concerns related to excessive weight being given to the polygraph testimony by the jury did not seem justified, and in fact, it was felt that the relevancy was high and its use would protect both society and the defendant. While it was felt that only minimal standards exist for polygraph examiners, it was believed that a court appointed polygraphist would eliminate this weakness. Taking the examination and admitting the findings as evidence was not seen as a violation of the privilege against self-incrimination. Employing the polygraph technique, it was believed, would result in fewer cases reaching trial, in that more cases would be dismissed and a probability of pleas being increased. These indirect results of polygraphy were viewed as beneficial to the innocent and to society, and polygraphy testing would serve to eliminate many cases from the court. No concern was felt that the jury would be too influenced by the polygraph findings because Judge Joiner believed that juries were much more aware and knowledgeable than in the past and able to evaluate the evidence appropriately. He did feel, however, that the statements supported by the opinion of the polygraphist appear to be hearsay, but indicated that this evidence could be admitted as an exception to the hearsay rule because of its high degree of trustworthiness. Accordingly, the polygraph evidence was admitted into evidence.

Another of the federal cases that admitted polygraph· testimony heard before a jury was *U.S.* v. *Dioguardi*.[62] The defendant, charged with falsifying a loan application, claimed that the handwriting was not his, while another person admitted that it was he who had filled out the form. The defendant attempted to introduce polygraph testimony on both himself and the other person. Judge Weinstein ruled that if the two men agreed to submit to an examination by a court-appointed examiner, the results would be admitted. The test findings on both men were found to be truthful, and the government agreed to a dismissal of the charges.

In *U.S.* v. *Hart*, another case heard by a jury, two former federal narcotics agents were accused of soliciting bribes.[63] The principal government witness, a confessed narcotics dealer, revealed that he had taken a polygraph examination at the request of the government. When the court learned that the findings were indicative of deception, he ordered the results disclosed to the jury without holding an evidentiary hearing. The government dismissed the indictment with no appeal. This case was different from most in that the test had been conducted on a witness rather than the defendant.

Some state courts have also admitted unstipulated polygraph evidence. In *State* v. *Alderete* in New Mexico, the court ruled that polygraph testimony was admissible at the court's discretion, but a proper foundation must be established.[64] The examiner must be qualified and the test used must be acceptable to his profession and be reasonably precise. In the Alderete case, the defendant was not allowed to enter the polygraph results because only the results, not the charts, were presented. The findings, therefore, were viewed as hearsay evidence. In this instance, the polygraphist did not qualify to testify, and the testimony did not establish that the polygraph was accepted as a scientific technique in the expert's profession.

The circuit court of the eleventh judicial court for Dade County, Florida, in *State* v. *George Curtis* allowed a defendant's motion for the admissibility of the results of two polygraphists.[65] One examination was conducted by an examiner selected by the defendant, while the other was administered by a court-appointed expert. The court indicated that in future cases, polygraph opinions would be admitted if a stipulation were requested by the defendant. If the state rejects the stipulation, the defendant may apply to the court who will appoint one or more qualified examiners.

In *People* v. *Cutter*, the court allowed the polygraph to be used at the pretrial stage in a suppression hearing.[66] The defendant had been charged with possession of Marijuana. The arresting marshall admitted that he had no warrant to search the defendant's bags, but he claimed that he had his consent.

The court concluded from an evidentiary hearing that the science of polygraphy had developed more sophisticated instrumentation, standard procedures, training of examiners, and had made great and significant advancements in the last ten years. Recent laboratory and field research had established that reliability and validity had exceeded 90 percent and it was seen as accepted by researchers and examiners and among psychologists and physiologists. The polygraph was also being employed by defense and security agencies of the government. The judge indicated that the courts have sufficient authority to control and limit the introduction of polygraph testimony so that an emphasis will not be placed upon it. The court, in consideration of these findings, elected to accept the polygraph findings and granted the motion to exclude the marijuana seized.

In a similar suppression hearing in Oregon in 1976, polygraph evidence was also admitted over the objection of prosecution.[67]

The Massachusetts Supreme Court in *Commonwealth* v. *A Juvenile* in June of 1974 allowed the admission of polygraph evidence without stipulation.[68] The court held that under certain circumstances and at the prerogative of the trial judge, polygraph examination results will be admitted into evidence.

In *State* v. *Donna Sonnie* in the Court of Common Pleas for Lake County, Ohio, the court ruled that the testimony of two polygraphists would be admitted, but conditioned its ruling on the defendant's taking another examination by an examiner selected by prosecution and subject to the approval of the court.[69]

A set of five rules were developed in New Mexico for the admissibility of polygraph evidence in court in the case of *State* v. *Lecaro:*[70]

1. Both parties would stipulate to the test and its admission as evidence.
2. No objection to its admission would be offered at trial.
3. The court would hear evidence of the qualifications of the examiner to establish his expertise.
4. Testimony to establish the reliability of the testing procedure would be heard to determine whether it is approved by authorities in the field.
5. Validity of the tests would be established.

A year later, in *New Mexico* v. *Dorsey* on February 12, 1975, the court found that the first two requirements listed above were impossibly restrictive,[71] and thereby opened the door to admitting polygraph evidence over objection.

In New York in 1972 the Niagara County Commissioner of Social Service filed a paternity suit on behalf of a welfare mother. The court allowed the defendant to introduce into evidence the results of a polygraph test that showed that the woman was lying in her claim that the defendant was the only man with whom she had sexual relations prior to the child's birth. In this case, *Stenzel* v. *B.*, the court indicated the difficulty in obtaining reliable testimony in paternity suits and its favorable experience in making a judgment through pretrial orders of a polygraph examination.[72] The polygraph approach was not seen as a substitute for judge or jury, but only an aid in making a decision. The court, on hearing the polygraph testimony, concluded that the plaintiff was lying and dismissed the case.

Polygraph evidence was admitted in a New Jersey trial court in *State* v. *Watson* in a posttrial motion on sentencing.[73] The defendant had been found guilty of contributing to the delinquency of a minor. Prosecution had submitted an affidavit indicating that the complaining witness stated that the defendant had threatened her life. In order to bolster his denial of this accusation, the defendant offered the results of a polygraph test that had been conducted by the state. The court agreed to admit the results to show facts not decided by the trial jury nor material to their deliberations. No problem was seen in utilizing polygraph evidence in a nontrial situation where the issue to be determined related to sentencing.

After fifty years, polygraph testimony appears to be approaching acceptance in the courts, that is somewhat comparable to other scientific evidence. Such acceptance is certainly not universal, for some courts still refuse to admit polygraph evidence even on a stipulated basis. The Georgia Court of Appeals on February 25, 1975, in *Famber* v. *State*, in which polygraph results had been stipulated, found this evidence inadmissible and having no probative value.[74] While many courts have ruled against admission,[75] in many jurisdictions polygraph testimony on a stipulated basis has been readily admitted,[76] and there is a definite indication that the courts are beginning to admit over objection.

The use of the polygraph approach in other countries varies considerably. In November of 1972, in Ottawa, Canada, the case of *Phillion* v. *Her Majesty The Queen* was heard. The defendant, who was charged with the murder to which he had earlier confessed, denied the truthfulness of this admission and sought to have polygraph testimony admitted to verify this claim. The court, however, ruled that this was inadmissible as evidence, and on appeal this decision was upheld by both the Ontario Court of Appeals and in 1977 by the Supreme Court of Canada. More recently, in November 1976, polygraph testimony was again admitted in the Province of British Columbia. In the Supreme Court of British Columbia in the case of Her Majesty the Queen against William Wong, the court admitted polygraph testimony over objection in a murder case.[77] The court concluded that the emotion-body reaction sequence has been established; the body responses are to a degree autonomic; the responses can be measured; and the control question technique seems to bring fairly accurate results where a positive result is attained. Some doubt was found related to the degree to which the polygraph has been accepted as a scientific instrument or technique among psychophysiologists.

It is of interest in the Wong case that while the polygraph findings indicated that the subject was truthful in his denial of any involvement in the murder with which he was charged, he was found guilty in spite of this.

Abrams reported that in Japan the polygraph is an accepted investigative tool that has been received in evidence by the lower courts since 1959 and more recently has been admitted by the Japanese Supreme Court at the discretion of the judge.[78]

The polygraph also has been admitted into the courts in Poland, where there is no ruling by the high court to prohibit its admission. It is employed in Yugoslavia and admitted by the Swiss courts, but there it cannot be the only evidence in the case. There is also an indication that in the Soviet Union, attitudes based on the research findings arguing against its usage in the past have now changed.[79] Barland and Raskin have reported that it is known to be used in

Mexico, Brazil, Argentina, Puerto Rico, France, Israel, Iran, Nationalist China, Thailand, and the Philippines.[80] In Holland there is no law restricting polygraph use, but the Court of Appeal (Hague) in 1952 ruled that because of the lack of experience with the approach in Holland and the differing opinions of experts, the results of polygraph tests would not be admitted as evidence.[81] Polygraph is not used at all in England, Australia, Denmark, Norway, Sweden, Finland or Ireland. In Germany, the West German Supreme Court (Bundesgerichtshof) in 1954 reversed a conviction in which polygraph evidence had been admitted.[82] The court prohibited the use of polygraphy in that it was viewed an encroachment upon the freedom of the defendant to make a decision and to act according to his own will. Moreover, law enforcement agencies were given no greater freedom in utilizing the technique than the courts. It was concluded that while a person may be voluntarily giving answers in the test, his true answers and the fact of his guilt are obtained against his will.

There has been antipolygraph legislation in the United States as well, but it has been directed at the use of the approach in employment situations. Generally, polygraphy has served two functions in business: that of evaluating job applicants (preemployment testing) and as a deterrent to theft (periodic testing). In the case of the former, the potential employee is asked a series of questions related to such issues as absenteeism, drug or alcohol use, theft, and so forth. Through a rather rapid test, a quick determination is made as to the suitability of the person for employment. In this technique, control questions are not employed, but rather, the response to each question is compared to the subject's reactions to the other questions asked.

Where this procedure has been used as a deterrent to theft, there is a great deal of evidence of its effectiveness.[83] The employees are informed that they are to be examined at regular and routine time periods and will be questioned as to whether they have been involved in any thefts during the preceding time between tests. When the employees become aware of this prospect, they do not steal, and dramatic savings are brought about through the reduction in losses due to internal thefts. This polygraph procedure has been successful enough for Lloyds of London and other bonding companies to reduce their rates when employees were routinely tested. The unions, however, have viewed the procedure in a very negative manner and have been responsible for fostering antipolygraph legislation in various states. There are no states that prohibit the use of polygraph per se, but fifteen states have enacted legislation to limit the use of the procedure in commercial, business and industrial settings. They are Alaska, California, Connecticut, Delaware, Hawaii, Idaho, Maryland, Massachusetts, Minnesota, Montana, New Jersey, Oregon, Pennsylvania, Rhode Island, and Washington.[84] The statutes essentially read the same way: No employer shall cause (require, demand, request) an employee or prospective employee to take a polygraph examination as a condition of employment or continued employment. Ten of these states exempt law enforcement agencies and a few exclude government employees and those dealing with drugs.

A police officer in Washington resisted the demand by a superior that he take a polygraph examination, but the Washington Supreme Court ruled that he was required to submit to an examination under penalty of dismissal.[85] The basis for determining on whom polygraphy will be employed would seem to be related to the importance of the person to the safety of society. Rulings against the use of this approach are not determined by any question of its validity, but rather to the issue of the greatest good for the greatest number.

It would seem likely that the union organizations and the American Civil Liberties Union will continue to attempt to prohibit the use of polygraphy in employment situations. Barefoot has pointed out, rather ironically, that the unions themselves do not hesitate to utilize polygraphy when the need exists.[86]

Throughout the years, while the courts have refused to admit polygraph results, they have often indicated that it is an effective investigative tool for law enforcement agencies.[87] Applying this procedure, police are not only able to eliminate innocent suspects, but they have been most successful in attaining confessions from the guilty. Some of the critics of polygraphy have argued that admissions accomplished in this manner should be viewed as coerced and should be excluded. The courts generally have ruled to the contrary. In *State* v. *DeHart*, the defendant appealed a murder conviction and stated that his confession made following a polygraph examination was not voluntary.[88] The Wisconsin Supreme Court upheld the trial court's decision to admit the confession into evidence. An admission of guilt made prior to a polygraph test was also held admissible by the Virginia Supreme Court.[89] In another situation, a defendant's confessing to crimes other than the one under investigation, the court ruled, did not make the confessions either invalid nor inadmissible.[90] In *Tyler* v. *U.S.*, the examinee admitted to involvement in a murder after he was informed that his polygraph tracings were indicative of deception.[91] The District of Columbia Court of Appeals affirmed the lower court's ruling that the confession was admissible. A similar conclusion was reached in *Commonwealth* v. *Hipple*.[92] The Pennsylvania Supreme Court found that since no promise, force, or threats were made, the mere use of a polygraph did not render a confession inadmissible. A similar decision was made in *Pinter* v. *State,* where it was stated that the threat of a polygraph examination was not seen as an undue influence in attaining an admission.[93]

In contrast to these decisions, confessions attained in association with polygraph examinations were ruled inadmissible in *Bruner* v. *People*[94] and *People* v. *Sims*.[95] In the former, the Supreme Court of Colorado ruled that the defendant's confession was involuntary and therefore inadmissible because the polygraph examination, as administered, constituted a punitive situation. Reportedly, the instrument and its components were kept on the defendant for twelve hours, and he was informed that the testing would persist unless he gave them the information they wished. In the second case, a seventeen-year-old girl confessed to a murder after a polygraph examination. The guilty decision of the lower court was reversed by the Supreme Court of Florida because the polygraph approach was employed without the consent of her attorney.

References made at the trial regarding the refusal or willingness of the defendant to take a polygraph examination have generally been considered improper as either lacking probative force, violating constitutional privilege, or inviting prejudice. Generally, it has been considered harmless error. In *Rank* v. *State*, reference to taking a polygraph examination was made by a state witness.[96] Since no objection to the comment was made at trial, the court considered that the right to claim the admission of the comment was an error on appeal and was waived. In some cases, such references have been considered as harmless errors.[97] While in contrast, in other instances it has been held to be a reversible error to even mention that the defendant or a witness took a polygraph test or was willing or refused to take one.[98] In *Commonwealth* v. *Saunders*, the defendant, accused of murder, attempted to introduce evidence that he had expressed a willingness to take a polygraph examination.[99] The Supreme Court of Pennsylvania affirmed the trial court's refusal to admit this willingness as evidence.

In an attempt at pretrial discovery of polygraph results, in *State* v. *Thompson*, a ruling by the Delaware Supreme Court stated that the accused had no due process right to pretrial disclosure.[100] Similar findings were reported in *State* v. *McGee*,[101] where the court found that the defendant was not entitled to pretrial discovery of polygraph findings because it could not be used in evidence. Similarly in *Anderson* v. *State*, the Court held that where polygraph results are inadmissible into evidence, the defendant will not be allowed to discover test results of those who testified against them.[102] In contrast, in *Ballard* v. *Superior Court*, the appeal court decided that the generally inadmissibility of the results did not preclude their use in pretrial discovery.[103] The defendant, accused of rape, was able to attain the polygraph results of the complaining witness.

Since the 1970s, there has been a growing awareness of the probative value of polygraph findings. The polygraph approach is clearly admitted into evidence by the courts much more frequently and in a wider variety of cases. The implication of this trend is that polygraphy will be admitted in the near future in the same manner as other scientific evidence. Polygraph testimony will be granted judicial recognition in some jurisdictions, and the expectation is that the extent of this recognition will broaden with time. Perhaps McCormick's statement of 1927 is finally being heard: "If science bids fair to furnish a fairly effective technique for the exposure of deception, we should not merely welcome it when it comes but stimulate and encourage efforts to speed its coming."[104]

Notes

1. *U.S.* v. *Frye*, 293 F. 1013 (D.C. Cir. 1923).

2. McCormick, C.T., *Handbook of the Law of Evidence* (St. Paul: West Publishing Co., 1954).

3. *People* v. *Williams*, 164, Calif. App. 2d, 858,331 P. 2d 251 (1958).

4. Boyce, R.N., "Judicial Recognition of Scientific Evidence in Criminal Cases," *Utah L. Rev.* 8 (1963-64): 313-27.

5. 167 Misc. 51,3 N.Y.S. 2d 348 (Queens Cty Ct 1938).

6. 279 N.Y. 204, 18 N.E. 2d 31 (1938).

7. Sell, W.E., "Deception, Detection and the Law," *U. of Pittsburgh L. Rev.* 2 (1950): 210-27.

8. Langley, L.L., "The Polygraph Lie Detector: Its Physiological Bases, Reliability and Admissibility," *Ala. Lawyer* 16 (1955): 209-24.

9. Silving, H., "Testing of the Unconscious in Criminal Cases," *Harvard L. Rev.* 69 (1956): 683-705.

10. Richardson, J.R., *Modern Scientific Evidence* (Cincinnati: W.H. Anderson, Co., 1961).

11. 324 F. Supp. 339 (D.C. Ariz 1970).

12. Md. Ct. Spec. App. 9969 (1969).

13. 356 F. Supp. 1363 13 CLR 1251 (C.D. Calif. 1973).

14. 356 F. Supp. 27 (M.D. Fla. 1973).

15. 27 Ore. App. 115 (1976).

16. 413 F. 2d 769 (10th Cir. 1969).

17. 435 F. 2d 686, 687 (7th Cir. 1970).

18. 361 F. Supp. 510 (D Md 1973).

19. 179 F. Supp. 278 (S.D.N.Y. 1959).

20. Va. Sup. Ct. (10/11/71).

21. 151 Neb. 368, 383, 37 N.W. 2d, 593 600 (1949).

22. 300 Mich. 562, 565-66, 2 N.W. 2d 503, 505 (1942).

23. 25 N.Y. 2d, 511, 515, 255, N.E. 2d, 696, 698, 307, N.Y.S. 2d 430, 433 (1969).

24. 210 Wisc. 651, 246, N.W. 314 (1933).

25. 343 Mich. 348, 373, 72, N.W. 2d 269, 282 (1955).

26. Mich. App. 255, 175, N.W. 2d 893 (1970).

27. 94 Okl. Crim, 45, 53, 230 P. 2d, 495, 503, Cert. denied, 343 U.S. 898 (1951).

28. Garvey, P.J., "New Jersey Supreme Court Committee on Criminal Procedure in Polygraph Tests—A Review," *Polygraph* 2 (1973): 116-21.

29. *People* v. *Jacobson*, 71 Misc 2d, 1040, 337 N.Y.S. 2d 616 Sup. Ct. Queens Cty (1972).

30. *Peterson* v. *State*, Tex. 247 S.W., 2d, 110 (1952).

31. 542, Wisc. 416, 8, N.W., 2d, 288 (1943).

32. 476 P. 2d 474 (Alaska 1970).

33. 27 Ill. 2d 302, 189, N.E. 2d, 260 (1963).

34. 306 S.W. 2d, 825 (Ct App. Ky. 1957).

35. *State* v. *Sanchell* 216 N.W. 2d 504 (Neb. 1974).

36. 188 So. 2d 24 (Fla. App. 1966).

37. 288 So. 2d 421, 36, ALR 3d 1274 (Fla. App. 1969).

38. *Butler* v. *State*, 228 So. 2d 421 (App. Ct. Fla. 1969).

39. *State* v. *Davis*, 188 So. 2d 24 (App. Ct. Fla. 1966).

40. 163 Kan. 622, 185 P. 2d 147 (1947).

41. 85 Cal. App. 2d 686, 695, 193 P. 2d 937, 942 (4th Dist. 1948).

42. 151 Neb. 368, 37 N.W. 2d 593 (1949).

43. 98 Cal. App. 2d 124, 219, P. 2d 70 (1950).

44. 331, Mich. 606, 50 N.W. 2d 172 (1951).

45. Inbau, F.E., and Reid, J.E., *Lie Detection and Criminal Interrogation*, 3rd ed. (Baltimore: Williams & Wilkins 1953).

46. Reid, J.E., and Inbau, F.E., *Truth and Deception: The Polygraph ("lie detector") Technique* (Baltimore: Williams and Wilkins, 1966).

47. 252 Iowa, 19, 104 N.W. 2d 568 (1960).

48. 91 Ariz. 274, 371, P. 2d 894 (1962).

49. Ill. 2d 302, 189 N.E. 2d 260 (1963).

50. 80 N.M. 786, 461, P. 2d 919 (1969).

51. N.J. Sup. Ct. 297 A. 2d 849 (1972).

52. No. 75-1170, U.S. Ct. of App., 8th Cir. (10/31/75).

53. 216 N.W. 2d 8 (S. Ct. Wis 1974).

54. 210 Wisc. 651, 246, N.W. 314 (1933).

55. 413 F. 2d 296 (10th Cir. 1969).

56. 356 F. Supp. 27 (M.D. Fla. 1973).

57. Kaplan, A.G., "The Lie Detector: An Analysis of its Place in the Law of Evidence," *Wayne L. Rev.* 10 (1964): 381-414.

58. Tarlow, B., "Admissibility of Polygraph Evidence in 1975: An Aid in Determining Credibility in a Perjury Plagued System," *Polygraph* 4 (1975): 207-64.

59. 350 F. Supp. 685 (DDC) (D.C. Cir. 11/9/72).

60. 348 F. Supp. 1377 (S.D. Cal 1972).

61. 350 F. Supp. 90 (E.D. Mich. 1972).

62. Crim. No. 72-1102 (E.D.N.Y. 1972).

63. 344 F. Supp. 522 (E.D.N.Y. 1971).

64. Ct. App. N. Mex. 15 CLR 2028 (2/27/74).

65. No. 70-5585 (1/31/73 Fla.).

66. 12 C.L.R. 2133 (Cal. Sup. Ct. 11/6/72).

67. *State* v. *Flaherty* 76-9-76 Cir. Ct. (Ore. 11/29/76).

68. (No. 1) 15 C.L.R. 2323 (Mass. 1974).

69. No. 23 C.L.R. 100 (Ohio 6/20/74).

70. 86 N.M. 686, 926 P. 2d 1091 (1974).

71. Beatty, T., Admissibility Rules Eased in *New Mexico* v. *Dorsey*, *Polygraph* 4, 339, 1975.

72. 71 Misc. 2d 719, 336, N.Y.S. 2d 839 (Family Court, Niagara Cty. 1972).

73. 115 N.J. Sup. 213, 278, A. 2d 543 (Hudson Cty Ct. 1971).

74. Ansley N., "Stipulated Admissibility Reversed by Georgia Appellate Court," *Polygraph* 4 (1975): 340.

75. *U.S.* v. *Salazar-Gaeta*, 447 F. 2d 468 (9th Cir. 1971). *U.S.* v. *Sadrzadeh*, 440 F. 2d 389 (9th Cir. 1971). *U.S.* v. *Rogers*, 419 F. 2d 1315 (10th Cir. 1969). *U.S.* v. *Tremont*, 351 F. 2d 144 (6th Cir. 1965). *McCroskey* v. *U.S.*, 339 F. 2d 895 (8th Cir. 1965). *Marks* v. *U.S.*, 260 F. 2d 377 (10th Cir. 1958) Cert. denied, 358 U.S. 929 (1959).

76. *State* v. *Brown*, 177 So. 2d 532 (Fla. Ct. App. 1965); *Herman* v. *Eagle Star Life Insurance Co.*, 396, F. 2d 427 (9th Cir. 1968); *State* v. *Ross*, 7 Wash. App. 62, 497 P. 2d 1343, 53 ALR 3d 997 (1972); *State* v. *Fields*, 434, S.W. 2d 507 (Mo. 1968); *State* v. *Freeland*, 255 Iowa 1334, 125 N.W. 2d 825 (1964); and *State* v. *Galloway*, 167 N.W. 2d 89 (Iowa 1969).

77. Vancouver Registry No. CC 760628 (Nov. 3, 1976).

78. Abrams, S., "The Polygraph in Japan," *Polygraph* 2 (1973): 36-41.

79. Widacki, J., "Polygraph Examination and its Practical Usage in Some Countries," *Krakowskie Studi Prawnicze* 9 (1976): 49-70.

80. Barland, G.H., and Raskin, D.C., "The Use of Electrodermal Activity in the Detection of Deception," in W.F. Prokasy and D.C. Raskin (eds.) *Electrodermal Activity in Psychological Research* (N.Y.: Academic Press 1973).

81. Merjes, P., "Scientific Criminol. Investigation Techniques Under Dutch Law," *J. Crim. Law, Criminol., and Police Science* 51 (1961): 653-60.

82. Kaganiec, H.J., "The Lie Detector Tests and 'Freedom of the Will' in Germany," *Northwestern U. Law Rev.* 51 (1956): 446-60.

83. Menocal, A.M., "Lie Detectors in Private Employment: A Proposal for Balancing Interests," *George Washington L. Rev.* 33 (1965): 932-54; "Lie Detectors for Employees," *Business Week Magazine*, September 16, 1939; McEvoy, J.P., "The Lie Detector Goes Into Business," *The Reader's Digest*, January 15, 1941, pp. 69-72; Barefoot, K.J., *The Polygraph Story,* American Polygraph Association, N.Y. 1974 (available through Cluett Peabody and Co., 510 5th Avenue, New York 10036).

84. Romig, C.H.A., "State Laws and the Polygraph in 1975," *Polygraph* (1975): 95-107.

85. *Seattle Police Officers Guild* v. *City of Seattle*, 80 Wn. 2d, 307, 474 P. 2d, 485 (1972).

86. Barefoot, The Polygraph Story.

87. *State* v. *Sanchell*, 216 N.W. 2d, 504, (Neb. 1974); *McCain* v. *Sheridan*, 324 P. 2d 923 (1958); and *Davis* v. *Stile*, Tex. Crim. Ct. of Appeals, 308 S.W., 2d, 880 (1957).

88. 8 N.W. 2d 360 (Wisc. 1943).

89. *Jones* v. *Commonwealth*, Va. 204 S.E. 2d 247 (1974).

90. *Weston* v. *Henderson*, 279 F. Supp. 862 (ED Tenn.)

91. 193 F. 2d 24 (D.C. Cir. 1951).

92. 333 Pa. 33, 3A 2d 353 (1939).

93. 34 So. 2d 7236 (Miss 1948).

94. 113, Colo. 194, 156 P. 2d 111 (1945).

95. 395 Ill. 37, 69 N.E. 2d 336 (1946).

96. 373 P. 2d 734 (Alaska 1962).

97. *Johnson* v. *State*, 166 So. 2d 798 (Fla. App. Ct. 1964); *Smith* v. *State*, 402 S.W. 2d 412 (Ark. 1964); and *People* v. *McLaughlin*, 3 Mich. App. 391, 142, N.W. 2d 484 (1966).

98. *Leeks* v. *State* 245 P. 2d 764 (1952); *People* v. *Carter*, 312 P. 2d 665 (1957); *State* v. *Chang*, 374 P. 2d 5 (1962); *Commonwealth* v. *Johnson*, 44 Pa. 237, 272, A. 2d 467 (1967); and *State* v. *Kolander*, 52 N.W. 2d 458 (Minn. 1952).

99. 125 A. 2d 442 (Pa. 1956).

100. 50 Del. 456, 134 A. 2d 266 (1957).

101. 91 Ariz. 101, 370 P. 2d 261 (1962).

102. 241 So. 2d 390 (Fla. App. 1970).

103. 44 CLR 291 (1965).

104. McCormick, C.T., "Deception Tests and the Law of Evidence," *Calif. L. Rev.* 15 (1927): 499-500.

8   Critique of Polygraphy

The court decisions to exclude polygraph testimony have included a long series of objections to its admission and its critics extended these even further. A lack of acceptance by the scientific community was the reason for rejecting this evidence in the precedent-setting Frye case.[1] While it is still being excluded on this basis in contemporary court cases,[2] the surveys of both Cureton and Ash have demonstrated that both behavioral scientists and attorneys now view polygraphy in a more favorable light.[3] In contrast to these findings, the Committee on Detection of Deception of the Society for Psychophysiological Research in 1974 reported that they were stalemated in regard to a conclusion of polygraph validity and whether its findings should be admitted into court.[4] The Forensic Section of the American Psychiatric Association was more definite in their report.[5] In 1946, this group indicated that valuable results could only be obtained with the polygraph when it was employed by ". . . thoroughly trained physicians and psychologists who will evaluate these data derived by applying other available methods and making use of all independently obtainable evidence." Lykken, apparently in agreement with this view, stated that polygraphy was a role for trained clinicians, but then added that he believed law enforcement should use it.[6]

In the modern concept of evidence, the general acceptance principle requires that the people using the particular scientific technique or those researching it are the only ones who need approve it, not the profession as a whole. This concept is particularly pertinent for polygraphy because its parent sciences of psychology, physiology, and medicine have become disinterested, and their members are generally unaware of the procedures, uses, and the research that has been conducted. If acceptance from the scientific community is to be derived from the opinions of practicing polygraphists and those scientists who are actually investigating the approach, its approval is assured. Thus, refusing to admit polygraph evidence on this basis is no longer appropriate.

Smith stated that a scientific technique must have as a foundation a theory and be developed through experimentation with its findings expressed in statistical terms, and it should utilize the best tools available and be refined through continuing experimentation.[7] None of these, he claimed, was true of polygraphy. A question of the soundness of the underlying theory was also raised in *Wisconsin* v. *Bohmer*,[8] but there should be little debate over this issue. While the exact pathways of neural excitation may not be known, there is little doubt as to the psychophysiologic basis of the technique and that it is generally accepted by the sciences. The act of lying during the examination causes an emotional reaction that in turn results in sympathetic arousal. The physiologic changes that occur, although they vary somewhat among persons, are sufficiently consistent during a deceptive response to allow for an interpretation. Skolnick's concern over the low correlation among autonomic variables[9] does not negate either the theory underlying polygraphy, nor its usefulness. While people do vary in their emotional response to lying and in their physiologic reactions that follow, these differences do not imply that the body changes are uninterpretable.

From reading the history of polygraphy, the pathway that experimentation has taken can be readily ascertained. Moreover, continued research is being conducted at research centers in Japan, Israel, and in the United States. Therefore, Smith's objections to polygraphy's lacking the requisites of being a science are unfounded. It is true, however, that the procedure has not generated much interest among scientists so that there are only a relatively small number actively involved in the investigation of this technique. The instrumentation employed is far less sophisticated than that utilized in laboratory settings. Lykken has stated that polygraphy is twenty years behind psychophysiology,[10] and Skolnick has emphasized that there are imperfections in the instrumentation.[11] Sternbach et al., in agreement with this opinion, view the instrument as being primitive, and they wrote that no attempts have been made to determine whether other techniques might offer better results.[12] In contrast to this statement, Ellson, et al., Ansley, Jacobs, Decker et al., Barland, and others have studied various transducers in an effort to improve the procedures.[13] There has been a tendency to remain with those sensors that have been effective, but cost factors and the need for a portable unit have probably inhibited the incorporation of additional components as well.

Improvements have been made in both instrumentation and technique and this has been recognized in *People* v. *Cutter*[14] *U.S.* v. *Debetham,*[15] and *U.S.* v. *Wainwright.*[16] The plethysmograph, cardioactivity monitor, and amplified cardio and pneumograph have been added to the system. The standards for membership in the American Polygraph Association have been raised, and licensure at the state level has been fostered. Standardization of training and technique have been carried out, and the training time has been extended. In addition, a numerical scoring system has been developed that greatly adds to the objectivity and reliability of the approach. Thus, statements such as those made by Smith that the polygraph has not changed since the 1920s[17] and in *People* v. *Jacobson,*[18] which cited the lack of technical improvements as a reason for exclusion, are not wholly legitimate criticisms.

The lack of validity frequently has been raised as the reason for the exclusion of polygraph findings,[19] but is quite inconsistent with the reliability and validity findings reported in Chapter 6. It must be recognized that a very direct relationship exists between the level of accuracy attained and the expertise of the examiner. No random sample of the effectiveness of polygraphists has ever been conducted, so it cannot be assumed that examiners in general reach validity in the 90 to 95 percent range. In fact, considering the results of Horvath's study in which 63 percent accuracy was reported,[20] it can be assumed that some polygraphists do not attain a desirable level of competence. Part of this can be attributed to a lack of experience as was demonstrated in Horvath and Reid's study in which inexperienced polygraphists were correct in 79 percent of their judgments as compared to 92 percent in those examiners who had been practicing for more than a year.[21] It is likely that the average polygraphist falls between these figures and the 95 percent accuracy reported in many field studies.[22] The many highly competent examiners, however, would be expected to be at the upper range between 90 and 95 percent validity. Inbau and Reid's evaluation of polygraph operators would seem to continue to be true. Some examiners are incompetent.[23] Unfortunately, incompetency exists in any profession whose members represent a wide range of experience, training, and ability, and in polygraphy this factor should not present a major problem for either attorneys or the courts since cross-examination will reveal the examiners who have weaknesses and the court can always appoint an examiner to readminister the test if there are doubts as to the findings.

Sternbach et al. have indicated that there is no good scientific research to demonstrate the claims of high validity reported in field research.[24] They specifically attacked the claims of Reid and Inbau and point up the low level of verification that was achieved. In their paper, which was published in 1962, they indicated that there is no public body of knowledge to support the claims of high validity. Since their report was published, however, investigations have been conducted that corroborate such findings—that is, with accuracy in the 90 percent range. Silving has pointed out that scientific evidence need not be conclusive to be admitted into court.[25] If the jury has been properly instructed, it need not be prejudicial. If the polygraph were, in fact, infallible, it would then usurp the jury's role, but since it is not, the jurors have to first decide whether it is accurate in the particular case and then use it as an aid in their decision of guilt or innocence.

Skolnick indicated that polygraphists have a wide range of rather sophisticated roles to play for which they are ill equipped.[26] They must rule out medical and psychologic conditions as well as function effectively as interviewers and as interpreters of the test results. They attempt to do so, he said, without any significant medical or psychological training. Six weeks of polygraph school do not prepare the operator to perform the high-level tasks that are required of him. Some have pointed out that less study is required than in vocations such as barbering, which demands decisions of much less importance. Both Langley and Burkey have also been most critical of the qualifications of polygraphists and have expressed the view that had operators been better trained or if psychologists or psychiatrists administered the examinations, polygraph testimony would likely have been admitted into evidence years ago.[27]

Since the time of these criticisms, the American Polygraph Association has added the requirement of a college degree in order to obtain membership in the organization. It does not, however, specify that the degree has to be in psychology or physiology. A grandfather clause was written into the requisites so that those persons who had been in the field, but did not have a baccalaureat degree, would not be forced out of polygraphy. For new members, a degree will be required. The same degree prerequisite is part of some of the state licensure laws and an entrance requirement for some of the polygraph schools.

Improvements have been made in school curricula as well.[28] At the Reid College of Lie Detection in Chicago, the course consists of six months of course work and internship, and admission requirements include a bachelor's degree. The polygraph course at the University of Baltimore is composed of 256 hours of class work over a thirty-week period. The American Institute of Polygraph Technology and Applied Psychology in Dearborn, Michigan, has a nine-week course of 360 hours in addition to an internship and two weeks of advanced training. The applicant must have a baccalaureat degree or an associate degree and five years of law enforcement investigative experience to be admitted into the program. The majority of the other schools provide only about 260 hours of class work.

At each school, the applicant must take a series of psychometric tests, have a background check, and generally pass a polygraph screening examination. These requirements represent an attempt to insure that students of sufficient intelligence and of good moral caliber enter polygraphy. While the length of school varies, the course work is fairly standard. A number of different polygraph techniques are taught along with courses in psychology, physiology, instrumentation, question formulation, interpretation, interviewing, and legal status.

While a very considerable difference must exist between a school of six weeks and one offering six months of training, one frequently gets the impression that the critics of polygraphy will be satisfied with nothing less than a doctoral degree in medicine or psychology. Skolnick implied that it was necessary to have a degree in medicine to recognize the existence of medical problems in the examinee.[29] Highleyman indicated that persons with heart disease, excessively high or low blood pressure, or respiratory disorders are not testable.[30] Turner, echoing these notions, stated that people with cardiovascular dysfunction are not fit subjects for testing.[31]

These writers apparently are unaware that the simplest way to determine whether an examinee is a suitable candidate for a polygraph examination is to test him. If adequate tracings can be obtained, regardless of his medical condition, he can be examined. It is highly unlikely, for example, that hypertension will result in a cardio tracing that is uninterpretable. It is quite conceivable that a respiratory problem might exist that would preclude a reading of the tracings of that component, but the cardio and galvanometer readings would be sufficient for a determination of truthfulness or deception. The major concerns insofar as medical problems are concerned are to avoid the testing of a subject in pain or in a state of physical exhaustion. The polygraphist, in questioning the subject about his medical state, will also be cautious of any disorders that might be exaccerbated by the stress of the examination. An asthmatic attack, a seizure, or even an attack of angina could be precipitated by the situation. In general, there are relatively few persons who are untestable due to medical problems.

In 1950, Floch wrote that psychopaths, psychopathic liars, and those with circumscribed amnesia could not be accurately examined.[32] Highleyman added psychotics, neurotics, and children to this list, while Eliasberg reported that the hardened criminal tended to be immune to polygraph testing.[33] The unlikelihood of accurately examining the incorrigible criminal because of the "ice water in his veins" was described by Turner, while Lykken stated that "...a psychopathic killer, who cares little about the test will pass it."[34]

The psychopath, whether he is characterized as having "ice water in his veins," being incorrigible, or a hardened criminal still possesses the same personality traits as other people. Psychopaths have little or no conscience and so feel no remorse. They are impulsive, crave excitement, are unable to establish relationships and are quite able to use anyone to satisfy their own needs. The psychopath, however, does not desire to go to the gas chamber or be imprisoned any more than anyone else, which, then, is his Achilles' heel. Psychopaths do not want their lies to be detected and that is the very thing that makes them detectable, as has been demonstrated in the research of Raskin and Barland and Raskin who reported that psychopaths were as accurately tested as any other subject.[35]

If the statement that neurotics are untestable were true, a very large portion of our population would be eliminated from polygraphy. This, however, is not the case. Occasionally, a person is so anxiety ridden that his tracings are too erratic to interpret, but such people tend to be rather rare. Neurotics, psychopaths, and people with other personality disorders in general can be examined without any great difficulty. Psychotics[36] and retardates,[37] however, cannot be tested without a significant risk of a loss of validity. Other authors have expressed the concern that the polygraphist would be unable to recognize personality disorders since psychologists and psychiatrists appear to have considerable difficulty in doing so themselves.[38] However, in the case of the polygraphist, if the subject's condition is not obvious, it would only infrequently create a problem because the tracings are typically too erratic to score. The result is simply an inconclusive test.

Insofar as the testing of children is concerned, there has been relatively little research in this area, but a study by this author demonstrated that average children age twelve or over could be tested with a high degree of accuracy.[39] Below this age, accuracy decreased.

Burack stated that there was a risk of the innocent subject responding more to a question to which he is being truthful but that threatens his life (relevant) than to a trivial question to which he is lying (control).[40] Lykken cautioned that the frightened innocent person would fail the test.[41] It would indeed be unusual for any person, innocent or guilty, to be free of anxiety when being examined. The innocent would of course be threatened by the accusatory question, but with proper polygraph procedure his attention will be directed to the control question. If the questions were not developed in this manner, distinguishing truth from deception in anyone, guilty or innocent, would be impossible.

Some concern has also been expressed that a suggestible innocent subject who was misdiagnosed as deceptive might confess. While both Eliasberg and Skolnick were fearful that confessions from the innocent might take place,[42] this could occur only on very rare occasions. One such case was reported by Dearman and Smith.[43] During the periodic polygraph testing of bank employees, one of the vice presidents was found deceptive when he denied stealing from the bank. An audit of the books revealed no such loss so the examination was readministered. Again the subject continued to react to the question: "Have you ever stolen any money from the bank or its customers?" Another examination was administered in an attempt to determine the amount stolen. A series composed of different amounts of money was presented to the examinee, and he showed large reactions to $800 and $1,100. He, reportedly, was convinced after that that he could not mislead the polygraph and so signed a confession and indicated a method that he thought he would have used had he really embezzled the funds. Another audit of the books showed no such shortage and also that he could not have stolen the money as he had described.

Because of the confusion, the bank officer was then referred for a psychiatric examination and then psychotherapy. It was learned that he had been involved in some financial dealings with his wife and mother for $800 and $1,100 for which he felt some guilt. Of particular interest was the fact that both his wife and mother were customers of the bank. It is evident that the examinee believed he had stolen from them, which explained his deceptive reaction to the questions, but not his confession. Obviously, if a person believes he committed a particular act, even if he is completely innocent, he will demonstrate a deceptive pattern if he denies it.

This type of response was demonstrated in a study by Weinstein et al., in which subjects were hypnotized and told they had stolen a sum of money.[44] They were instructed to deny the mock theft when asked questions related to it during a polygraph examination. In each case, the subject was diagnosed as deceptive and the examiner successfully determined what denomination of bill the examinee was hypnotized to believe that he had stolen. Thus, a false positive could result in a case of this nature.

Another area of criticism of the polygraph involves truth and deception, which have been described as being on a continuum. Polygraphy only allows for a "yes" or "no" answer, and thus it reportedly does not take into account the various possible gradations of truth or lying, for example, associated with degree of involvement or guilty knowledge. It was also believed that such factors as memory loss, rationalization, suggestion, and imagination could play a role in distorting the tracings because a simple "yes" or "no" response is required.[45] There is no doubt that the subject must be able to respond with an unequivocal answer or else inaccuracies are inevitable. This requirement should not, however, create any problems for the examiner who should be quite able to phrase the queries in a manner that meets it. Backster writes of the need for clarity of issue in the formation of questions.[46] If, for example, five men were beating up another man and the victim died, the suspect could not be asked whether he killed the man. He would not know whether he definitely struck the killing blow, and therefore, he would not be able to respond unequivocally. In these instances a false negative or false positive could result. The question should be asked: "On June 5th were you one of the men who struck John Smith?" In this manner, problems that would result in inconclusive findings can be dealt with quite easily.

Floch reported cases of "circumscribed amnesia" in which the act that had been committed was so reprehensible that the person completely repressed it, which thus resulted in amnesia for the experience.[47] While such amnesia is an extremely rare occurrence, conceivably a situation of this nature could cause a false negative reaction. Nevertheless, it is also possible that the unconscious reaction would be strong enough for sympathetic arousal to result and the suspect's being appropriately diagnosed as deceptive.

Inbau and Reid estimated that 20 percent of guilty subjects attempt some means of "beating the test."[48] Highleyman and Skolnick were both concerned that polygraph subjects could successfully do so.[49] A wide variety of techniques, in fact, have been employed in an attempt to mislead the polygraphist; these range from spur-of-the-moment responses to well-thought-out plans that require researching the field of polygraphy and physiology. The vast majority of countermeasures, however, tend to be quite obvious and easily detected and at the most cause only an inconclusive diagnosis. While labeling a subject who uses countermeasures as being deceptive is tempting, if indications of deception are not present, the distortions in the tracings that result can only be considered as inconclusive findings. An excellent review of countermeasures was written by Barland and Raskin, in which they divided the various techniques into such categories as mental, physical, and chemical countermeasures.[50]

There has been a good deal of concern related to the use of pharmaceutical measures to defeat the purpose of the examination. These measures can only be successful to the extent of creating an inconclusive finding because there simply is no drug that can cause a reduction in the subject's reaction to the relevant questions and not affect the controls. When the subject does not react to any question, he simply cannot be examined, whatever the reason for this unresponsiveness. In most instances, unless excessive dosages of drugs are used, which becomes quite obvious from the examinee's behavior, truth and deception can still be determined.

Reportedly, some drugs affect the galvanometer responses, as manifested in a plunging traceline, so that no measure can be made through this component.[51] Zimmerman has suggested that this problem can be dealt with in some instances by placing the electrodes on the toes rather than on the subject's fingers.[52]

Depressants, analgesics, sympatholytics, and parasympathomimetics in particular effect the tracings, but there is general agreement that inconclusives rather than false negatives result from excessive drug use.[53]

A covert attempt at movement is a rather typical approach in trying to mislead the operator. Muscle contraction of the arm on which the blood pressure cuff is applied causes such a large and abrupt increase in the cardio tracings as to be easily discernible from the physiologic changes that occur with sympathetic arousal. More subtle reactions can be brought about through the contraction of smaller muscle groups such as the anal sphincter or pressing down with the fingers or toes. The effect that results varies with the activity, the person, and even with the same person at different times. Since the examinee has no feedback as to the effect of these movements, he cannot determine whether the reactions are very large and obvious countermeasures or if there are no changes in the tracings at all. This technique is thus less than valuable to the subject since he may make his efforts to "beat the test" apparent. The opinion of the majority of examiners is that these approaches do not accomplish the subject's purpose. In contrast, Kubis demonstrated, in an experiment of countermeasures, that when the examinees' pressed their toes against the floor, the accuracy attained in his study was reduced from 75 percent to 10 percent.[54] However, in a replication of this study, More reported no loss of accuracy when the same procedures were utilized.[55] While this discrepancy in the findings is difficult to explain, it quite possibly could be related to the expertise of the examiner.

Attempts to control breathing have been rather ineffectively used to distort the test findings. Larson actually incorporated the respiration component into the polygraph to discover whether subjects were trying to effect the cardio tracings through their breathing.[56] Since the operator can easily compare the cardio and GSR reactions in relation to a subject's respirations, irregular breathing or deep breaths can easily be picked out and a determination made as to whether they are affecting the cardio and GSR tracings. While controlled breathing can cause an inconclusive finding, the result is more likely to be only that the questions will have to be repeated until readable charts are obtained.

Creating a very regular and rhythmic series of respirations is difficult to achieve since it requires a degree of concentration that would be difficult to maintain during the questioning. Even if the subject were successful in continuing this effort throughout the examination, the only result would be that the tracings of that one component being difficult to interpret. Whatever method the examinee tries will be further complicated by the polygraphist's comparing his breathing pattern during the examination to those periods between tests. Often subjects who alter their respirations, only do so during the questioning and their attempt to mislead the operator becomes quite obvious. The overall result is that this measure has not been an effective means of "beating the test."

Pain, like a number of the emotions, causes sympathetic arousal. Through such devices as biting the tongue, pressing down on a tack that the subject has placed in his shoe, or applying pressure to a sore, changes in the tracings similar to that found during deception are created. As in the case with movements, the examinee, without feedback, has no way of knowing whether he is overreacting or not responding at all. Thus, in using this countermeasure, he again risks the possibility of giving himself away.

In contrast to these physical countermeasures that tend to be observable, a variety of mental maneuvers have been tried. Kubis has studied the effects of relaxation and attempts at dissociation as a means of reducing sympathetic dominance.[57] His results indicated that this approach was not very successful. The threatening question impinges on the awareness of the subject and distracts him from his purpose. Similar difficulties are met when the subject tries to concentrate on counting or staring at an object. More success has been achieved with the opposite approach of conjuring up a stimulating image during the control questions. Sexual or hostile fantasies can cause physiologic changes resembling deceptive reactions. Kubis found that accuracy was reduced from 75 percent to 25 percent, while More's validity findings were lessened from 95 percent to 80 percent when exciting imagery was employed.[58] While the use of imagery is impressively effective in laboratory research, it is highly unlikely that except in rare cases any significant results would be attained in an actual examination.[59]

When a suspect faces imprisonment if his lie is detected, utilizing these distracting procedures effectively becomes most difficult. While empathizing with the subject and feeling the emotional and physical reactions of which he is literally aware when he is lying is not easy, the reader might try to picture himself taking a peak of tension test. Knowing that the fourth item to be presented is critical, try to imagine attempting different distracting techniques while the voice of the examiner penetrates through your imagery. With the presentation of each item, you become increasingly aware that the polygraphist is about to read off the key question. As much as you try to concentrate on sex or blood, the worry of whether you can accomplish your aim impinges on your thoughts until the significant item is presented. You can feel your pulse literally pounding against the blood pressure cuff, and the sensation of uneasiness in your stomach is all too apparent. Then the question is passed, and your whole body relaxes, and you almost sigh with relief and then hope that the examiner did not see it. But, he does not have to observe such reactions in the subject's behavior, everything is all in the tracings, from the change in heart rate to the deep sigh. Although this description may seem to have been over dramatized, it is rather similar to what many persons have described as their feelings during the procedure.

Another mental mechanism described to thwart the polygraph procedure is rationalization. In psychological terms, rationalization implies the unconscious process of giving a good reason in place of the real one. When the term is employed to mean a countermeasure, it is clearly a conscious procedure with its goal being to lie without being detected. An example of rationalization is a case in which the subject had been the driver in an armed robbery. When he was asked during the examination whether he had robbed the store, he responded "no" and showed only a very slight deceptive pattern. A very different reaction occurred when the wording of the sentence was changed. After the test, he admitted that he had concentrated on what he tried to make a fact for himself: that he did not actually rob the store, he only drove the get-away car.

A competent examiner is very cautious in formulating the questions so that this should not present a problem. Amounts of money stolen, for example, are handled carefully because if the examinee is asked if he stole $625 and he had only gotten $600, he would be truthful when he denied stealing the $625. Being aware that the questions may be understood by the subject in a very literal sense, the polygraphist develops them in a manner that minimizes the likelihood of any attempts at rationalization being successful.

Hypnosis can be classified as another mental technique that might successfully mislead the polygraphist. Floch wrote of long-term prisoners who managed to convince themselves through hypnotic procedures, that they had actually not committed the crime for which they have been imprisoned.[60] Attempts to demonstrate that hypnosis can actually achieve this objective have been partially successful in laboratory research. Once again, the reader should be wary of generalizing from the laboratory to a real situation.

Weinstein et al.[61] were able to deceive a polygraphist, at least partially, by telling their subjects under hypnosis that they had not taken part in a mock crime in which they had participated. The subjects were also instructed to feel no guilt or anxiety about the act or in regard to the test. The results were not completely achieved because the examiner did not find them nondeceptive, but the tracings were sufficiently disturbed to force an inconclusive diagnosis. The charts appeared deceptive to the operator, but he stated that he could not indicate this finding with a good deal of assuredness. Had this been an actual investigation, in all likelihood the hypnosis would not have been sufficient to inhibit the emotions to the same degree. In a somewhat similar study, Germann, although he interpreted his findings differently, demonstrated that hypnosis somewhat decreased detectability of deception by causing a greater number of inconclusive charts to be obtained.[62] In neither study were deceptive charts labeled as nondeceptive.

In an investigation by Bitterman and Marcuse, subjects were hypnotized and an amnesia was developed for particular words.[63] While the subjects in a conscious state had no recall of the word, they reacted more to it during a polygraph examination than they did to a series of other words. In contrast to the other research, this study indicated that hypnosis was not effective as a countermeasure to polygraph examinations.

Whatever the method employed to counter the test, much is dependent upon the subject's belief in its effectiveness. If he is thoroughly convinced that it will work, this belief could serve to considerably reduce the fear of detection and result in his deception becoming more difficult to determine.[64] While this placebo effect certainly does exist, this author has talked with many subjects who failed the examination, but stated that they were certain, before the test, that they could "beat it."

In general, countermeasures are not very effective in accomplishing anything but producing inconclusive results. Moreover, their devices are very apt to be discovered, which would certainly place the onus of guilt upon them even though the results of the test would not be reported as deceptive.

Another weakness frequently attributed to polygraph has been the lack of standardization of instrumentation, training, theory, and technique.[65] Skolnick stated that the approaches employed were so dissimilar that it was not possible for operators to read one anothers' charts.[66] While they may have not been able to do so in the past, this is no longer the case. The tendency now, particularly in major cases involving courtroom testimony, is to obtain the opinions of several examiners. Standardization has been emphasized by the American Polygraph Association so that, at this time, there are essentially few differences among polygraphists in any of these areas.

The New Jersey Supreme Court Committee on Criminal Procedure on Polygraph Tests indicated a concern that the admission of polygraph testimony would result in frequent battles of the experts.[67] As it is, attorneys tend to view expert witnesses in a less than favorable light in recognition of the fact that some typically give testimony for prosecution or the plaintiff, while others are biased toward the defendant. There is a good likelihood that bias will not occur in polygraphy, because the charts can be interpreted by a number of examiners and reliability is high. As has been indicated, a typical procedure in cases in which the evidence will be admitted into court is to obtain the opinion of several polygraphists to ascertain whether the procedure is appropriate and whether the charts have been accurately scored. Along these lines, Houts has suggested that since there are concerns that polygraph testimony might have too great an impact on the jury, the results always should be evaluated by several polygraphists.[68] A good example of this was the Patricia Hearst case. Her attorneys, Al Johnson and F. Lee Bailey, not only had her polygraph examination administered and interpreted by a team of four examiners, but sent copies of her charts to a number of other experts to be certain that they were in agreement with the results. The latter is not an overly expensive procedure since the outside examiners do not have to be present during the testing itself.

In California, a group of experts has made itself available to evaluate any charts in which differences of opinion exist so that these can be dealt with prior to trial. Another means of dealing with discrepancies is for the court to appoint one or more examiners to evaluate the charts or reexamine the subject. Frequently the defense attorney will request that a private examiner check the charts of his client on a test that was administered by a law enforcement agency. Since examinations are frequently administered on an ex parte basis by a private examiner prior to a stipulated test by a police examiner, those charts that are found nondeceptive likewise are available to the law enforcement polygraphist. Because polygraphists are few in number and since they belong to the same societies and attend the same seminars, there is a feeling of comaradery regardless of whether they typically work for prosecution or defense. Their major motivation, probably because there has been so much difficulty in furthering the case of polygraphy, is to improve the lot of their field. Therefore, they work well together even though they are on different sides of the courtroom. It is felt that any battles of experts that do occur will be minimal.

The complaints that there are some examiners who are unethical is probably as true as in any other field. There is no way of knowing how many, but there are probably few. The number of polygraph examinations that are referred to an operator is dependent on his competence, and an attorney will quickly discontinue working with a polygraphist if his results tend to disagree with the findings of others. The unethical and incompetent are soon out of business. It should be recognized, however, that it would be a simple matter to produce charts so that they would appear deceptive or nondeceptive. The inflection used when presenting a question would be sufficient to cause a reaction that resembles a deceptive response. Even questioning a subject between tests on only the relevant questions will give him the feeling that he is doing poorly on these items and increase his concerns and therefore his reactions to them. The opposite effect would occur if the emphasis were placed on the controls. An unethical examiner could quite easily ask neutral questions in place of the control items and create a chart that clearly looks deceptive or even more easily substitute another person's chart. Risks of such unethical behavior are probably quite small and can be easily eliminated by using observers, recording the entire process, and having the charts signed by the subject after the examination. Finally, if any questions of the conduct of the operator exist, a reexamination by an independent polygraphist could be conducted.

Concerns about the impairment of cross-examination and the inability to question the polygraph instrument itself seem rather inappropriate.[69] It is the interpretation of the tracings that are of primary importance and on which depends a diagnosis of truth or deception. This situation is exactly the same as the expert in cardiology testifying as to his interpretation of the electrocardiograph findings or the neurologist diagnosing epilepsy with the electroencephalograph. Since this medical testimony has not been found to impair cross-examination in the courts, then certainly the same should be true for polygraph evidence. The issue of excluding the polygraph findings as hearsay evidence was raised in *U.S.* v. *Stromberg*[70] and dealt with by Judge Joiner in *U.S.* v. *Ridling.*[71] As previously indicated, he felt that the statements made by the subject and supported by the opinion of the polygraphist would appear to be hearsay. He added that despite this factor, polygraph testimony should be admitted as an exception to the hearsay rule.

The privilege against self-incrimination frequently has been raised as an issue, but in *People* v. *Houser,*[72] the court indicated that the Fifth Amendment is always subject to waiver and may be affected by the accused's consent to take a polygraph examination. It has been recognized that a person cannot be directly coerced into subjecting himself to a polygraph test for he could easily distort the results through constant movements. Both Coghill and Burkey, in contrast, take issue with the description of the test as being voluntary.[73] They emphasized the many subtle pressures that are brought to bear on the person that force him into taking the examination. Refusing to be tested might suggest guilt, for example, and Silving noted that once polygraph testimony was offered on a more routine basis, the jury also would assume guilt if it were not presented.[74] Here, too, the arguments against polygraphy that were promulgated in Germany have been presented. Free will precludes the deliberate suspension of the conscious for the purpose of exploring the unconscious. The theory of the German courts was that the unconscious mind, as measured through the physiologic changes, was answering involuntarily if the person were lying to avoid the discovery of his guilt. To take away the person's right to deny his culpability, even though he consents to a polygraph examination, was viewed as an involuntary act and a loss of the privilege to avoid self-incrimination. Falick stated that any attempt at penetrating the inner being violates human dignity and the right to privacy.[75] Protection against unreasonable search and seizure includes, in his thinking, the penetration of the inner domain of the individual person. Silving also ascribed to this the loss of human dignity, which she said is assigned to good and wicked, innocent and guilty alike.[76] Truth was characterized as being only a means to achieve justice; but dignity was the end itself. Quite obviously, Silving feels that it is better for justice to suffer rather than to detract from the dignity of man. Somewhere in this attempt to preserve dignity, the victim and the victims that will follow must be considered. It would be most unfortunate if, in our endeavor to protect the dignity of the accused by avoiding techniques that might search out the truth, we failed to protect society. The price of dignity would be too high if it served to add to the list of victims. There is no argument with John Adams' statement that it is better ". . . that many guilty persons should escape unpunished than one innocent person should suffer."[77] However, today our purpose is not punishment but rehabilitation and protection. The innocent must be protected, but so too must the innocent victims who stand to lose if the guilty are released. Perhaps some degree of dignity must be sacrificed if truth is to be found, and if polygraphy opens the door to the truth, then it should be utilized. Wicker stated: "There is today in our courtrooms entirely too much intentional perjury . . . usually difficult, and often impossible for even an experienced trial lawyer to expose on cross-examination many of the lies of false swearing witnesses," and further indicated that "polygraph interrogation is now the best available method of detecting deception."[78] Frederick Barnett described the polygraph approach as "the great equalizer" because it dispensed justice, unlike the courts and jurors, without bias,[79] and is not effected by the subjects, race class, demeanor, or intelligence. In this way too, the dignity of man is maintained.

Further criticisms of the technique include Skolnick's statement that the test is based on a lie when people say that it detects lies.[80] Smith wrote that to say the polygraph is infallible is to use a lie to detect a lie, while Eliasberg indicated that the jury will believe in its infallability and so be influenced by that.[81] Lykken emphasized that the determination of guilt or innocence is the role of the jury, but if the polygraph were admitted into evidence, it would make this decision for them.[82] The polygraph also has been described as attacking the heart of the matter under investigation—the credibility of the witness—and thereby usurps the role of the jury.[83] To this, Roper added that the credibility of the witness is for the jury to decide.[84] If the polygraph decides truth or deception, what is left for the jury? The result then is that the question to be answered rests on the credibility of the examiner, not the defendant.[85]

No competent and ethical polygraphist would claim that the polygraph detects lies, is infallible, nor decides guilt or innocence. Even before Keeler's statement in 1934,[86] emphasis has clearly been placed on the fact that the term *lie detector* is a misnomer. Operators in their explanation of the approach typically present their description in terms of the measurement of physiologic changes that occur in the nervous system because of the fear of a lie's being detected. Infallibility will never be attained, and in fact, if it were, then the concerns related to usurping the role of the jury would be even greater. As it is, there has been very little study in this realm, with the exception of cases being cited in which the court or jury decided in opposition to polygraph findings. These cases, of course, demonstrate little except that in some instances the polygraph did not have that great an impact. The impact would be obviously difficult to analyze because much of the effect of the testimony would be dependent on the expert witness' ability to present his testimony in an effective manner. The acceptance of the testimony by the juror is in part based on the polygraphists' credibility just as is the case with any other expert witness. Other factors that would greatly influence the jury's attitude would be the instructions given to them by the court and the effectiveness of the attorney's examination and cross-examination of the expert witness.

Barnett[87] obtained the court's permission to interview the jurors in *U.S.* v. *Grasso*,[88] in which the defendant had been charged with selling cocaine. The results of a polygraph examination were admitted into evidence, and the examiner testified that the defendant was truthful in his denial of this act. The jury found him innocent, and then the eight of the twelve jurors who were available were questioned as to how they had reached their decision. They indicated that while they were impressed with the foundation testimony and were convinced that the procedure could differentiate truth from deception, the results were put aside while they considered the other evidence, which they found to be sufficient to declare a not guilty verdict. They did report that if the decision had been more difficult, the polygraph testimony would have been viewed as sufficient evidence to raise a reasonable doubt. In this instance, the polygraph testimony did not in any manner invade the province of the jury. In the case of *Wisconsin* v. *Loniello and Grignano*,[89] Inbau reported that the court questioned the jury as to whether the polygraph testimony were helpful in making a decision.[90] The jurors agreed that it assisted them in determining the credibility of the witnesses and the defendants.

Forkosch[91] polled the jurors in the 1938 case of *People* v. *Kenny*.[92] In this instance, Reverend Summers has tested the defendant with a galvanometer and found him to be nondeceptive. While none of the jurors based his decision on this evidence alone, five of the ten interviewed indicated that they accepted this testimony without question. Four of the ten stated that if they were to serve on a jury again, they would accept this type of evidence as conclusive. Only one of those interviewed expressed the opinion that he would be prejudiced if the defendant refused to submit to the examination.

In a further attempt to evaluate the impact of polygraph testimony on a jury, Koffler had some law students make a decision of guilt or innocence in three hypothetical cases.[93] In the first instance there was slight evidence of guilt, and no polygraph test had been administered. In the remaining two cases, deceptive polygraph findings along with the minimal evidence of guilt were reported. In the second case, testimony indicated that polygraphy was reported to be 85 percent accurate, 14.5 percent inconclusive, and .5 percent in error. Accuracy in the final case was presented at 99.5 percent, while the level of error was at .5 percent. Koffler concluded from the reactions of the students that a person could be convicted on little more than fragmentary evidence and adverse polygraph findings. As the margin of error reported for this procedure was reduced, less was required in terms of other evidence to convict the defendant.

At this time, the impact of the polygraph testimony upon the jury is felt to be the major reason for excluding polygraph testimony. And the greater the demonstration of its accuracy, the more this objection will be raised. The issue actually is whether judicial instructions can be presented in a manner that will allow a jury to appropriately evaluate polygraph testimony. Too strong a warning could easily negate its probative value, while little or no instructions could result in too large an impact on the jurors. The recommendations made for the court's instructions to the jury in *U.S.* v. *Valdez* are felt to be sufficient to accomplish their purpose.[94] Neither will the jury be overly impressed by the testimony, nor will they ignore it. Thus, this author believes that admission of polygraph evidence will not impinge on the province of the jury.

In *U.S.* v. *Urquidez*, the court indicated that it would be overburdened by the many variables involved in polygraph testimony and the examination and cross-examination that would take place would significantly lengthen the trial process.[95] This, however, would only be the case in the early stages of admissibility for when polygraph testimony is admitted under judicial notice, only the requirements for the presentation of any scientific data would be needed. The operator would be qualified and subject to examination and cross-examination.

At the present time, the majority of criticisms that have been leveled against polygraphy are no longer viable: Some of the weaknesses have been corrected, while other complaints were never appropriate. There is no doubt, however, that a considerable need for improvement exists. Undoubtedly, the weakest link lies in the lack of competence of some of the examiners and the inability of the American Polygraph Association to keep these people from practicing. It should be recognized that unless there is a breech in ethics, this control cannot be effected any more than in any of the other professional groups. A change that could be fostered, however, would be to certify those polygraphists who can demonstrate a greater level of expertise. With a list of such examiners, the courts and attorneys would be in a better position to select one with a high level of experience and ability.

Further emphasis should be placed on elevating the prerequisites for membership in the professional societies, admission into the polygraph schools, and for attaining licensure. A baccalaureat degree with a major in psychology or physiology would be desirable, and the schooling should be expanded and definitely should include an internship in residency. The 260 hour programs seem insufficient when compared with those of longer duration, and attempts ought to be made to extend their curriculums.

More research is required in a broad range of areas including the area of instrumentation. There is no doubt that more sophisticated sensors are available, but these have to be studied to determine their effectiveness in lie detection. Attempts should be made to evaluate the impact of polygraph testimony upon the jury and how it is influenced by the court's instructions and the role of the attorneys. Ideally, the sciences should become more involved in both studying and actually administering polygraph examinations to criminal suspects, for without the latter, they cannot appreciate the many variables that influence the results. Because the doorway to admissibility in the courts has been opened, it is expected that behavioral scientists and attorneys will begin to develop enough interest in this field to take the necessary training and become involved in polygraphy itself.

Notes

1. *U.S.* v. *Frye*, 293, F. 1013 (D.C. Cir. 1923).

2. *U.S.* v. *Debetham*, 348, F. Supp. 1377 (S.D. Cal. 1972).

3. Cureton, E.E., "A Consensus as to the Validity of the Polygraph Procedure," *Tenn. L. Rev.* 22 (1953): 728-42, and Ash, P., "A Survey of Attitudes on the Polygraph," *Polygraph* 2 (1973): 200-23.

4. "House Committee Calls for Ban on Government Use of Polygraphs," *Amer. Psychol. Assoc. Monitor* 7 (April 1976).

5. Eliasberg, W., "Forensic, Psychology," *Southern Calif. L. Rev.* 19 (1946): 349-409.

6. Lykken, D.T., "Guilty Knowledge Test: The Right Way to Use a Lie Detector," *Psychology Today*, March 1975, pp. 56-60.

7. Smith, B.M., "The Polygraph," *Scientific American* 216 (1967): 25-31.

8. *State* v. *Bohmer*, 210, Wisc. 651, 246, N.W. 314 (1933).

9. Skolnick, J.H., "Scientific Theory and Scientific Evidence: An Analysis of Lie Detection," *Yale Law J.* 70 (1961): 694-728.

10. Lykken, D.T., "Psychology and the Lie Detector Industry," *American Psychologist* 29 (1974): 725-38.

11. Skolnick, "Scientific Theory."

12. Sternbach, R.A., Gustafson, L.A., and Colier, R.L., "Don't Trust the Lie Detector," *Harvard Bus. Rev.* (1962): 127-34.

13. Ellson, D.G., Davis, R.C., Saltzman, I.J., and Burke, C.J., *A Report of Research on Detection of Deception*, Contract No. N6 onr - 18011, September 15, 1952, Office of Naval Research (available through Indiana University, Bloomington). Ansley, N., "Capillary Responses as a Polygraph Channel," in N. Ansley (ed.), *Legal Admissibility of the Polygraph* (Springfield, Ill.: Charles C. Thomas, 1975). Jacobs, J.E., "The Feasibility of Alternate Physiological Sensors as Applicable to Polygraph Techniques in N. Ansley (ed.), *Legal Admissibility of the Polygraph* (Springfield, Ill.: Charles C. Thomas, 1975). Decker, R.E., Stein, A.E., and Ansley, N., "A Cardio Activity Monitor," in N. Ansley (ed.), *Legal Admissibility of the Polygraph* (Springfield, Ill.: Charles C. Thomas, 1975), and Barland, G.H., "Use of Voice Changes in the Detection of Deception," presented at the 86th meeting of the Accoustical Society of America, Los Angeles, October 31, 1973 (available through Department of Psychology, University of Utah, Salt Lake City).

14. 12. CLR 2133 (Cal. Sup. Ct. 11/6/72).

15. 348 F. Supp. 1377 (S.D. Cal. 1972).

16. 413 F. 2d 296 (10th Cir. 1969).

17. Smith, "The Polygraph."

18. 71 Misc. 2d 1040 337 N.Y.S. 2d 616 Sup. Ct. Queens Cty Ct. (1972).

19. *Skinner* v. *Commonwealth*, Va. Sup. Ct. (10/11/71); *Boeche* v. *State*, 151 Neb. 368, 383, 37, N.W. 2d 593, 600 (1949); and *People* v. *Becker*, 300 Mich. 562, 565, 566 2 N.W. 2d 503, 505 (1942).

20. Horvath, F.S., "The Accuracy and Reliability of Police Polygraphic (Lie Dector) Examiners' Judgments of Truth and Deception: The Effect of Selected Variables," unpublished doctoral dissertation, Michigan State University, East Lansing, 1974.

21. Horvath, F.S., and Reid, J.E., "The Reliability of Polygraph Examiner Diagnoses of Truth and Deception," *J. Crim. Law, Criminol. and Police Science* 62 (1971): 276-81.

22. Abrams, S., "Polygraph Validity and Reliability: A Review," *J. Forensic Sciences* 18 (1973): 313-26.

23. Inbau, F.E., and Reid, J.E., *Lie Detection and Criminal Interrogation* 3rd ed. (Baltimore: Williams and Wilkins, 1953).

24. Sternbach et al., "Trust the Lie Detector."

25. Silving, H., "Testing of the Unconscious in Criminal Cases," *Harvard L. Rev.* 69 (1956): 683-705.

26. Skolnick, "Scientific Theory."

27. Langley, L.L., "The Polygraph Lie Detector: Its Physiological Basis, Reliability, and Admissibility," *Ala. Lawyer* 16 (1955): 209-24, and Burkey, L.M., "The Case Against the Polygraph," *American Bar Association, J.* 5 (1965): 855-57.

28. American Polygraph Association Newsletter, July-August 1976.

29. Skolnick, "Scientific Theory."

30. Highleyman, S.L., "The Deceptive Certainty of the 'Lie Detector'," *Hastings L.J.* 10 (1958): 47-64.

31. Turner, W.W., "Invisible Witness: The Use and Abuse of the New Technology of Crime Investigation," (Bobbs-Merrill Co. 1968).

32. Floch, M., "Limitations of the Lie Detector," *J. Crim. Law and Criminol.* 40 (1950): 651-52.

33. Highleyman, "The Deceptive Certainty," and Eliasberg, "Forensic Psychology."

34. See Turner, "Invisible Witness," and Lykken, "Guilty Knowledge Test."

35. Raskin, D.C., *Psychopathy and Detection of Deception in a Prison Population*, Report No. 75-1, NI 99-001 (available through Department of Psychology, University of Utah, Salt Lake City, and Barland, G.H., and Raskin, D.C., "Psychopathy and Detection of Deception in Criminal Suspects," presented at the Society for Psychophysiological Research, Salt Lake City, Utah, October 25, 1974.

36. Abrams, S., "The Validity of the Polygraph with Schizophrenics," *Polygraph* 3 (1974): 328-37.

37. Abrams S., and Weinstein, E., "The Validity of the Polygraph with Retardates," *J. Police Sciences and Admin.* 2 (1974): 11-14.

38. Beck, A.T., "Reliability of Psychiatric Diagnosis: A Critique of Systematic Studies," *Amer. J. Psychiatr.* 119 (1963): 210-16, and Pasamanick, D., Dinitz, S., and Lefton, M., "Psychiatric Orientation and Its Relation to Diagnosis and Treatment in a Mental Hospital," *Amer. J. Psychiatr.* 116 (1959): 127-32.

39. Abrams, S., "The Validity of the Polygraph Technique with Children," *J. Police Sciences and Admin.* 3 (1975): 310-11.

40. Burack, B., "A Critical Analysis of the Theory, Method, and Limitations of the 'Lie Detector'," *J. Crim. L.* 46 (1955): 414-26.

41. Lykken, "Guilty Knowledge Test."

42. See Eliasberg, "Forensic Psychology," and Skolnick, "Scientific Theory."

43. Dearman, H.B., and Smith, B.M., "Unconscious Motivation and the Polygraph Test," *Amer. J. Psychiatr.* 37 (1963): 1017-20.

44. Weinstein, E., Abrams, S., and Gibbons, D., "The Validity of the Polygraph with Hypnotically Induced Repression and Guilt," *Amer. J. Psychiatr.* 126 (1970): 143-46.

45. *People* v. *Leone*, 25, N.Y. 2d, 511, 515, 255, N.E. 2d, 696, 698, 307, N.Y.S., 2d 430, 433 (1969).

46. Backster, C., Technique Fundamentals of the Tri-Zone Polygraph Test (available through 645 Ash Street, San Diego, California 92101).

47. Floch, "Limitations of the Lie Detector."

48. Inbau and Reid, "Lie Detection."

49. Highleyman, "The Deceptive Certainty," and Skolnick, "Scientific Theory."

50. Barland, G.H., and Raskin, D.C., "The Use of Electrodermal Activity in the Detection of Deception," in W.F. Prokasy and D.C. Raskin (eds.), *Electrodermal Activity in Psychological Research* (New York: Academic Press, 1973).

51. Hess, C., "Observations Regarding the Effects of Specific Drugs on Polygraph Tracings," *Polygraph* 4 (1975): 314-28.

52. Zimmerman, C., Personal Communication (available through Scientific Security, 80 Boylston Street, Boston, 02116).

53. Berman, M.A., "Prescription Drugs and the Polygraph," *Polygraph* 4 (1975): 329-38.

54. Kubis, J.F., *Studies in Lie Detection: Computer Feasibility Considerations*, Technical Report, 62-205, Prepared for Air Force Systems Command, Contract No. AF 30(602)-2270, Fordham University, New York, 1962.

55. More, H.W., Polygraph Research and the University, *Law and Order* 14 (1966): 73-78.

56. Larson, J.A., "Manipulation of the Marston Deception Test," *J. Crim. L.* 12 (1921): 390-99.

57. Kubis, "Studies in Lie Detection."

58. Ibid.; see also, More, "Polygraph Research."

59. Abrams, S., "The Polygraph: Laboratory Vs. Field Research," *Polygraph* 1 (1972): 145-50.

60. Floch, "Limitations of the Lie Detector."

61. Weinstein et al., "The Validity of the Polygraph."

62. Germann, A.C., "Hypnosis as Related to the Scientific Detection of Deception by Polygraph Examination: A Pilot Study," *Intern. J. Clin. Exp. Hypn.* 9 (1961): 309-11.

63. Bitterman, M.E., and Marcuse, F.L., "Autonomic Response in Post-hypnotic Amnesia," *J. Exp. Psychol.* 35, (1945): 248-52.

64. Gustafson, L.A., and Orne, M.T., "Effects of Perceived Role and Role Success on the Detection of Deception," *J. Appl. Psych.* 49 (1965): 412-17.

65. Sell, W.E., "Deception, Detection, and the Law," *U. Pittsburgh L. Rev.* 2 (1950): 210-27.

66. Skolnick, "Scientific Theory."

67. Garvey, P.J., "New Jersey Supreme Court Committee on Criminal Procedure in Polygraph Tests, A Review," *Polygraph* 2 (1973): 116-21.

68. Houts, M., "Team Testing Will Bring the Polygraph Safely into Court," in N. Ansley (ed.), *Legal Admissibility of the Polygraph*, (Springfield, Ill.: Charles C. Thomas, 1975).

69. *Boeche* v. *State*, 151 Neb., 368, 37, N.W. 2d 593 (1949).

70. 179 F. Supp. 278 (S.D.N.Y. 1959).

71. 350 F. Supp. 90 (E.D. Mich. 1972).

72. 85 Cal. App. 2d 686, 193 P. 2d 937 (1948).

73. Coghill, M.A., "The Lie Detector in Employment," Industrial and Labor Relations Library, Key Issues Series No. 2, July 1968 (available through Public Information Center Industrial and Labor Relations Library, Cornell University, Ithaca, N.Y., 14850), and Burkey, "The Case Against the Polygraph."

74. Silving, "Testing of the Unconscious."

75. Falick, P., "The Lie Detector and The Right to Privacy," *N.Y.S. Bar J.* (1968): 102-10.

76. Silving, "Testing of the Unconscious."

77. "The Founding Fathers: John Adams," *Newsweek* 1972.

78. Wicker, W., "The Polygraph Truth Test and the Law of Evidence," *Tenn. L. Rev.* 22 (1953): 711-27.

79. Rapaport, D., "The Greening of the Lie Detector," *The Washington Post*, April 15, 1973.

80. Skolnick, "Scientific Theory."

81. See Smith, "The Polygraph," and Eliasberg, "Forensic Psychology."

82. Lykken, "Guilty Knowledge."

83. Richardson, J.R., *Modern Scientific Evidence* (Cincinnati: W.H. Anderson Co., 1961); *People* v. *Davis*, 343, Mich. 348, 373, 72, N.W. 2d 269, 282 (1955); and *People* v. *Sinclair*, Mich. App., 255, 175, N.W. 2d, 893 (1970).

84. Roper, R.S., "The Search for Truth at Trial, An Argument Against the Admission of the Polygraph Test Results at Trial," *Polygraph* 5 (1975): 130-38.

85. *Henderson* v. *State*, 94, Okl. Crim. 45, 53, 230, P. 495, 503, Cert. denied, 343, U.S. 898 (1951).

86. Keeler, L., "Debunking the Lie Detector," *J. Crim. Law, Criminol., and Police Science* 25 (1934): 153-59.

87. Barnett, F.J., "How Does a Jury View Polygraph Examination Results?" *Polygraph* 2 (1973): 275-77.

88. Cir. Ct. Green Lake Cty. Wisc. (1935).

89. *U.S.* v. *Grasso*, U.S.D.C. Boston, Mass. (1973).

90. Inbau, F.J., "Detection of Deception Technique Admitted as Evidence," *J. Crim. L.* 26 (1935): 262-70.

91. Forkosch, M.D., "The Lie Detector and the Courts," *N.Y.U.L. Quart. Rev.* 117 (1939): 202-31.

92. *People* v. *Kenny*, Misc. 51, 3 N.Y. (Supp.) 2d, 348 (1938).

93. Koffler, J., "The Lie Detector, A Critical Appraisal of the Technique as a Potential Undermining Factor in the Judicial Process," N.Y.L.F. 146 (1957): 3123-39.

94. 91 Ariz. 274, 371 P. 2d 894 (1962).

95. 356, F. Supp. 1363, 13 CLR, 1251 C C.D. Cal. (1973).

Appendix

Appendix:
Establishment of a
Foundation for Court

Foreword

The testimony you are about to read was gathered by Attorney F. Lee Bailey, and his staff which included attorneys Gerald Alch, Mark Kadish, John Truman, A. Johnson and the undersigned in support of introducing polygraph evidence to corroborate and confirm statements made by Captain Ernest Medina regarding the highly publicized My Lai Massacre investigation in August 1971, during the trial by Courts Martial of Captain Ernest Medina.

It was introduced in an effort to lay a foundation of scientific credibility of the art and science of the detection of deception technique, and its significance cannot be overlooked by legal practitioners, scholars, investigators and polygraph examiners.

Here you have the questions and answers by recognized practitioners, and the legal approach and argumentation upon which to lay a foundation for a technique from which the legal community demands 100% infallibility.

Many examiners have been called upon to advise or to enlighten attorneys, not familiar with the technique, as to how to present the results of a polygraph examination (also see *Criminal Law Library, F. Lee Bailey and Henry B. Rothblatt, Investigation and Preparation of Criminal Cases, Federal and State*, Lawyers Cooperative, Bancroft-Whitney, Rochester, N.Y. 1970, page 299-329).

It is even more difficult when examiners are being called upon to advise attorneys on what questions to ask during cross-examination, once an examiner has been allowed to testify.

The question as to how to present polygraphic evidence is extremely important in each and every case and can only be answered in one way: "As long as there is no considerable recognition in the Appellate Courts and as long as courts still use the language of *Frye vs. U.S.* 293 F 1013 (1923) which in effect, even that far back, demonstrated its exteme value in supporting the veracity of *Frye's* denial (Frye was released and exonerated after serving three years of a life sentence, after a person had confessed to the actual killing . . . *New York Judicial Counsel, 14th Annual Report*, 265 (1948)), every effort must be made to see to it that courtroom exposure of the technique must stand the test of Scientific Proof of Credibility."

Over the years I have had occasion to conduct polygraph examinations for

The material in this appendix is reprinted with the kind permission of Charles Zimmerman from his book, *The Polygraph in Court* (B.H.F. Printing P.O. Box 83 Auburndale, Mass. 02166, 1972). It consists of the expert testimony presented before the Court in the trial by Courts Martial of Ernest Medina regarding the My Lai incident.

Mr. F. Lee Bailey, Esquire, in all of the cases that were made subject to an attempt to lay a foundation of scientific credibility. I have had the great fortune of assisting in such preparations of the techniques since 1960. In doing so I observed that while such preparations started out with tremendous "skull sessions," hours and hours of reading and writing in *Commonwealth of Massachusetts vs. Willard Page*, 1961, to a rather routine "setting" in the trial by *Courts Martial of Captain Ernest Medina*, re: My Lai Massacre, 1970/71.

From these various presentations (*Commonwealth of Massachusetts vs. Fatalo*, 1963—*People of New Jersey vs. Dorothy and Harold Matzner*, 1968 and *State of Michigan vs. Peter Lazaros*, 1970, among others) I learned and recognized that the most outstanding legal and scientific presentation must include:

1. Recognition of physiological aspects of the technique—the opinion of such experts as to its possible value in verifying truthfulness . . . (usually by recognized Psychiatrists, Psychologists, or Physiologists experienced in the field.)

2. Historical Developments, Statistical Data, Scope of use, Professional Organizations . . . (by recognized examiners, not connected with the case at bar)

3. Use of the technique in the same State by Federal, State, or Municipal Agencies . . . (by local examiners . . . stressing the fact that it is used during the initial process of the investigation . . . that instruments and training are supported by public funds and whether or not they are aware of any person eliminated by the technique but subsequently charged or tried for the crime in spite of the examination result)

4. Last, but not least, the examiner who conducted the examination (who testifies to his own expertise and background in the field, test construction employed, and reasoning for his opinion)

With such a presentation the examiner conducting the examination would not have to make any self-serving statements as he would testify only to his own examination and leave all of the needed testimony in support or recognition of the technique to case-disinterested witnesses/experts.

It is with that thought in mind that I conceived the idea as to the usefulness of this transcript in printed format, since it represents an effort to afford practitioners the proper introduction of this extremely valuable technique to the legal community.

I am indebted to Messrs. F. Lee Bailey, Dr. Basilio, G.J. Swidler, Gordon H. Barland and Dr. Raskin for their contributions, advice and consent.

Charles H. Zimmerman
Boston, Massachusetts

Testimony

(The court was called to order at 0912 hours, 19 August 1971.)

MJ: Court will come to order.

TC: Your Honor, all parties to the trial who were present when the court recessed yesterday are again present with the exception of the members of the court. Our reporter today is Specialist Anderson who has been previously sworn.

MJ: Let the record reflect that we are in an out-of-court hearing, in fact, and we'll proceed this way during the day. I think the record should also reflect that this is a, in effect, a motions hearing; that there are certain witnesses who are, with the consent of both parties and the military judge, not sequestered but, are, in fact, in the courtroom and will apparently lend support, one to another, to get a complete picture of the position taken by the defense. Since the defense is perfecting its record, I'll give you the opportunity to so proceed.

TC: Sir, before the defense proceeds, can I just be certain of what, for the record, what we're litigating today? As I understand you have denied an evidentiary hearing to the defense on the—have decided not to allow them to present evidence on the reliability of a polygraph pursuant to Rule 1, Paragraph 142e, of the *Manual*. As I understand that you have made this ruling and that particular ruling is final and that the purpose of today's session is to allow the defense for the purpose of the perfection of a record and for the building of a record to present evidence of the reliability of a polygraphic test for the purpose of demonstrating its credibility and admissibility into evidence. Their purpose in doing this is to state that your following the clear rule in the *Manual* is an abuse of discretion that reaches Constitutional proportions so that the purpose of today's hearing is merely to allow the defense to perfect this particular issue for appeal. Am I correct in understanding that is the purpose of today's session?

IC: My recollection is somewhat at variance, Your Honor. As I recall, I motioned before you to bring in at Government expense certain witnesses to establish the authenticity and reliability of this technique of truth verification whereupon, pursuant to the flatout provisions of the *Manual*, you ruled that you had no discretion. And, certainly, it's never been contended that any abuse of discretion by this court was conducted at Constitutional level or any other levels. Because of that rule, the expense was not warranted and an offer of proof would be accepted, in view of the fact that the defense did not have the funds to produce the witnesses at private expense. On the other hand, due to the fortuitous circumstance that the American Polygraph Association happens to be having an Annual Convention at the Regency Hotel in downtown Atlanta, I requested that we be allowed to put this testimony in the record for several purposes. Number one, because we think the provision in the *Manual*, if it is properly construed to deny to an accused the use of this evidence, is an error of Constitutional dimensions and should be preserved for appellate or other reviewing consideration. Second, it would be possible, it may indeed be possible to obtain a clarification of the rule favorable to the accused from that authority which has the power to rewrite the *Manual* at its discretion in Washington. And third, it may well be that the prosecution, through its efforts to bring out certain conversation with the defendant, could open the door so that the evidence becomes admissible for reasons quite apart from its general admissibility. And, for that reason, I have asked for this hearing. It is my purpose to show, first, that the technique, as a science, is a reliable technique with a creditable history particularly in the military and that the use of such evidence would benefit the administration of justice and in this particular case render more likely the fact that the truth will emerge and justice will be done to this accused and, of course, the United States. The second question presented is whether the particular examiner who ran the test is qualified. I suspect we'll have a stipulation on that since the examiner was employed by the Government and still is but, if not, he can stand on his own qualifications. That phase of it I won't go into until such time as for one purpose or another the evidence might become admissible. Today's hearing is to establish for Your Honor and for this record that the technique is venerable, time-tested, well-structured and reliable to the extent that judicial admissibility should be granted, period.

MJ: Since I see no variance within my understanding between the two positions of the parties, I'll say, "Yes, that's exactly what we're going to go into today." And you may proceed, Mr. Bailey.

DC: Mr. Backster, please. If you will come down and be sworn by the prosecutor.

(Mr. Cleve Backster, civilian, was called as a witness for the defense, was sworn and assumed his seat on the witness stand.)

DIRECT EXAMINATION

Questions by Major Eckhardt:

Q: Would you please state your full name?

A: Cleve Backster.

Q: And what is your residence and address, please?

A: 165 West 46th Street, New York City.

Q: And your occupation, please, sir?

A: Polygraph examiner.

TC: Mr. Bailey, your witness.

Questions by Mr. Bailey:

Q: Mr. Backster, would you give the court a little of your background generally and particularly in the field of polygraph examination.

A: I entered in the field of polygraph interrogation and polygraph examination back as early as 1948. In fact, since that time, I've been full time involved in research in the polygraph field, the administering of polygraph examinations and the conducting of a school in New York City that trains primarily police officers in the use of the polygraph. Also, the technique that has been taught for a number of years at Fort Gordon Polygraph School involves a great deal of material that is a result of the research that was conducted during my eight years as Research Chairman for the entire polygraph field.

Q: Prior to your entry into the polygraph field in 1948, what background did you have?

A: Prior to that, I was in the Counterintelligence Corps as an interrogation instructor at Fort Holabird and prior to that, I had a commission in the United States Navy.

Q: Where did you receive your initial training in polygraph examination?

A: The initial training was received from the Leonard Keeler. This is back in the time of the start of the organized course of instruction at the Keeler Polygraph Institute.

Q: Is that in Chicago?

A: In Chicago, Illinois.

Q: And what is the name of the school that you now operate?

A: The Backster School.

Q: And how long has that been in operation?

A: The Backster School has been in operation since 1949 or I'm sorry, 1959.

Q: For the record, would you give us the address where your offices are located?

A: 165 West 46th Street.

Q: Now, Mr. Backster, starting with the instrument itself, would you explain to the court, what are the components of the instrument that is commonly called the polygraph?

A: The instrument called the polygraph really is not an invented instrument. It is the collection of three standard recording components that have many other uses in the psychological field and the field of physiological research. And the three that are the primary components of the present day version of the polygraph involve the respiratory section that makes a running recording on chart paper of the breathing of an individual, the respiratory pattern and changes. Also, there is a section that utilizes the blood pressure cuff assembly that is popularly used in the medical profession today but, this cuff assembly actually is attached through a connecting pneumatic tube to a tambour arrangement that makes a running recording of each pulse beat of the individual and relative changes in blood pressure during the polygraph examination. The third component is called galvanic skin response and, in fact, this is widely used in psychology departments as an indicator or reflector of emotional changes within an individual. The popular explanation of the cycle galvanic reflex or galvanic skin response is that it records resistance changes within the individual being tested that relate to emotional changes.

Q: And how are these three components allowed to record what is happening in an individual?

A: The three components, two of them being pneumatic in nature, namely the breathing unit and the heart and blood pressure unit, are connected to tambours that through a mechanical linkage position a pin on a moving chart paper and also the galvanic skin response is connected through an electronic arrangement to another recording pin; but, these pins are positioned in alignment with each other so that they record simultaneously on the moving chart paper.

Q: At what speed does this chart paper move?

A: The popular speed of the—of most polygraphs, in general, use the six inches a minute.

Q: And what polygraph instruments recognized by the profession, to your knowledge, are currently in production or in use?

A: I'd say the instruments primarily in use are the Stoetling deceptograph and the Keeler polygraph.

Q: And are there in fact some modifications of these instruments that have been developed from time to time by examiners in the field?

A: Yes. The fact that there are two popular sources for the instrumentation has created a lively competitive situation where there have been continual improvements and refinements of the instrument where they're considered quite adequate even by the most strict scientific standards as far as a recording instrument for these physiological changes brought about by emotionality within the subject.

Q: All right. Now, with view toward assessing eventually in your testimony the accuracy of the technique, what problems, if any, arise as to the instrument itself? Is there any problem of reliability in taking the information, physiological information, produced by the body and getting it on to the chart paper or is that a generally reliable method?

A: This I think is considered, again by even the strictest scientific requirements, as something that can be accomplished successfully with present day equipment but, if there is some kind of mechanical or electronic failure it becomes extremely obvious that the failure is present. There are methods of testing the sensitivity of the polygraph and the proper functioning of each of the instrument components that are very sound and leave very little to be desired as far as the equipment itself is concerned.

Q: Now, in connection with your training as an examiner, have you had some background in both physiology and psychology?

A: Yes, I have.

Q: Can you give the court just a little of your sources of learning in those two areas?

A: Well, I was a psychology major in college and also have been exposed to a good bit of physiology also through some extended research in other areas where the galvanic skin response is utilized other than the polygraph field.

Q: If we may then infer from your testimony that here is supposedly some cor-rolation between deception and what is recorded on the three components of the polygraph, would you, component by component, explain to the court what is happening when interrogation is conducted with the polygraph attached and what the examiner is looking for, first with the pneumograph than with the blood pressure cuff, because the technical term is a little longer than I can handle this morning and then, with the galvanic skin response.

A: First I might mention, in order to clarify the term interrogation while the instrument is activated, that the interrogation is reduced to a procedure where questions are asked that where it is appropriate to receive a yes or a no answer rather than a narrative on the part of the subject because extensive talking be-yond a brief answer will distort the readings for reasons other than those related to emotions tying in with the particular fear of detection that is utilized as a principal part of the polygraph technique. But, when a question is asked and these questions I might add are spaced approximately 20 to 25 seconds apart in the breathing although a person may ordinarily think that they can consciously control the breathing, any attempt to force a breathing pattern is recognizable by a trained polygraph examiner and the breathing pattern involves very dra-matic suppressions and then compensations for the loss of oxygen during this suppressed period when the person was under the localized emotional stress of a question that was bothersome to him. So, these suppressions in the breathing pattern and compensations where a person is oxygenating to make up for the oxygen lost during the time that there was suppressed breathing, form a very readable pattern that has one of higher reliabilities in the three components of the instrument. In the heart section, or the blood pressure—pulse section of the polygraph, primarily, we are interested in looking at relative changes in blood pressure in the individual, relative changes in the amplitude of the pulse beat and relative changes in the rate of the pulse of the individual. And during recent years research has been conducted that has allowed us to formulate rules for the interpreting of these charts. Rules that would allow us to enunciate why we're looking at a chart and seeing that which we consider to be a significant reaction. In past days I think this was less exact but now we are able to describe beat for beat and assign tracing characteristic terms to that which is occurring on the chart that can be, I think, made clear even to a layman in that particular technique. In the galvanic skin response, the apparent resistance change that occurs at the time that a person is under emotional stress is a well-validated aspect as far as years and years of psychological instruction are concerned utilizing this very component, but, usually with a visual needle indicating the changes in psychology labs all over the world and, of course, in the classroom instruction. And when a person is under emotional stress there is an apparent relative change in resistance where the needle will sweep very dramatically toward the top of the chart and recover. If properly understood and properly utilized this also can be a very valuable contribution to polygraph technique.

Q: Now, each of these components is in some manner registering a reaction, is it not?

A: Yes, sir. It is.

Q: And the reaction is stimulated by some kind of question in each case?

A: Yes, yes, it is.

Q: Now, can you give the court in brief summary and without a full blown lecture in physiology what the phenomenon is that begins as a psychological stimulus and winds up as a measurable and recorded physiological response?

A: Yes. First, I might mention the steps that seem apparent in the use of this instrumentation, the particular use for which it's being applied. First, a question is asked that requires appropriately a yes or a no answer and I might state that these questions are divided into several categories, categories that involve a non-lie question, a possible lie question, a probable lie question, and perhaps another category not widely used, a known-lie question. Now, the question that is asked that is relevant to the issue during a polygraph examination is a relevant question and is a possible lie question where there may be deception. Now, the mechanics of eliciting a meaningful reaction in this structured testing situation involves the asking of a relevant question where the subject answers. Now, let us assume that in that particular example the subject is attempting deception. Fear is an emotion that is easily reflected on the polygraph chart, but, there are many varieties of fear and the testing technique is structured carefully so that the fear that is recognized and is appropriate in this particular testing configuration is the fear of detection and the fear of detection, of course, is stimulated by a deception answer to the relevant question. So, that when a person is asked a question that relates to the incident or crime involved and answers with deception, there is a fear, psychologically, within the individual, a fear of detection and the consequences of detection, not from the polygraph examination per se, but how it may guide the investigation to look further into the matter to unearth additional collaborating information. Now, this emotion of fear; the structured pressure of the emotion of fear, causes many physical changes in the body, many physiological manifestations exist, and of these, the selected ones that have been mentioned just previously actually it will show sometimes in all three tracings or two of the three tracings but there will be a consistency that is very recognizable. So, we have the asking of the question and hypothetically the answer with deception, the fear of being detected in that deception, fear of bringing about physiological changes in the form of relative rise in blood pressure and recovery, the slowing down of the pulse rate, the beat or the pulse rate during the actual time immediately after the question, the breathing suppressions that are present many times and the galvanic skin response needle excursion representing an apparent relevant change, a relative change in the skin resistance of the individual.

Q: All right, if the question is answered truthfully, that is without deception, are these responses or changes absent in the subject?

A: This depends on the competency of the examiner administering the examination. Now, if the only possible lie question asked during the structure of the polygraph examination is the relevant question, and there is no other question type that could elicit an emotionally involved reaction, this would be unreliable as far as present day standards are concerned in polygraph. But, if we place nearby the relevant question, a question that we call a control question, a question that has some appropriate emotional involvement to the individual, if the individual is not attempting a deception to the relevant question, we then can reliably interpret the absence of reaction on the relevant question. In other words, this whole procedure I think ties into a very acceptable psychological concept, a psychological set. In other words, a person's attention is geared into that which can most affect his well-being and if the psychological set of the individual is geared toward the relevant question then the control question will be of no immediate importance to him. Now, if the individual is being truthful to the relevant question and there is a control question located nearby that has some stigma but not enough to dampen out the pertinent reaction of an individual attempting deception to the relevant question, the individual will wait for the control question and actually be relieved on the relevant question and then show a reaction on the nearby control question. So, if these two questions are used in companionship with each other then when a person answers a relevant question and there's a lack of reaction, we have reliability.

MJ: Are you going to go into what is a question that is of concern to the individual but is not a relevant question? My mind goes along with you and it seems that you're saying, "Did you commit the larceny?" would be the relevant question. "Are you having marital problems with your wife?" might be something that would be also emotionally involved but _____ .

WIT: Your Honor, this is a no no in polygraph.

MJ: Well, I would assume that it would be.

WIT: No, we must keep the classification of the control question in the same category as that that's being utilized for relevant questions in the test. And let's use the example of the test question, we might say, "During the first 18 years of your life, did you ever steal anything from somebody?", you know _____ .

MJ: I see.

WIT: It's a sort of naive question but it's one that could only stimulate a person to concern if they were not emotionally involved because of a fear of detection on the relevant question. So, it's a balance and the psychological set will switch from one to the other in an appropriate manner if the examiner is skillful in constructing these questions.

MJ: I don't want you to do this, but I'm just getting myself orientated. I get the impression that really the body's reaction, other than this galvanic skin response, is when a person attempts deception he, in effect stops. His breathing slows up, he is trying to hold himself back, his heart slows down, the pulse obviously slows down as if he caught his breath and caught his internal involuntary body actions and then it relaxes as he gives the answer. Is that something of the sort that occurs?

WIT: Yes, sir. I believe, for instance, if we take the breathing tracing as an example, when a person is asked a question he may exert the same effort to inhale a cycle of breathing but the tenseness and the reservation throughout his rib cage, et cetera, and the muscular complex around the rib cage, will cause him to actually inhale less volume of air from the same effort and he does not realize this because here the psychological factor is actually taking over and dominating the physiological necessity.

MJ: If there's an emotional tenseness it causes a physical tenseness?

WIT: Yes, sir. It's based on the fight-flight-holding mechanism and psychological concept and at that particular brief period of time, the psychological reasons of the then current problem during the 20 or 25 seconds supersedes or really overrides the physiological needs of the body.

Further questions by Mr. Bailey:

Q: In connection with that, Mr. Backster, and in order to learn whether or not a person could successfully control those responses upon which you depend to to diagnose deception, if any is present, would you explain to the court generally what the sympathetic nervous system consists of?

A: Yes, the—actually the entire phenomenon that we're interested in reading tie into let's say involuntary processes of the body. In other words, processes that we are not usually consciously able to control with rare exception. Now, there's some research now showing that some learned people from the east, under certain circumstances, can manipulate physiological functions. But, they can usually produce reactions but not prevent oncoming reactions. So, involved in the sympathetic nervous system is that part of the physical complex that is not readily under the control of the individual unless they're awfully specialized in pretty high level areas and these people don't seem to get in too much trouble.

Q: If a stimulus is applied, a psychological stimulus perceived by the senses of the individual, is the sympathetic nervous system involved in the transmission of that stimulus to a physiological reaction?

A: Would you repeat your question, the first part of it?

Q: Yes. To what extent is the sympathetic nervous system involved in transmitting the stimulus, in this case a question, to the physiological reaction that you've described and depend upon?

A: Well, first I think that we must translate the question into the fact of whether it be a threat to the individual or not and then we throw in very conventional and well understood processes that involve the fight-flight-holding procedure and then there's a whole complex orientation as far as the sympathetic and parasympathetic nervous system is concerned that goes into play. And these things pretty well establish physiologically—but the thing psychologically we must establish is that we are indeed creating a threat at that very block of say 20 or 25 seconds to the individual that will actually throw into gear the fight-flight-holding mechanism involving a real complex—the reason I probably don't wish to enter into too much detail is that I don't really think that we know as much as we may thing we do about this inner and very complicated complex of sympathetic, parasympathetic nervous system action. It's like electricity, we flip the switch and the light goes on and we certainly know it's there and we assume many things as far as the pattern of reaction is concerned from the psychological stimulation to the physical happening at the time. We know there is a complex involvement of the involuntary portions of the body and this does occur and it occurs reliably with consistency when the person is—feels in threat as far as their well-being is concerned.

Q: Mr. Backster, you've made reference to the fight-flight-holding mechanism. Would you tell the court briefly what you mean?

A: Yes, I mean that if there's a threat to your well-being at the time you have to make a definite decision. Whether you're going to stand there and just worry or whether you're going to pursue that which is threatening you or whether you're going to run like you know what. I mean this is fight-flight-holding. It is a basic decision. But all of them involve a keying up of the body to get ready for action and the action that you take may, of course, be selected but the physical process and preparation is pretty similar in all cases.

Q: All right. Now, you've indicated that there may be less than perfect certainty about the entire theory of participation of the sympathetic nervous system and the physiological responses which event. Can you tell us just generally what the empirical exprience of the profession has been about the dependability of those responses appearing when deception is attempted?

A: Yes. I would again compare this to throwing that light switch. Very seldom do we fail to get light and we know what to do in that case. And the reliability— first the validity of the use of this as a system I think is extremely high and the reliability so far as arriving or receiving this type of response each time is extremely high. In other words, I think we must have validity plus reliability from the scientific stance in order that this is meaningful. And there's been plenty of groundwork done in the psychology lab to show that there is both validity and reliability as far as recording mechanisms of this type are concerned in accurately reflecting the phenomenon. So, borrowing these concepts, these validated concepts, from primarily the field of psychology, we have been able to properly utilize them.

Q: To what extent are there methods that an individual might take to deceive an examiner, and I suppose the instrument although that would appear to be inappropriate, but to deceive an examiner into thinking that there were no responses when, in fact, deception was being attempted? Would drugs or any kind of conditioning operate to deceive an experienced and qualified examiner in your opinion?

A: I might mention that there are a lot of rumors that are passed around as to how you can beat the polygraph, a great variety of things. And some of the misinformation involves the attempt to produce reaction and, of course, anyone that produces reaction is not in anyway fooling the polygraph examiner. In other words, the person, in order to adequately fool a polygraph examiner would have to prevent an oncoming reaction. And frankly I've been in this field and as I say for well over 20 years and I, myself, could not "beat" the polygraph. So, I don't worry about this. This has never been an actual problem; it's only been a theoretical problem. There are safeguards that can be put into the polygraph technique. For instance, anything that would cause the person not to react properly would eliminate the reaction on the control question as well as the relevant question. Now, if we do not see a capability of reaction during the actual polygraph examination, let's say within one or two questions on each side of the relevant question, where we can actually compare the lack of reaction on the relevant question to a presence of, on the control question, on one side or the other, we would come to no conclusion whatsoever. We would say that temporarily that person was not a fit subject for examining and continue the examining at a later time. So, the person has not at all beat the examiner in anyway. He has merely prolonged the examination procedure.

Q: If drugs of some kind were ingested which could, and there are such drugs, interfere with the pulse beat or the blood pressure or the rate of oxygenation, how would the examiner know that the person was under the influence of these drugs and therefore not suitable for an examination?

A: Actually, again, unless the person was under the effect of some type of drug to the point where it was extremely obvious from external senses, I don't look at it as being a very significant problem. People have come to me and I've found out they've taken various forms of tranquilizers in order to try to fool the examiner and I've told them they'd better change their brand because it really wasn't having much success because if anything it was putting them in a better state for. the polygraph examination. We've had people that have tried to use stimulants but all that does is exaggerate the size of the present reaction that would exist anyway and it just is no problem.

Q: All right.

A: So, if there are such drugs I'm not aware of them.

Q: Now, with reference to various kinds of individuals, and I refer now to mental condition, supposing a sociopath or a person who congenitally has a low level of social concern, in other words, really doesn't care or feel badly about what he's done, even though it's criminal, supposing he encounters a polygraph examination, is there any reason to believe that because of his state of mind, that he would not respond in a fashion that would enable you to diagnose deception?

A: I think this gets into the situation of the very basis upon which the polygraph successfully operates. In other words, if we must rely on making a person remorseful or let's say feel ashamed for what they have done, I think the polygraph wouldn't have gotten off home base. In other words, we are not relying at all on the repentance of the individual or the shame for that which has occurred. We must remind the individual as part of our pretesting situation that regardless of how they feel, in other words how careless they may be in feeling that that which they have done is justified, that society feels differently and that there is some kind of inconvenience that is in store for that individual if they are first, let's say, detected by the polygraph which leads to additional evidence that's presented into court or reinforces other evidence. So, it isn't at all that we have to rely on the social standards of the individual. We must remind the individual of the social standards that are then prevalent and that which is in store for the person. So, the idea of the person feeling justified or rationalizing in any way is not allowed to interfere with the deceptional nature of the technique.

Q: Is there anyway to administer a polygraph examination to a subject that doesn't wish to take one?

A: In the first place, any person that is a qualified polygraph examiner wouldn't think of doing this because it's completely voluntary situation and the person that is taking a polygraph examination, even if they pretend to be cooperating, all they have to do is move and shift—they're not—in other words, they may vocally agree to take the examination but he can always prevent a meaningful reading even if they felt obliged to sit in that chair. Now, there is no way that I know of at all, and it's grossly unethical to have the person take an examination against their wishes. Now, the entire time that I've been in the polygraph field, I have never tested a person that has not beforehand in a manner that I felt was sincere, reflected their consent to take the examination and given their written statement accordingly. Now, I think that, of course, this involves a basic fairness to your fellow man and I always give a person an opportunity to reject the polygraph examination if somehow they have been maneuvered into a position that's caused them to volunteer for something they really did not wish to participate in. And I think most polygraph examiners certainly that meet these ethical requirements are not abusing people by "forcing them" to take polygraph examinations. In the first place this is a physical impossibility.

Q: Now, Mr. Backster, what kinds of cases have you as an examiner, apart from your teaching and research, worked on since 1948, what classes of cases?

A: Well I think just about the whole gamut of polygraph testing from homicides and the criminal work right on down. We've been quite active because we train primarily police officers at our school in being helpful to them in their departments sometimes, on the consultant basis, after the individual leaves the school. So, we've been exposed quite a deal to the use of the polygraph in criminal cases; but also my background having been intelligence, I've been very active in the military and the intelligence use of the polygraph. And, in that regard, I think I've had probably as close an exposure as most. I think I've been a consultant to almost every Government agency that's made use of the polygraph and I've even helped to design the now current techniques that are used in those areas.

Q: Now, in that connection, you said that you have been a consultant to many branches of Government including the military. Are you familiar with the educational course given at Fort Gordon?

A: Yes, I am.

Q: Would you tell the court just a little bit about it? That is, who comes to be trained, what they are taught, and what happens to them, from your own personal knowledge?

A: Just from my own personal knowledge over a rather extended period of time. In the first place the requirements, which I think there are better sources than I for the exact requirements, but they have been extremely high by the standards of the field. We've felt that they've been extremely careful in those that they test. And I've also visited a number of classes during the actual conduct of the classes and have talked to these people that are in the midst of training; and of course it is a lengthy course; in fact, I would say it's the longest course of actual classroom instruction type course that exists in the field today and also, of course, there's a lot of practical phases of the course. And I think the only course that exceeds it in length is John Reid's course in Chicago that involves a great exposure to the actual practice of the application of the polygraph in addition to theory. But by all standards in the field, and this is to the best of my knowledge and source of information, this course far exceeds, as far as the concentrated theory that's administered plus the opportunity for applying the polygraph in not only hypothetical but actual cases, is by far the top of the heap.

Q: What kinds of subjects are taught, individual subjects such as psychology and physiology, if you know?

A: Right. Now, during the course the subjects of psychology, physiology, mechanical aspects of the polygraph, are taught. The related interview or interrogation processes that are—that lead up to the obtaining of the basic information required in the administering of the test to the subject are taught. There's a great deal of practical application of the polygraph in laboratory situations and actual situations and a great deal of work is done in chart interpretation because no matter how skillful a person is at structuring an examination and giving the examination under the appropriate set of circumstances, if they can't read the charts, why, as far as we're concerned they're failures as polygraph examiners. The technique has been structured in a way that these charts that—where the questions have been deleted and only a code is used to show the kind of question that is asked at the time can be utilized not only for training purposes but where a system is set up where remote supervision can be exercised over examiners where the person that is reviewing the work of another examiner does not have to have been there during the time of the actual examination. In other words, the degree of standardization has been worked toward and I feel now achieved to where one expert in the field should adequately be able to read the charts of another expert with no significant deviation as far as their conclusions are concerned.

Q: Has this been your experience over the past several years, that you're able to read others charts, and they're able to read yours with a high degree of reliability?

A: Yes, sir, it certainly has. In fact, this has been the main thrust of my research efforts in the field of polygraph.

Q: Now, Mr. Backster, will you tell the court the manner in which a polygraph examination, and I mean the entire process, not just the few minutes that the instrument is running with its chart recording, the manner in which a polygraph examination is given and take, for instance, a hypothetical homicide case where you're presented with someone denying that he committed a murder that has been committed by someone, and he is a suspect. How do you go about it?

A: Yes, sir. This is my own personal experience but I don't think it varies greatly from the average examination administered in the field. Now, the first thing that I as an individual do in this type of testing would involve myself in what I call a preexamination reliability estimate. In other words, I would try to estimate, and we actually have a numerical scale on which we can do this where it could be subjected to scientific scrutiny to see if it meets the strictest scientific requirements, we would estimate the effectiveness from three standpoints of the pending case. Do we have adequate case information to conduct a polygraph examination. Do we have a degree of strength of issue that would motivate the person into showing a significant response.

MJ: A degree of what?

WIT: *Significance of issue or strength of issue.*

MJ: Strength of issue?

WIT: Right. In other words, a *fear of detection would be to a degree based on this*. And, then, do we have distinctness of issue. In other words, if the person is attempting deception, do they *know that they are attempting deception* at the time? So, we would make an estimate of these three involvements and we would decide that at best would we have reliable polygraph results regardless of that which was indicated on the chart. In other words, this is a safety factor that's built into the procedure. Should we even be testing that individual at all?

MJ: Let me—I don't want to interrupt—but consider in this also the other side; a person who is accused of a homicide believes himself to be innocent and wishes to demonstrate this by the polygraph. In other words, obviously the approach must be different. One you suspect there's a consciousness of guilt, the other you're not certain, but at least it's represented that there is no consciousness of guilt. Would your approaches be different?

WIT: No, sir, because we don't know which is which at that time. This is the purpose of the examination, to see in our opinion who's attempting deception. But, again, consciousness of guilt is something that I think that we would be very careful to avoid because we're not relying on consciousness or the guilty conscience of the individual because of the guilt. We are reminding the person, if they be involved _____ .

MJ: No, when I say conscious _____ .

WIT: Or awareness of guilt.

MJ: Awareness.

WIT: All right. So this would tie in then to the distinctness of issue. In other words, let us utilize two examples, if we had a person that was on the ground during a street fight and ten people were kicking him while he was down, each of the ten people would like to think that the other nine kicked harder and caused the death of the individual. This would lack _____ .

MJ: That's a good example.

WIT: This would lack the distinctness of issue. On the other hand, if we had something that was much more abrupt and outright and a person did know that they indeed pulled the trigger of the gun that caused the death we would have a high distinctness of issue. So, does that answer—may I continue with the sequence?

MJ: Yes. In other words, what you're saying is your approach to determine whether or not a—what made me ask the question, you stated, "Is there an issue?" You're presented with the facts of the case and apparently the police would in one case say, "We think this man did it." The other case, the individual, through his attorney perhaps, has come to you and said, "My client says he didn't do it, I kind of believe him and I'd like you to verify it for me." It seems to me your approach could be different; I don't know.

WIT: Well, now, in the first place, if there is an issue, for instance in the case of the homicide which you asked, the body is found, that is the issue. It has nothing to do with the later selected subjects or volunteers to take the polygraph examination. So, the issue has nothing to do with the potential subject that may volunteer or be asked to take the examination later. So, the evidence in the case information would show that there indeed was an issue. Otherwise we wouldn't know how to approach this because again we would be presuming in advance a degree of involvement which we certainly try not to do. Now, after the preexamination evaluation estimate the next step would then be, and also through that we would select a target that would seem to be the appropriate target or issue to approach first. Now, the thing we try to do is take the more intense issue first and then work down the line if there is to be additional phasing of the test.

(At this point two gentlemen entered the courtroom.)

MJ: Are these gentlemen also prospective witnesses?

IC: Yes, sir, they are, this is Mr. Brisentine.

MJ: Brisentine, I recognize Mr. Brisentine. Maybe these gentlemen would like to sit up here also. We'll let you be the jury today. Sorry to interrupt you.

WIT: That's all right.

MJ: There would have been so much disruption, I wouldn't have been hearing all you said. Would you go ahead, please.

WIT: Yes, sir, I will. So in our sequence of approaching a polygraph testing situation, and the requested example is that of a homicide case, we would first do our preexamination reliability estimate to see if we have adequate case information, if we have strength of issue, if we have the distinctness of issue. The next thing that we would do is to take that prime target, the thing that seems most intense in the case there were more than one factor involved in the test, and we would then start to construct test questions. Now, the first questions that would be constructed would be the relevant questions and these relevant questions and the technique approach that's in wide use would involve the formulation of at least two very direct and to the point relevant questions that relate to the issue concerned or that which we call a target. Now, these questions and the formulation of these questions, of course, involves, in fact, reflecting back on that which is involved in course instruction, involves a lot of instruction on the proper formulation of nonambiguous questions, questions that are to the point, where semantics is quite an issue of clearly formulating the questions so that the person taking the test will understand the question. Now, the way we double check the understandability of these questions is to read the question as they're mutually formulated. Now we even allow the subject to be involved to any degree necessary to formulate the question that will not allow him to sidetrack the issue that is involved. We will then read the question that seems to be the finished product to the subject and ask him to explain back to us that which is meant by the question just to double check the fact that he is really aware of the meaning that's pertinent. And then once these two strong relevant questions or direct relevant questions that are very pertinent to the incident are formulated then the control questions are formulated. In other words, picking questions that are in a similar category and do not have an intensity that would in any way usurp or detract from the reaction to the relevant question if the person were attempting deception. These control questions are formulated and of course during the actual testing structure are located close by to the relevant question. Then other supporting questions are formulated. We have questions we call neutral questions. These are questions that have no—in other words they theoretically should be a nonlie question if we use that classification I mentioned earlier. In other words, questions that we feel certain of the answer in regard to which we feel certain to the answer, such as, "Is your first name John?", or, "Do you live in the State of Michigan?", or whatever it may be. Now, these questions are merely to orient the individual taking the test to any question being asked regardless of the type. And then we have—in fact in some—well, I'd say primarily, without making the matter too complex, these are the prime types of questions. We have neutral questions, we have relevant questions, and we have the control questions or formulated. Now, these questions are carefully reviewed with the subject taking the test, the person taking the test, and it is only with their consent that these questions are understandable and are pertinent to the examination that we then continue. And under no circumstances is a question injected into the testing procedure that is not previously reviewed carefully with the subject. In other words, there are no surprise questions whatsoever. And we found that there's a very good reason for this. If the person did not have confidence in the examiner regarding unreviewed questions that person may have some other incident on their mind that they're afraid will be injected into the testing procedure and if they did have this fear we feel they would not show reliably on the relevant questions being asked in that then current target or incident. Now, after these questions have been reviewed, then the person is—well, actually the questions are reviewed by category rather than the actual order that they're used. In certain types of tests that I mentioned, this may not be true; but in the principal chart, the principal test type that's used in a polygraph examination, the exact wording, word for word of the questions is known although the actual order may not be known. Now, then the test is administered and we run a number of these charts in order to have a consistency of that which exists as far as the presence of or a lack of reaction on the relevant questions. Now, the—actually, a minimal number of charts would be two, absolute minimal, and likely there would be three or four charts that were actually involved on those same two primary questions used or relevant questions. Now, in the system that I personally use, which I can best talk of, we then have a scoring system for these relevant questions and we use a numerical scoring basis for each of the questions. In other words, we have three tracings that are actually involved in the polygraph. We have at least two strong relevant questions, or pertinent relevant questions, which gives us six separate opportunities of interpreting that particular location on the chart in regard to truth or deception. So if you will multiply this times the four charts, or three charts even, we have at least 18 separate opportunities to determine truth or deception during the procedure. Now, if the person accidentally shows an extraneous reaction at one or two of these times this is compensated for by the number of times. In working for reliability, we have a presence of a lack of reaction. So, there are a great number of safety precautions that are built into the procedures in this regard as far as consistency is concerned. And then after the examination procedure, the chart interpretation is completed and the numerical tally, if the person is using the numerical tally system, is figured out and then this is converted back to a three—a reading that would have to fall into three possibilities. These possibilities would be that in the opinion of the examiner, the person was being deceptive, that they were being truthful, or that the test was inconclusive. Now, I think that basically covers it, sir.

Further questions by Mr. Bailey:

Q: All right. One thing I think that may not have been mentioned is the extent of the pretest interview, what the examiner is trying to accomplish, how long it's likely to take, and what it consists of.

A: Yes. Actually part of the pretest interview, in fact a significant portion of it, would be the construction of the test questions with the mutual consent of the subject and of course to the satisfaction of the examiner that the questions were adequate to serve the purpose of that particular examination. Aside from that, a number of basic questions are asked and explanations are made to the subject taking the examination so that this procedure is not an extremely unfamiliar one to him by the time the examination gets underway. There is of course quite a variety as far as the scope of this pretest examination is concerned. But any questions that are asked by the subject—an attempt is made to answer them to the subject's satisfaction regarding the procedure. There is a basic explanation given as far as the attachments are concerned that are utilized in the polygraph examination. Depending on the type of examination, I think that we would pretty much scope exactly what was asked in the pretest. Pretesting is a significant portion, of course.

Q: What would the practicability be of having a third party present, either a police officer if the case was brought by the police or a counsel if the case was brought by the accused himself, present during the pretest interview and the test itself?

A: I don't know that this would be disastrous but I'm not sure that it would be desirable. In other words, during—especially during the actual testing of the individual the examiner would have a certain continuity that he was trying to pursue. In other words, if the—I suppose if the attorney were to just sit there like a fixture or piece of furniture that it would not interfere during the pretest but if the attorney had to inject a great number of objections and tried to tell the examiner how to formulate the questions and things of that nature I suppose it could be quite dis—quite a distraction. Now, during the examination itself I think this becomes a greater problem. If the attorney is sitting in the room and doesn't have a real obvious or apparent reason for being there as far as an extremely pertinent part of the procedure is concerned, I think that if he clears his throat or if he moves or so forth and so on there's an opportunity that there will be extraneous reactions that will show up on the chart. So, I would say by choice it wouldn't be desirable although I don't say that it would be disastrous if it did occur.

Q: All right. Now, to what extent is it essential for an examiner to establish a rapport head to head and that is—I mean with the subject in order to define the perimeters of his language, articulation, and ability to communicate without the interference of a third party? Is that essential in some way to the procedure?

A: Yes, this is extremely essential because I think it's very pertinent to arriving at test questions that are mutually agreeable to the parties concerned. Number one, mutually—understandable by the subject and also agreeable to the examiner in the light of not avoiding the issue or somehow weakening the question to where it would be ineffective. And this rapport, this ability to work out questions on that basis, I'd say it's extremely important that this rapport be created between the examiner and the subject. I don't think you can have extraneous antagonisms that would exist if this were not the case, because antagonisms involve shades of emotion, and of course we have equipment that is indicating emotion in a tracing form. So examiners have had a wealth of experience in how to do this and what to do and what not to do in order not to stimulate extraneous emotional factors that would interfere or prolong the examination procedures. So, the ability for the examiner to have proper rapport with the subject with a minimum of interference during the actual part of the examination is pertinent. I would say it would be extremely helpful.

Q: All right. Now, you have told the court earlier that one of the important phases of structuring the test itself is to make sure that the questions are phrased in a manner that is not in any way ambiguous to the subject answering them and in his own language.

A: Yes.

Q: Assume, hypothetically, that Captain Medina were a subject that you were testing and in the pretest interview the answers that he gave you to questions you put were in part language that I advised him to use. Would this interfere with your putting together test questions? That is to say, he consulted me and I advised him on the phraseology of how he should answer you. Would that prevent you from putting questions together that you knew he understood personally and without my help?

A: I think this would, perhaps, add an extraneous distraction to the examination procedure. Although your explanation to him as to the terms at the time would be absorbed when the inner—there's always a slight stress in an examination, it's natural for anyone to be slightly stressed regardless of whether they are being truthful or deceptive to the relevant issue. In the time of this slight stress during an examination procedure I think he may quickly forget some of the explanations you gave him and I think that some of the phraseology might sound a little strange and just make the questions more vague and less meaningful. So, I think that it's extremely important to refine the questions down to language that is clearly understood by the subject and not to embellish it with legal phraseology which perhaps you would be tempted to do in the example you gave. This is extremely important.

MJ: Would this be eliminated though if you follow the procedure of having the—after the control question is formulated, to have the subject repeat it back to you in his own language and his own understanding? Wouldn't that tend to eliminate any probability of misconception?

WIT: Well, here again, I think that during the preliminary interview when, as I say, a sizeable length of time is consumed in the procedure, this may be mutually understandable. Now, during the polygraph chart we have about two and a half perhaps at the most three minutes that's involved and we have a question that is being asked every 20 or 25 seconds. And I just think under that procedure, when the actual equipment is in operation, and there is that degree of stress that would exist with any subject, I think that some of these mutually agreed upon extraneous technicalities, and I say extraneous only from the standpoint of the examiner, would be an unnecessary distraction from the examination. In other words, we steer tenaciously clear of professional or legal terms in the examination. We make sure it's something that is quite natural or spontaneous to the individual taking the test where we do not lose the meaning though of the target issue.

Further questions by Mr. Bailey:

Q: Now, let's come to the present day use of the polygraph. To what extent, first of all, do police departments, State and Federal around the country, make use of this technique in their investigations to your knowledge, personally?

A: Well, to my personal knowledge and this must be an estimate because I have a great reverence for statistics and I don't have the data immediately on hand for statistics, but there are hundreds of police departments throughout the country, in fact we've—well I've personally been involved in the training I would say at a minimum of five hundred police officers going out throughout the country to give thousands of examinations; and other schools that are involved in the training business could attest to I think an equivalent or even an excess to that amount. So, it is a widespread procedure that is utilized. I would personally feel it's a great advantage to police departments throughout the country.

Q: What about, now, the area of private examiners working for commercial fees in industry, criminal cases, and so forth; how many of these would you estimate are now practicing?

A: Well, here again I—it would be difficult to estimate; but there would be certainly several hundred of them throughout the country. But these, in many cases, are individuals who have retired from their police department duties or their military duties and have gone into the commercial application of polygraph afterwards. It's really hard to keep track of the actual numbers. I think perhaps the American Polygraph Association would be more helpful in that.

Q: All right. And for how long has the military engaged in the use of polygraph examinations, to your knowledge, personally?

A: Well, I'm personally aware of their involvement in the use of the polygraph from—well, well before 1950 and I think it is well before. But, actually the first classes, in fact, that were trained of military were while I was Director of Training at the Keeler Polygraph Institute in Chicago and this would date back to, oh, 1949-'50.

Q: Do you know off hand, and we have another witness who can, or several, who may be able to give us a more precise answer, do you have any idea as to how many military examiners are in operation on a daily basis?

A: No, sir, I really wouldn't know that with any degree of accuracy.

Q: From your involvement with the military, Fort Gordon, and your meetings with your association of whom I assume some are active military examiners, do you know the degree, if any, of reliance that is placed on this technique in the investigative phase of criminal cases?

A: My impression, as a party very much exposed to this, and of course involved in it from personal experience earlier in my career, I would say that a great deal of reliance is given to the use of the polygraph.

Q: Now, how do you statistically verify the opinions that may result simply from a polygraph examination? Are your tests in any way followed up or the tests that you supervise so that you can later demonstrate through independent criteria whether or not the examiner had reached the correct, that is, historically correct conclusion?

A: Yes, sir, this is a difficult task to do because sometimes the ultimate outcome of cases we're not aware of, and also, of course the standards that you're going to use for that which constitutes a verified case sometimes are somewhat ambiguous. But we do make a definite effort, in fact part of my personal experience is to follow up afterwards and try my best to see if it is ultimately a verified case and then go back and restudy the charts in a meaningful way at that time to see the comparisons between that which is involved in the polygraph test on those subjects and the ultimate verification. If you want to talk from a strict, scientific standpoint and you're talking statistics a statistician will tell you that you can never get statistics in regard to such a field of endeavor where the ultimate answer to each and every one of the cases is not known. This becomes a theoretical point because I think the estimates are extremely impressive and the estimates of effectiveness involve very high percentages.

Q: Well, if you were to clear, to borrow a term from the jargon, to clear a suspect and report back to a police agency or someone else, that in your opinion he was truthfully denying his guilt where later on evidence, including perhaps his own confession, were developed, which would demonstrate the inaccuracy of your conclusion, would you in the ordinary course of events, and I ask you now to reflect on your experience of over 20 years, be likely to hear about it?

A: That particular example, I think we would be likely to hear about, yes.

Q: All right. And how frequently does it occur that an examiner, either yourself or someone under your supervision, calls as truthful or deceptive—that is, reaches an opinion, in just for instance take criminal cases and is later demonstrated to be in error? How often does this occur as a practical matter?

A: I would have to think back some time. There may be one or two isolated examples, but fortunately they're far enough back, perhaps voluntarily repressed in my memory, but I'm sure they do exist, but in a minimum degree, in other words one or two at best in my over 20 years experience.

Q: How many tests are you currently running or supervising in the course of a year?

A: Oh, running—counting the tests run and supervised would actually get into the thousands because our students are going back and we supervise them for a period of two years after they go back to the police department. In other words, they're sending charts in, we're reviewing the charts, we're giving them whatever help or critique that we can after they leave the school. So, it would be in the thousands.

Q: And how frequently are those who are graduates, may we say "tyros in the field" sending in opinions which ultimately turn out to be contrary to the fact? Is this something that happens often?

A: This is an extremely scarce occurrence. Now, perhaps they're not talking about it but we certainly aren't hearing about it either, Mr. Bailey.

Q: The last question that I want to ask you is whether or not you can tell the court anything about the development in the past 20 years in the field of polygraph examinations that might have a bearing on the wisdom of using such information in an evidentiary capacity?

A: I personally, of course, have been very directly involved, as I said before, for a period of eight consecutive years in our professional organization. I was Chairman of the Research and Instrument Committee. Now, during this time the primary task was that of trying to combine and consolidate the various techniques in the field into a more or less standardized polygraph technique. And I think as far as the evolvement of polygraph technique is concerned, there has been a fantastic evolvement. In other words, the test technique originally involved just a relevant question. You just asked the person if they did it, whatever it was, and there was not skillful use of any control procedure whatsoever and this went through a number of years in the polygraph. And then, in fact, through the introduction of the Reid Control, and we have John Reid here who can talk more about this, we started to really enhance the validity of the polygraph by having a comparison of the person's capability of reaction located very close by the relevant question being asked during the polygraph procedure. And I would say that the validity in polygraph really rose to fantastic heights with the introduction of this one factor. And since then we've gone to a great extent, in fact this was before even my eight years in the research capacity, since then a great effort has been applied toward standardization so that one examiner can read another examiner's charts even though the person can be any distance away. Where we are utilizing standardized forms to where even through telephonic communication we know what the other examiner is speaking of. And my personal stress has been that this standardization has been very necessary to enhance professionalization of the polygraph and raise the reliability of it.

Q: To what extent does your profession police itself as to the individuals who are permitted to hold themselves out as experts?

A: There's been a great deal of effort in the American Polygraph Association to be very careful of the qualifications of individuals they accept into membership. And also there's, even aside from this, there's been a great deal of effort within the establishment of the users of the polygraph, such as the military, to have a whole procedure of qualifying an examiner to where they enhance their knowledge of his proficiency by insisting that a certain number of tests be run over a period of time and that he not be away from testing for a period of time. In other words, there are separate procedures for the individuals in the field. In general, American Polygraph Association has a very intense program on this and I have personal knowledge that the military has their own program of this type.

Q: Now, obviously a dishonest polygraph examiner could wreck havoc with the process if he were willing to prostitute his professional skill. Do you have any ethical controls over the membership of American Polygraph Association if that is to be regarded as a criterion of professional excellence which would protect the public against charlatans?

A: Yes, sir, I think in the past there's been somewhat of a tendency, I think perhaps a defensive tendency, years ago in the polygraph field to state that one examiner should not read another examiner's charts. This goes back, I'd say 15 to 20 years ago; and that one examiner shouldn't test after another examiner has tested. Now this has been almost completely thrown out. In other words, with rare exception, those people are certainly known and aren't taken too seriously. In other words, if a person—if a polygraph examiner were to engage—in other words, the only commodity he has to present is the truth and if he gives in one iota as far as the truth is concerned he has nothing left as far as his wares are concerned. And now in the field today there is no hesitancy for another examiner to reexamine an individual tested by another polygraph examiner. There's no hesitancy of another examiner to look at the charts of the person who claims to have been proficient in the initial test. So these taboos have been to the greatest extent completely eliminated.

Q: One of the judicial suspicions that has been raised from time to time is that perhaps, as in the profession of psychiatry, litigation of a polygraph question would result in a battle of the experts, whereas in the litigation of, for instance, fingerprints, experts rarely disagree. What has been your experience of two qualified experts testing the same individual on the same issue and coming up with conflicting opinions about his truthfulness or deception?

A: This has been extremely rare. It's certainly the exception more than the rule. It's something that can be resolved because if an impartial referee that has extensive experience in the field is called in to examine both sets of charts I think it becomes quite apparent where this discrepancy did enter into the situation.

Q: Do you know of any court case where two polygraph examiners have presented conflicting opinions on a single issue?

A: I don't have that information at my finger tips. I should imagine there might be a case, yes.

Q: And have you been involved in courts in connection with the polygraph in the past 20 years?

A: Yes, sir, I have.

Q: To what extent?

A: Last how many years?

Q: Last 20 years.

A: Oh, yes, I have, especially in military hearings and Government Agency hearings, disciplinary boards, and labor management prearbitration procedures. There's quite a variety of exposure to that—even psychiatric review board.

Q: What branches of the United States Government, aside from the military, make frequent use, according to your personal experience, of the polygraph?

A: Well, there's historically been extensive use in Central Intelligence Agency, National Security Agency. In fact, there's quite a list of users of the polygraph in addition to a number of, of course, the military intelligence organizations. Now, the current extent and just how much these—I think there are better sources than I on that at this moment.

Q: Very well, all right, your witness.

MJ: Do you want to take a recess?

TC: Yes, let's give the court reporter a break.

MJ: Yes, I think he's had a workout. Let's take a shorter recess, though I think. Let's take a ten minute recess. We have a lot to cover.

(The court recessed 1020 hours, 19 August 1971.)

(The court was called to order at 1039 hours, 19 August 1971.)

MJ: Court will come to order.

TC: Your Honor, all parties to the trial who were present when the court recessed are again present.

MJ: Let the record further reflect that Mr. Backster's still on the stand. Sir, you're reminded you're still under oath.

CROSS-EXAMINATION

Questions by Captain Wurtzel:

Q: Mr. Backster, you've been in polygraph examination for a long period of time, have you not?

A: Yes, sir.

Q: And approximately how many examinations have you given?

A: I would say I've been involved in over 50,000 examinations, from then I sort of lost count.

Q: And approximately what percentage of those have been conducted pursuant to police interrogations or at the request of police departments?

A: Well, of my involvement in examinations as far as the review and help in the construction of the exams, it's a little hard to delineate my actually administering the exam versus involvement, but I would say, oh, 20 to 25 percent. That's an estimate, not a statistic.

Q: All right. And of the 20 or 25 percent, how many of those did you personally administer and construct the examination and administer and examine the test results?

A: This again is an estimate that I would—I would state perhaps over five thousand.

Q: And of those five thousand the subject of those examinations were oftentimes suspects, were they not?

A: Yes, sir, they were.

Q: The majority of the time they were suspects?

A: Yes, they were.

Q: Suspected of some criminal involvement?

A: They—this is in the police-type case you're talking of?

Q: Yes.

A: Yes, I'd say in most of the cases they were.

Q: And the purpose of the examination was to determine as much as possible whether they were criminally involved?

A: The prime purpose of our examination is to establish the truthfulness of the individual.

Q: But in asking your questions, your relevant questions were to determine the degree of criminal involvement, if any, is that correct?

A: Yes, sir. And the controls are to determine the truthfulness.

Q: And the majority of those times those suspects were represented by counsel?

A: Yes, sir.

Q: Now, in order for you to conduct a valid examination the subject has to be willing to take a test, doesn't he?

A: Yes, sir.

Q: He has to voluntarily take the test?

A: Yes, sir. This is a requirement.

Q: You can't force him to take a test and get a valid result?

A: We can't force him to take the test, period. It's a double question. The second, we wouldn't get a valid result.

Q: All right. And if the suspect's or the subject's attorney didn't want him to take an exam, he could have prevented the examination. You of course wouldn't give the examination, right?

A: That's correct.

Q: Now, it's true, is it not, that the ideal manner in conducting an examination is when you and the subject are alone in the room, is that correct?

A: Yes, sir.

Q: And that's for the purpose of establishing a rapport between you and the subject so he can get to know you and understand you and you can understand him?

A: Well, primarily the purpose of being alone in the room is that any unnecessary ingredient as far as the person present would be an intrusion and perhaps resented even on the part of the subject. Now, there are exceptions especially with an interpreter where we must have the third person in the room. But they're very pertinent to the examination.

Q: The majority of these times the examination room itself has a bugging device of some sort so that the test is monitored from the outside?

A: Well, many times I wouldn't be aware of that. Sometimes there has been monitoring systems.

Q: And you, of course, make the subject aware of that fact, don't you?

A: Well, if the subject asks if there is a listening device in the room or a two-way mirror we would very, very quickly tell him there was. In fact, this I'd have to—I would have to say that the tenacity in which this is done, especially up to and including recent years, the situation has changed a lot. I think in the past that there, perhaps was surreptitious viewing and listening. But with the present day polygraph this has gotten to be quite a taboo thing.

Q: But if the subject learned during the course of the examination that there were surreptitious monitoring he would lose confidence in you, wouldn't he?

A: It depends on the examiner. In the first place, surreptitious monitoring, if it didn't have a purpose, would certainly incur the loss of confidence on the part of the subject. Now the—there can be a purpose for surreptitious monitoring or a purpose for monitoring that could be initially surreptitious, particularly in the earlier days of polygraph in the connection with the female subject being tested. In fact, many times it's been desirable to have a matron behind the observation post.

Q: The point is that if you're—if you're giving an examination to a suspected criminal offender of some nature and he's represented by counsel; his counsel, if the room is bugged, has the opportunity to either listen in or be present doesn't he?

A: If the room is bugged, you mean if there _____ .

Q: If there's a bugging device, if there's a listening device, that counsel could listen to—in the outside, if he wanted to, couldn't he?

A: Well, what you mean is if there's an inner communications setup.

Q: If there's a monitoring device?

A: Yes. Yes, and if he requested it, certainly.

Q: And if it was present and it was available to him he could listen to it if he wanted to?

A: Well, it—in any examination that I've administered, this is the case. Now, I can't speak for other examiners.

Q: How many examinations of suspected criminals have you given where the counsel has been present in the room, during the examination?

A: Quite a few, in fact, upon any request of the counsel, to you're saying being present in the room?

Q: Yes.

A: I'm sorry—I'm thinking still of the monitoring. I haven't given any tests with the counsel present in the room, but I do have available or could establish a monitoring facility for the counsel and I've given many examinations and tests with that set of circumstances.

Q: Well, during the course of your pretest interview when you're counstructing the questions with the subject, you could construct your questions with the presence of the attorney so that they're understandable to the subject, couldn't you?

A: Let me explain that in this manner, first we have a lengthy interview with the attorney in which they are to present the information as they see it. This is their opportunity to clearly present the information. Now, only the phase just prior to the administering of the charts is the sort of critical phase that we're mentioning as to the desirability or lack of desirability of having the counsel in the room. The counsel is usually nearby and even if not monitoring the procedure they're available for conference, in fact a conference after every chart in effect, and certainly before the start of the charts the questions are shown to the counsel.

Q: So, the counsel knows exactly what questions are being asked?

A: There's absolutely no reason—in my test, he does. Now, there's no reason he shouldn't in other tests.

Q: And if he doesn't want a particular question asked you, of course, wouldn't ask it?

A: Absolutely not.

ATC: Nothing further.

IC: Questions by the court?

MJ: I have some.

EXAMINATION BY THE COURT

Questions by the military judge:

Q: I'm only concerned with—well, actually I won't say I'm unconcerned—I'm concerned with several factors. One, you've been in the business for 20 odd years. I would question, based upon your testimony, why the courts have been reluctant to accept the high degree of accuracy and professionalism which you've demonstrated here? May I ask this, has the art or the science improved significantly say in the last ten years?

A: Yes, sir. And just to regress a bit, in fact anyone that had asked me personally, in fact even before they've asked many times, why the polygraph examination results could not be brought into court as evidence over the objection of either party, I would have said, "This is the worst thing that could happen." In fact, this would've been my answer up until I would say perhaps eight or ten years ago because the evolvement of the technique and the evolvement of the ethical standards as such did not allow us to know who competent examiners were. In other words, it would be disastrous that if in a blanket fashion the polygraph was admitted and then some inept individuals were involved in examinations it could set the polygraph back 50 years.

Q: What you're suggesting then is that the—I'll preface it with this. The equipment itself is fairly basic and I believe, perhaps, the skin attachment is more recent. But, the equipment itself is scientifically valid and it doesn't vary particularly from one examiner or one location to another. In other words, what I'm really suggesting is that the machinery, if it's working properly, is going to be identical with the same subject regardless of who's examining the subject because the machine, in effect, doesn't lie.

A: Well, let me perhaps use an example for this. If any of us were to go into a surgical supply store and buy the best scalpel in the store, I would fear for being on the table if one of us were to try to use it. In other words, the equipment, at a minimum, should function properly. In other words, there are many checks to see that it is doing that. The technique is what is important.

Q: I think the technique is the thing that I was eliminating from the question. In effect, what I was really saying is that the sharp scalpel in the hands of a butcher or in the hands of an excellent surgeon is still the same sharp scalpel.

A: Yes.

Q: It's just the way it's used. In other words, the equipment itself is dependable under scientific standards today?

A: Yes, like a thermometer is not an appendicitis detector. In other words, it's used for many things; except it can be used as a part of the procedure.

Q: Now, accepting the fact then that the equipment itself has reached a state of development that is, if it's functioning properly, is highly reliable.

A: Yes, sir, and it's very apparent if it's not functioning properly.

Q: My question then would relate, as to admissibility and the position of admissibility by courts, apparently would not rely on the machinery itself but rely on the people administering the tests?

A: Yes, sir, I think that's correct.

Q: Now, am I to understand from your testimony that part of the problem existing prior to—this goes back to your answer earlier. Part of the problem as of ten years or more ago was that there was no sufficient degree of control or professional control that you could verify within your profession the competence of the operator and now you feel you can?

A: Yes, sir. In fact, this has required perhaps some drastic standards to enforce because actually the latest step that I personally have done is to allow the incorporation of the entire technique, in fact the F. Lee Bailey, Henry Rothblatt book on preparation of cases. And this will allow the defense attorneys throughout the country to at least state to the polygraph examiner that may be on the other side of the testimony, "Now look, we don't expect that there's one technique only; but what have you done that is equivalent to the competency that is exhibited in the structured polygraph technique, that we have here before us in this book?" And it allows them to piecemeal and go through as far as ingredients of sound technique is concerned and completely discredit the person that is trying to give polygraph testimony where there is incompetency involved or where there's neglect even though they are competent in a particular set of circumstances.

Q: Well, what we're getting to then is that we're dealing, as opposed to the scientific capabilities of this procedure, we're dealing with the subjectivity of the operator and of the subject. These are the two matters where we can have variation?

A: Yes.

Q: All right. Now, would I be correct in—first starting off with this position, based again on your earlier testimony, an accomplished examiner will take the case file and the material, perhaps even discuss this matter with counsel, and he evaluates the material that he has and he decides whether, as you stated, there was a degree of specificity as to the issues and matters of this sort. Now, since the operator makes his determination as to the specific issues that must be examined and the specificity of those issues, is this one of the possible areas where the subjectivity of the examiner can affect the ultimate results? In other words, if he puts the emphasis on the wrong subject or the wrong specific matter to be covered, he is going to affect the ultimate outcome of the test?

A: Yes, sir; in fact, in my personal structured testing technique we take each possible distinct target or subject that could be covered as an individual factor in a complex case, a rape, robbery, murder, for instance, and we would do an analysis of the presence of adequate case information, strength of issue, and distinctness of issue on each of the possibilities as far as that which should be approached first. Now, it's important to approach the more intense one first or that can dampen out and cause to be less reliable or unreliable the remaining.

Q: Now, that is a matter of choice that you make yourself though based on the matters submitted to you?

A: Yes, sir. Of course, there's a variance in competency in doing that.

Q: All right. Now, that's what I'm driving at. In other words, if one of your students with two years experience were faced with the same degree or the same set of facts it is possible that we would come up with slightly different conclusions then yourself?

A: The difference—now, I can only speak of the people that I've been instrumental in training as so forth—we have an actual numerical system and we have a scale, in other words a five position scale, where we would place case information as very inadequate at the number 1 end of the scale up to nearly complete at the number 5 end of the five position scale. And these are translated into values that are then added up for a total. In other words, we would watch the total of each of these possible targets and approach that target first. Now, even though there may be a few points difference in the students at least that we've trained, I doubt if one target could supersede the other. It could compete with it on about an equal plane but as far as it being extremely troublesome, with this careful approach, I don't think so. But I can't state for the general technique.

Q: Would—I accept that as certainly a more than adequate answer. You have recognized the problem and are attempting to eliminate it.

A: Definitely.

Q: What about Mr. Reid's school or the school at Fort Gordon? They're all, of course, highly competent and I'm aware of their reputations. But, do they use the same techniques for evaluating and arriving at what is important in a particular case?

A: I can speak for the Fort Gordon school where the prime emphasis of their course of instruction is built around this carefully weighted and scientifically structured test. Now, Mr. Reid is here and certainly can speak for himself but I think he has an equivalent for this fancy deal I've devised.

Q: Although I'm speaking of these gentlemen, I'm not really necessarily limiting it to them. Just generally what I'm really suggesting is, has the profession reached a degree or the science reached a degree of professionalism that with a very high degree of probability if a given set of facts were presented to a number of operators or examiners, would they most likely come to the same consideration or arrive at the same conclusion that these are the important issues and these are, with a variation of wording, these are the relevant questions and control questions we should be asking? So, that if you were to walk into a case you could probably, after having reached a rapport with the subject, use the test questions with slight modifications perhaps but certainly reach basically—has it reached that degree of competence?

A: Sir, there is certainly a significant portion of the field that has that I'm knowledgeable about personally. And, of course, this has become a problem now of the fact that it theoretically or actually can be done to enhance or expand the number of examiners in the field that are using that degree or level or competency and technique. Now, if this person does not or uses something that is short of that, at least we alarm attorneys through publishing this information with a manner in which to point out the inadequacies of the technique used by the other faction.

Q: And I gather from that what you're suggesting is even if those persons who do not use this degree of selectivity in choosing the examining questions, nevertheless their competence is high enough that we're talking about the credibility and not the admissibility of the evidence as being totally deficient in scientific capability or scientific approach?

A: Well, I think you'd find that the other examiners that have arrived at their training through other sources and so forth will have a very capable equivalent of these things that I happened to have structured in this particular approach.

Q: Now, let me pass on—I believe, in addition to this selectivity then or subjectivity of the examiner himself, I believe you stated that the hostility or lack thereof of the subject himself can affect—in other words, what I'm envisioning is we may have a subject who is hostile but covertly hostile so that the examiner is not so completely aware that he would go ahead and take the examination anyway and this could affect the results.

A: This definitely would show up on the charts. In other words, hostility does involve strong emotion and therefore you would get emotion but not in the pattern that isolated itself to a given type of question. It would be throughout the entire pattern.

Q: So, again, you're suggesting even though hostility may affect the ultimate test that it is apparent and therefore can be considered by the examiner?

A: Yes, sir.

Q: He's not to be misled by it?

A: Oh, not at all. In fact, the charts would be a mess and he would state that it's an inconclusive case at that time or he would talk to the person and question him.

Q: Of course, I'm envisioning here not the person who is so completely hostile but the one who is hostile only to the extent that he is distorting to some degree the results. Does it happen at all and if it does does it happen often enough to render the results questionable?

A: In my opinion, it wouldn't render the results questionable. It would prolong the examination procedure. It may cause indefinites but indefinites are not errors. In other words, we have a three position scale. A person is either, in our opinion, truthful, deceptive, or indefinite or an incomplete test at that time.

Q: Well, would I be correct then in saying—you've indicated you normally can come up with a conclusion the subject is untruthful, he's truthful, or we have no conclusion. Am I to assume that under most circumstances you can take the inconclusive results and with an appropriate amount of time you will get a positive result?

A: Yes, sir. In fact, with a proper pre-test, and again this gets back to the importance of the pre-test, this hostility should've been neutralized before even the first chart was in process.

Q: Now, let me ask about this, we've mentioned the subject; would an examiner who has an abrasive personality or where the rapport never reaches the desired level, will this not also have an effect on the examiner's results?

A: Not on the examination's results. I think on the career of that examiner. These people don't stay in the field too long.

Q: This is one though that we cannot really reach the results except by the knowledge of his own compatriots, I would assume.

A: Well, of course, when this becomes a problem, an abrasive personality on the part of the examiner, we again have extraneous emotions exhibited in the form of general nervous tension. Hostility, of course, does not relegate itself to any one type of question and therefore we know we've got problems and that examiner should never have arrived at a conclusion and if he did erroneously he can be called upon very easily by review.

Q: I see. Well, I think you've, in effect, answered my question. You state you monitor your ex-students for instance and I'm sure there are other cases where these examinations are reviewed. What you're suggesting is that if there is a personality problem it's going to be reflected and even if the examiner is refusing to acknowledge it the other examiners in association with him are most likely to pick this up?

A: Yes. And not only that; but this examiner soon becomes disillusioned by his degree of inconclusiveness and gets disenchanted with the polygraph.

Q: Now, I suppose the only other matter would be the, this goes back to the first problem, perhaps, but would be the expertise of the examiner himself in developing the relevant question and the control question.

A: This is extremely important.

Q: And how does the profession guarantee to the extent of almost total reliability—we're dealing in criminal law and we must have reliability beyond a reasonable doubt in effect—how does the profession guarantee that the examiner who is preparing the relevant and control questions is, in fact, reaching the correct control and relevant questions?

A: Here, again, by review. In fact, in our standard approach that I've been personally involved in, we have a check list of questions that are applied to that relevant question which has been formulated to see if rules have been violated and from just a structural standpoint it becomes apparent under review. But, also, if the test question is ineffective, we have less than an ideal situation. In other words, in polygraph technique where we have at least two main components; that's the relevant question and the control question, we must receive a reaction either on the relevant question or on the control. There cannot be a reaction on both which would be the case if the control was too strongly formulated. Or we can't have a lack of reaction on both types of questions. We must demonstrate capability of reaction then and there within 15 or 20 seconds of the time the relevant question is asked. So, if there is an impropriety in the formulation of these questions, you will get such charts that will have reactions to both types of questions or to neither of the types of questions.

Q: If I understand your premise, the relevant question is the one that goes to the actual matter in issue?

A: Yes, to the target issue.

Q: The target issue. The relevant question also involves some degree of _____ .

A: Stigma.

Q: Stigma, right.

A: Yes, sir.

Q: So, basically you should get some reaction to both, should you not?

A: This is the fallacy, in fact the danger, where that is the only potentially emotionally important type question in the test. Let's say that again we got back to the non-lie questions, the possible lie questions, the probable lie questions. Now, the very purpose, the importance, of the control question, and Mr. Reid can attest—I think he will—to this because he is responsible for the introduction of this safety technique, is that we must have a factor in the examination structure that will detract from the natural nervousness, the natural stigma of the issue at stake, the natural slight resentment of the accusatory nature of the matter even being involved in the investigation. These factors must be detracted from and, in fact, this is done by putting in the control question that has enough stigma to override these other artificial stigmas that are not part of a structured examination. Now, the only thing that makes polygraph procedure a valid technique is the fact that it is carefully structured. Because you cannot look at a chart and identify one emotion from the other on the tracings you are receiving.

This has been known as a fact psychologically for many years. Now, the only reason that it becomes meaningful is that we have structured procedures that allow room only for fear, and of fear there are many varieties, the fear of detection to the particular incident that's at stake. So, if we do the rest of the structured examination in this manner we are inviting real problems.

Q: Well, I'm not sure I still understand completely what you're driving at. Let me take the case of the hypothetical individual who's charged with stealing money from his employer. You state you've narrowed down the issue to, let's say, "Did you take the money from the safe?" as the relevant question. "Have you ever stolen anything in the last 20 years?" And let's assume this individual used to steal watermelons from his neighbor's farm all the time when he was a kid. Would you not get a reaction to both of these if he said, "No." to both?

A: In this particular case we would assume that the person is, as later verified, involved. In the example you gave, in other words where he would be attempting deception to both types of questions. Now, in the control question which I personally call a probable lie question he will be attempting deception to both questions if he is involved in the crime that's involved in the testing. Now, even though he is lying to both questions he will show a lie only to the question that to a greater extent affects his immediate well-being. Now, the watermelon thing is out of the picture because he now stands a chance. He is jeopardized as far as his immediate freedom, mental state of well-being, whatever the situation happens to involve, by that then and now situation or here and now situation rather than the example, in fact I don't even overlap the times that the crime occurred with these earlier-in-life questions. I ask questions about—at least staying five years back. "The first 18 years of your life or between the ages of so and so and so and so did you do such and so?" Now, this might, and it's actually structured to evoke a reaction from that individual if he does not have fear as far as being detected is concerned on this argued issue. So, the balance of these questions is that that requires skill on the part of the examiner where the artificial stigma is eliminated by injecting the control procedure, close by. In other words, his psychological set, for the person that's involved, is waiting for the relevant question. In fact, he even relieves when you get on these other questions. But, on the other hand, if he were not involved in the crime he is tied up and concerned with the slight stigma of the control question and will relieve on the relevant question rather than show an artificial reaction.

Q: I follow that. One aspect needs to be clarified. You stated if you get a deception on both then you have to verify this later by the ascertainable results of that _____ .

A: No. If we get reaction to both types of questions and this is noticed, as it should be, at the end of the first chart, we know the remedial action that must be taken immediately because we know the problem that's involved. For instance, if we have a reaction to both a relevant question and a control question, we know our control is too strong.

Q: I see.

A: And we'll weaken the control question.

Q: Do you have to start all over again?

A: No, on the next chart we'd just make the adjustment between the _____ .

Q: Do you work this out with the subject?

A: With the subject every time. We don't change a word without talking it over with the subject.

Q: As regards whether he's consciously deceiving or not on the control question, you do not anticipate a particular reaction?

A: This is a probable lie question and the only time he should lie to this question is if his psychological set is not geared to the fear of detection because of involvement to the relevant question. We do indeed expect a reaction every time that he is not attempting deception on the relevant issue. In other words, he should show on that control question that he is not hiding something or is involved in the target issue or the relevant issue of the test. These questions are designed that way. They're designed as probable lie questions and we indeed do insist on a reaction being present on the control procedure if he does not react on the relevant question procedure. Otherwise a person _____ .

Q: What I'm suggesting is if you get a reaction on the relevant question and the control question is a probable lie, you nevertheless, since you have a reaction on the relevant question, do you expect relief and therefore no reaction on the control question?

A: Oh, that's correct.

Q: All right.

A: We expect no reaction. It's not a question of some on one and more on the other.

Q: Even though you have reason to believe that the control question is nevertheless a false answer?

A: That is correct.

Q: All right.

A: It's a built-in safety factor.

Q: Then I can understand then if he gives a correct answer, he relieves on the relevant question and reacts on the control?

A: Right, it must be an either or. It can't be both.

Q: And this is demonstrated by psychological as well as scientific results?

A: Yes, any psychologist who's analyzed this entire procedure is very quick to state that the psychological set process is involved which is a very valid psychological concept. It's indeed involved here. In other words, we are focusing the person's attention to that which more greatly threatens his well-being.

MJ: I have no further questions.

IC: I just have one further question unless you gentlemen have something further.

REDIRECT EXAMINATION

Questions by Mr. Bailey:

Q: Do you know Mr. Robert Brisentine?

A: Yes, sir, I do.

Q: Do you know of his professional reputation in polygraph?

A: Indeed, I do.

Q: Do you know Mr. Charles Zimmerman?

A: Yes, sir, I do.

Q: And do you know his professional reputation within the field?

A: I certainly do.

Q: What degree of confidence would you have as an examiner in an examination conducted by one with the other acting as a consultant or collaborator?

A: Well, I think indeed if I were in some kind of trouble, and I hope this doesn't occur, and I needed to ask to be tested I'd be very pleased to have either of these gentlemen do it.

Q: If you were guilty or innocent?

A: I'd hope I'd be innocent.

Q: Do you know of any technique _____ .

A: I think I'd go another direction, just to follow through on that, if I were guilty, and look for someone else.

Q: Do you know of any technique, method, subterfuge, or anything else that would enable the most sophisticated examiner, such as yourself, to deceive either of these gentlemen individually as an examiner?

A: No, sir. I've been an advocate, in fact I've been criticized at times for publishing information that's available to the general public about the intricacies of the technique. Now, I've always said, now, if we must depend in the polygraph field on secrecy of the technique in order that it enhances its success this technique is worth nothing whatsoever. In other words, it's a question of who got to the library first. The reliability would be shattered and the validity as well. So, I've always, in any contribution I could make in the field and my very involved research participation has been—if this is some procedure whereby being totally aware of it could cause me to in any way fool the polygraph, forget about it. And I, myself, and I think I said this earlier, have no feeling of security in taking an examination myself using the technique that I'm familiar with at least.

IC: I have nothing further from this witness, Your Honor. May we have Mr. Reid? I might say, by way of explanation, while Mr. Reid is being sworn, Your Honor, that it's not our purpose to be redundant to any extent. The additional experts in the field are to be called for the purpose of contributing their own experience. The fact that I omit the same background and explanation is simply to avoid redundancy.

MJ: Before the oath is administered to Mr. Reid, I suppose I should disclose that I had the pleasure of examining some of Mr. Reid's techniques when I attended Northwestern's school in Chicago. His office brought over some equipment. I'm sure Mr. Reid doesn't remember me. I remember him. He had a lot of students that day. I've heard a lot of his background and expertise and seen his equipment in operation and, in fact, he offered the detection device to all the students which I respectfully declined. These two gentlemen have both appeared in court (pointing to Mr. Brisentine and Mr. Presson). I believe they've both appeared in my courts before. Certainly, when I was an instructor in military law in the military justice field, they both appeared as qualified experts in their field and presented lecture material and demonstrations of their expertise to students of mine. So, I have personally met three of your experts and I'm aware of them already.

IC: Thank you, Your Honor. It would be most fortunate indeed if instead of merely sitting in the jury box they would have to decide the question; but, we'll proceed with the testimony.

MJ: All right. Mr. Reid.

(Mr. John E. Reid, civilian, was called as a witness for the defense, was sworn, and testified as follows.)

WIT: If I might, I'd start off by thanking you for your flattery.

MJ: It was intended as a simple statement of fact and privileges.

WIT: Thank you, sir.

DIRECT EXAMINATION

Questions by Major Eckhardt:

Q: Mr. Reid, would you please state your full name for the record?

A: John E. Reid.

Q: And your address, please, sir.

A: 7306 North Bell Avenue in Chicago.

Q: And your occupation, please, sir?

A: I'm a polygraph examiner.

IC: Your witness, Mr. Bailey.

Questions by Mr. Bailey:

Q: Mr. Reid, I'm going to be brief as to your background because it appears to be well-known not only here but elsewhere. How long have you been a polygraph examiner?

A: Well, since 1940.

Q: Have you operated a school teaching others to use the polygraph?

A: I have.

Q: For how long?

A: Since 1947.

Q: And is it still in operation?

A: It is.

Q: It was described by the previous witness as perhaps the longest course now given. How long do you take to educate, basically, an examiner?

A: Well, we have an internship type training and that takes six months.

Q: Now, Mr. Reid, are you the author of a volume called *Lie Detection and Criminal Interrogation* together with a Fred E. Inbau?

A: Yes, sir.

Q: Do you recall an edition of that book, which I believe for the record is published by the Williams and Wilkins Company in Baltimore, that came out in 1953?

A: That's right.

MJ: It's also been quoted by the Supreme Court, as I recall.

IC: It certainly has.

Further questions by Mr. Bailey:

Q: In the volume that I've described, in the 1953 edition, did you address yourself to the question of the wisdom of judicially using as evidence polygraph test results?

A: Yes, we did.

Q: And did you and Mr. Inbau express an opinion as to whether this should or should not be done?

A: It should not be done.

Q: Now, would you give the reasons that prompted you to make that recommendation to my profession and your own in 1953?

A: Well, we felt at that time that the examiner qualifications were possibly not the best, that the techniques certainly were not common among examiners, and that there was no control over the use of the instrument whatsoever.

Q: Did you, in 1966, publish a revised edition of the same work?

A: We did.

Q: And did you again address yourself to this same question about the use in court of these results?

A: Yes, we did.

Q: What position did you take in the volume five years ago?

A: In 1966, we decided, after examining the whole field, that the polygraph had not reached the stage where it should be considered by the courts with all other type evidence. And we made the proposal at that time in the edition itself that if the judge and the prosecutor and defense counsel believe that the test should be accepted and that they would agree upon the expert testifying and the one who did the test beforehand that that should be admissible as evidence.

Q: Mr. Reid, you're an attorney yourself, are you not?

A: I am, sir.

Q: And you have been involved over the years in a good number of cases that have been decided in one court or another, have you not?

A: Yes, sir, I have.

Q: Have you done testing, for instance, for police departments around the country?

A: I have.

Q: Have you done testing for individual counsel in criminal cases?

A: I have, sir.

Q: I want you to address yourself, if you will, to the question of handling evidence of this character and whether or not we have the machinery to do it in court. Are you familiar with other kinds of expert testimony?

A: Yes, I am.

Q: Fingerprints, ballistics or firearms identification, and so forth?

A: Yes.

Q: Do you feel that if a polygraph examiner were to testify in a case and render an opinion as to the truthfulness of say the accused or a witness who appeared, that the tools of cross-examination would be adequate to expose either an error on his part, incompetency, or the other things that experts are usually challenged on?

A: I believe so, yes.

Q: Are there sufficient standards of which the legal profession can learn to challenge an examiner who has not done a competent job in this very sensitive area of credibility?

A: I'm sure there are.

Q: And if, for instance, today we should have an examiner that appeared and rendered an opinion who was not a skilled professional, well-structured ethically, where could a lawyer reach to find rebuttal evidence within your profession? In other words, how would he go about persuading the court that the evidence should be disregarded?

A: Well, certainly there is sufficient information published on this subject. Of course, I have been the victim of cross-examination that I would certainly have sweated out terribly if I were on the opposite side of the fence and I didn't know what I was talking about. I believe that there is sufficient information, in the literature, to prove out the tenor of the man's testimony. If he hasn't got the background he shouldn't be on the witness stand and I think that he could reveal himself easily. It certainly is within the scope of the defense attorney to call another man to override his testimony such as Mr. Backster, Mr. Brisentine, Mr. Berman, a great number of the different men that are prominent in the field.

Q: The complaint is sometimes made that in malpractice cases we have trouble getting competent doctors to testify against incompetent doctors. From your experience in this field and your personal acquaintanceship with the leading experts, do you think there would be any hestitancy to appear and expose a charlatan or incompetent who was attempting to mislead a court with his opinion?

A: Absolutely not.

Q: You're also aware as an attorney, and when I say "our profession" I'm referring to yours and mine as opposed to yours and that enjoyed by these gentlemen, particularly in the area of psychiatry where we have the classic battle of the experts and both sides can usually get an expert to testify their way. In your own experience, not only in court cases but from dealing with other examiners over the years, what do you think is the likelihood that this would occur with any degree of frequency if we used this testimony as a matter of routine. That is, that one expert would say that he is lying and one would say he was truthful?

A: I think we'd stand out exceptionally if the experts were accepted properly and they had the credentials to start out with. I don't think we'd have a great deal of differences.

Q: Are you able to concur with Mr. Backster's opinion that in all likelihood one good examiner on one subject will come to the same conclusion as the other?

A: I do.

Q: And has that been your experience?

A: Yes, sir.

Q: And have you noticed any marked improvement in the overall standardization and professional skill of examiners generally within the past decade?

A: Oh, yes.

Q: And I take it this is to some extent responsible for the change of position of you and Professor Inbau?

A: Right, sir.

Q: Now, Mr. Reid, on the question of reliability which was discussed by the previous witness, can you tell me whether or not within the past year or so any studies have been done which would inform the court as to the demonstrable reliability of this technique?

A: Yes, sir, there were two studies that were done and they're exceptional in their scope in that they were done on actual case subjects where the results of the tests were known to the examiner—I mean to the one who conducted the test, myself and Mr. Horvett. We knew the results. We took ten of our examiners, seven were experienced men and three were not, three were in training, and we gave them these ten sets of records. We have five different charts that we run on each individual. So, that represented a great number of records for ten different cases. We took these records and chose out the most difficult of these records. We had one person who confessed and one person who is—no, we had one person in each one of these groups who was guilty. The examiner did not know anything about who was guilty, who was not guilty, or whether we had any guilty people in this group. They were given these sets of records. They then were to study the records—well, let me go back a bit. We have made an estimate then there's about 25 percent of the polygraph case records that are given that any examiner can point out to a person unacquainted with this technique that he could easily see the results. There's also 65 percent of the case records that are—really call for considerable intelligence and experience in order to come out with the proper result. And then there's about ten percent of the polygraph case records that are such that they're impossible to make a decision for some reason or another, such as physical disabilities on the part of the subject, mental, emotional, some sort of thing that would destroy the validity of the test. Now, we chose from this 65 percent, the hardest group, these records that we wanted to study. We submitted these records to these examiners and told them that they had one day to examine them and study them out and then make a definite determination. We held them down to two decisions on each question that was asked and each case that was asked, to come down to either a truthful or non-truthful. They had to calibrate these particular things. Now, getting away from the technique because we all have the same technique so there's no problem there. They knew exactly what questions were irrelevant, they knew which ones were relevant, and they knew which ones were the control questions from our technique. But they knew nothing more about this case whatsoever. They knew that this—they were given this much information—that this was a sabotage case, or this was a theft case, or this was this. Some—just the kind of case it was. They did have, however, they did not have the questions but they were told which ones were the relevant and which ones were not relevant. They were to examine these things then and come out with their decision. It was very amazing that these men were able, and it brings out a second point that we didn't look for, the seven experienced examiners came out with a tremendous, high accuracy that is reported in the *Journal of Criminology* right now, June issue. The three men that were in training came out with less accuracy. However, the least of them was 70 percent and the highest man in the whole group was 97 percent. This is without knowing anything about the subject, not seeing him, knowing anything about him, having any opportunity to see him at all. We almost feel that if all of these examiners were able to sit and talk with this person, know that he was a jittery person, he was something or other, to see him we could assist ourselves in increasing our accuracy even in that situation. That was the first one. The second one, sir, to follow on the reliability study, the second one that has not been published was the—Mr. Fred Hunter of our staff chose four examiners to study four sets of charts. He did not tell them he used the same formula that the others used, that Horvett and myself used. He did not tell them anything about them. He just told them, "Take these charts in and you hold it down to truth or non-truth." He didn't tell them that there was anybody guilty, didn't tell them who was innocent, whether they were all innocent or all guilty. Now, these were probably easier charts because he was seeking one additional thing. First, reliability of an examiner on the truthful side. To see whether or not there'd be any mistakes made by an examiner regarding a man telling the truth. And he also wanted to see if the examiner could take this set of charts, this group, examine them, make a decision on them with the bare facts, put them aside, leave, and then six months later he gave the same stuff back to these examiners and had them do it again. But this time he mixed them all up. They weren't coming so they couldn't even rely on their memory, didn't know that this was the same thing. He told them that this was another set of charts he'd like to have them work with and make a decision on. It's amazing the reliability that they came up with. First, there was none of them overall who called anybody guilty. They happened to be all innocent people and they all came out with that same decision. Some that incorporated error were indefinite. They couldn't make the decision exactly. So, there was an error point. I can't report on this exactly at this point but it was very, very slight. But the thing that impressed me most was that there was 96 percent that the examiner had marked truthful—all of the examiners—and then the next time around he became a little bit more conservative but he was 96.1 percent better. He was a little bit better the second time but they were exactly the same answers. They were all reported innocent individuals and they were. They were verified as innocent. On both of these cases, you might understand, we knew the answers because in his case, the latter one that we're speaking of, there was some bonds stolen from a bank. We had a great, great amount of subjects. Now, we found the man who did it after about 40 or 50 different people and we stopped the testing. They were anxious because it was a great number of bonds we're talking about. They were lost. Therefore, this bank said, "Look, we're going to go until we find them." And, so, we went along and we came to about 40 subjects and this one individual showed his guilt reactions. He was interrogated and then he confessed that he stole the bonds and brought them back. The second _____ .

Q: Were the charts you used taken from this group of innocents in the bonds test?

A: Yes, they were known. So, this is one of the things that were used. This is the thing that was used with the four examiners in the second situation. We only chose the innocent ones.

Q: I take it that in both of these experiments or studies the examiners were facing circumstances more adverse than in the practical administration of an actual case.

A: Indeed they were, yes.

Q: As to the low percentage of errors that did occur, if the matter were a subject of litigation and could have the full study by examiners hired by both sides, do you have an opinion as to whether even those errors would likely be eliminated?

A: I'm sure they'd be eliminated even without the additional help. If the examiner could examine the person on the spot himself, be able to observe him, whatnot and so forth, there's a number of things that could influence an examination that an examiner may have to eliminate the person or bring him back for reexamination because he's so upset the first day. These things we would take into account and face to face we would know the proper procedure.

Q: Very well. I'll put a final question to you. As you realize, we have highly compacted this testimony because we're trying to get through, perhaps, the cream of the industry in one day. As one involved for 30 some odd years now where the overall administration of justice and the desire to bring to it an accuracy of result based on a means of finding the truth, do you have an opinion, Mr. Reid, both as an examiner and as a lawyer and as one who has consulted frequently with prosecution authorities, as to whether or not the overall administration of justice would be bettered or jeopardized or hampered if the proper use of polygraphic evidence were to become a part of our system?

A: It would be bettered, sir.

IC: Thank you. I have no further questions of this witness.

ATC: No questions.

MJ: I don't believe I have any questions. I certainly thank you for your testimony, Mr. Reid. Again, I find the figures impressive. I would excuse you at this time back to your seat. Can we proceed on to the next witness?

IC: Yes, Your Honor.

MJ: All right. Thank you, Mr. Reid.

IC: Dr. LeMoyne Snyder.

(Dr. LeMoyne Snyder, civilian, was called as a witness for the defense, was sworn, and testified as follows.)

DIRECT EXAMINATION

Questions by Major Eckhardt:

Q: Would you please state your full name?

A: LeMoyne Snyder. L-E-M-O-Y-N-E S-N-Y-D-E-R.

Q: Dr. Snyder, where do you reside, please?

A: Paradise, California.

Q: And what is your occupation, please?

A: I'm a medical legal consultant.

IC: Thank you, sir.

Questions by Mr. Bailey:

Q: Doctor, would you give the court some of your education, training, and background? First, in the field of medicine.

A: Well, I am a graduate of Harvard Law School and I practiced general surgery for a good many years.

MJ: Just a moment, do you mean Harvard Medical School?

WIT: Harvard Medical School. Yes, Harvard Medical School.

MJ: I was going to say, I would appreciate the opportunity _____ .

WIT: There's quite a difference.

IC: I've known a few doctors who may have graduated from law school by mistake.

Further questions by Mr. Bailey:

Q: Would you continue, please doctor?

A: I practiced medicine and general surgery for a good number of years and then I did become admitted to the bar in Michigan and went into the field of legal medicine which is simply the application of medicine and science to the purposes of law. I have been in that field now since 1947 and have been doing that exclusively.

Q: Have you written some texts in the field especially with reference to pathology?

A: I wrote a book called *Homicide Investigation* and that came out first in 1944 in the English edition and has been reprinted ten times and revised.

Q: Doctor, you are familiar, I may assume, with a technique called polygraph?

A: Yes, I am.

Q: Would you tell the court when you first encountered the polygraph and in what capacity you encountered it?

A: I first rubbed shoulders with the polygraph in 1933 when I became acquainted with Leonard Keeler who is the person who more than any other single person perfected the polygraph, not only the instrument but the technique of the employment of the polygraph. Keeler and I became very close friends. During his lifetime we were together frequently on cases all over the country. At that time I was Medical Legal Director of the Michigan State Police. After I saw what Keeler could do with a polygraph, I became very much interested in it and I believe that it's true that I purchased the first polygraph outside of Chicago for the Michigan State Police in 1934 and we set up a polygraph laboratory almost 40 years ago. I'm not a polygraph examiner. I have never run cases myself but I have been experienced with it and know many of the people in the field. I have looked at thousands of charts. I've participated in the polygraph interrogation of thousands of persons, prisoners and suspects and whatnot.

Q: Doctor, I believe you've written a number of articles on the polygraph in law reviews and elsewhere, have you not?

A: Oh, a few, yes.

Q: Didn't you write one in the *Rocky Mountain Law Review* about 1940?

A: Yes, that was one of the first ones—giving our experience in the State Police with the polygraph after I think eight years. That was one of the very early articles I believe ever published on the experience with the polygraph in police organizations.

Q: Doctor, making specific reference to your experience and skill as a physician and your knowledge of the techniques and the things that people in that profession rely upon and also taking into account your understanding of the scientific basis of the technique that we're here discussing, can you make any comparisons as to reliability, for instance, between the recording and diagnostic technique of the polygraph on the one hand and on the other hand things like the electroencephalogram, the electrocardiogram, the X-ray spectrogram, and other things that we commonly use in court every day?

A: Well, yes, the—a thing that has always annoyed me about the public reaction to the polygraph is that they insist that the polygraph technique be infallible. They say, "Well, is it infallible?" Well, of course not. I don't know of anything in the field of medicine or physiology that's infallible. Take X-rays; courts welcome X-ray testimony and yet the radiologist can be totally in error in his interpretation of an X-ray plate. A physician can be totally in error on his interpretation of a blood test and yet these things are welcomed. And then when you get down to such things as personal identification; why, the polygraph is infinitely more reliable than personal identification. Take an ordinary thing— take a steel tape. "Why a steel tape is infallible." Well, is it? Supposing you start two inches from where you should have started to measure it or end up two inches short of where you're supposed to end up? There's a human error that'll go into anything and that includes the polygraph, of course,

Q: Now, doctor, making your specific reference, if you will, for a moment to an electrocardiogram which is a read out of physiological occurrences in the body. Can you compare the polygraph as an instrument, forgetting the individual and his technique, but the polygraph as an instrument and its dependability to the recognized dependability of the instrument that is the electrocardiogram?

A: Well, there, now, they say, "How accurate is the polygraph?" Well, the polygraph, the machine, is totally accurate assuming that it is in operating condition. If there's nothing wrong with the machine, there's nothing wrong with the electrocardiogram or a clinical thermometer. But it depends on the interpretation of the graph that is made by this instrument.

Q: Now, given an accurate instrument and assuming a skilled interpreter of the electrocardiogram which results from the operation of that instrument and an equally skilled, on a comparative level, interpreter of a polygram would you expect the degree of reliability to compare favorably as between those two?

A: I would certainly think so, yes.

Q: Have you as perhaps, I won't say a sideline but as an endeavor on your part, I believe together with Earl Stanley Gardner and others, ever been involved in a project to check the actual guilt of people who suffered court conviction?

A: Oh, yes.

Q: And to what extent, if any, in the course of pursuing this kind of case where innocence was claimed after a judgment was rendered, did you and your associates rely on the use of the polygraph for screening out those who just wanted to get out of jail?

A: Well, the way we used it—we had a great number of convicts write in from not only the United States but Europe claiming that they had been unjustly convicted. Well, there are all sorts of angles to the thing. For instance, a person may have been convicted of first degree murder when he actually was guilty of manslaughter or maybe not guilty of anything. So, where we would start would be with the polygraph and these prisons actually welcomed us into the place and would have them all set up for us and we would run these people on the polygraph. After going over the thing two or three times you would have a very substantial idea whether there was any use in proceeding any further with that particular individual. And, of course, we got all sorts of results. Some of these people were innocent and we were able to do something for them. Many of them weren't.

Q: Now, putting on your hat as an attorney for a minute, in those cases where you did find sitting within the prisons people who were innocent of the charge for which they stood trial even though the judgment was one of guilt and I assume these resulted from false confessions, misidentifications, and a variety of things that happened in court causing the system to misfire, do you have an opinion as to whether or not a skillfully administered impartial polygraph test could, in any substantial number of those cases, have prevented the mistake in the first place had it been received by the court?

A: Yes, I have no doubt at all that most of them could've been avoided.

Q: Doctor, you have been pretty close with what is now the American Polygraph Association through the years when it evolved from a number of associations, have you not?

A: Yes, I have.

Q: And do you, through annual meetings and other sources of communication, keep fairly well abreast of developments in the field such as professional ethics, skill standards, and so forth?

A: Yes, yes, I do.

Q: Can you note within the past decade, for instance, any substantial improvement in the area of standardization?

A: Oh, yes, and particularly if you'll go back further—go back 25 years—there's just all the difference in the world. Comparing it to that time and to just ten years ago, there's been very substantial improvement.

Q: Is it correct to say then that whereas there have been for many years individuals of the stature of perhaps Mr. Reid and Mr. Keeler whose results were almost always accurate there were also a number of individuals of much lesser competence whose standardization couldn't be defined?

A: Yes, that's perfectly true. Of course, the polygraph was a very attractive thing for people to get into who didn't know anything about it and in the very early days a lot of those people did the whole science no good at all. But that has changed now and people who are in the business, who have been in the business, who are experienced, who belong to these professional organizations and get the literature and the meetings, I think by and large are very competent examiners.

Q: Doctor, you have been, certainly at least since your days with the Michigan State Police and your entry to the bar, a person concerned with the accuracy of our system of justice. Do you have an opinion as to how it would be affected if we made use of expert testimony from polygraph examiners the same way we use other experts who have instruments to aid them in their diagnoses? Do you think it would help or hurt the overall administration of justice?

A: Oh, I think it would be extremely helpful to the administration of justice.

MJ: I only have this one observation, as a lawyer principally than as a doctor, I can foresee the use of this as a device to prevent injustice. My concern, perhaps, is what about the individual who is probably guilty and elects to exercise his Constitutional right to remain silent in the courtroom but has somehow or other been foolish enough to take a polygraph examination. Would you feel that it would be in the best interest of justice to allow the prosecutor to introduce the results of a polygraph examination indicating that he was examined on the question of his guilt and the questions indicated he denied it and that he was lying?

A: Well, of course, I think one of the great features of the polygraph technique is that there's no way in the world that anybody can be forced to submit to a polygraph test. In many respects it's a good deal like a witness taking the Fifth Amendment. He puts himself in a bad light by refusing to take a polygraph test, that's true. But, on the other hand, supposing the court allows some bank clerk who six months ago was in the bank when it was held up and come in and say, "Why, that's the man sitting right over there." Why, as compared to admitting the polygraph test which I think is infinitely more reliable assuming that a qualified person administered it _____.

MJ: Well, as a matter of trial tactics and in the interest of justice since this is what the question related to, would you consider that the admissibility, assuming it was admissible at all, of a polygraph examination should be restricted to—where it inculpates an individual it should be restricted to impeachment?

WIT: Well, after all, I think that the polygraph test is just one of a whole variety of types of evidence that can be introduced to convict a person. Take blood tests in a paternity case for example, take firearms identification, take fingerprint examinations, take all the rest of these things. I don't think that the polygraph test should supplant all of those at all. But I think that it ought to be taken into account along with these others.

MJ: I gather from what you're saying, sir, that you feel that when a subject voluntarily subjects himself to a polygraph examination he should be bound by the results and it can be used either for him or against him regardless of whether he exercises the right to remain silent in court.

WIT: It would seem to me that that's reasonable.

Further questions by Mr. Bailey:

Q: This then is similar to an individual who agrees to submit to any other kind of scientific test that he can't be compelled to submit to it?

A: Yes.

Q: He rides the result. As a practical matter, doctor, from your experience, in how many cases are we likely to wind up with an individual who's tested reacted, and everything shuts down at that point as against the number of cases where we either have admissions or something to put into present day evidentiary terms the indications of the reactions in the first place?

A: Well, I'm not sure that I get the thrust of your question there.

Q: All right, let me rephrase it. In most polygraph examinations where deceptive reactions are noted by the examiner and interrogator which he invariably is, is the matter left there or is the matter likely to be reduced to those kinds of admissions which we use every day rather than just the reactions on the chart?

A: Well, if I understand your question, in—I'm not sure I understand the question.

MJ: The way I understood the question was—you have a person who's examined and he says, "No, I didn't do it." and you confront him with this result and you say, "This shows that you're lying." The individual looks at it and then he says, "Well, all right, I did." That admission is then reduced to writing and the admission becomes admissible against him rather than the result of the polygraph examination.

WIT: Yes.

MJ: Now, the other side of it is where the individual says, "No, I didn't," you confront him with the fact that he's lying, and he insists that he's still—in the machine's wrong and he's right, he didn't do it. I think this puts the coin on both sides.

WIT: Yes.

Further questions by Mr. Bailey:

Q: What I asked you, doctor, was whether as a practical matter we frequently run into a situation where we have reactions and nothing else or whether admissions usually follow hard on.

A: Well, admissions don't always follow. When you're fairly convinced that the person is lying and, of course, that's one of the things that I object very seriously to is people trying to put a percentage of accuracy on the polygraph. I think it's totally impossible to do such a thing because, after all, if the examiner runs a test and the indications tell him that this person is withholding the truth or evading the truth or lying and the subject says he's telling the truth and nothing ever subsequently turns up to solve that riddle, how are you going to classify that? It's just that the polygraph said he's lying and he said he isn't and nothing ever happens. Well, how are you going to fit that into a percentage of accuracy? You can't.

Q: You'd have to term that an unverified opinion.

A: You can't use it at all.

Q: But is it true, that many opinions of examiners, due to later developments, are verified one way or the other either by confession or exculpation?

A: Yes, that's true.

Q: And as against the verified results where verification appears _____.

A: Sometimes years after, the verification appears.

Q: Where you have then something for comparison to assess the accuracy, what degree of accuracy would you say is usual in verified results?

A: I don't like to speculate on degree of accuracy at all. I say this, that an examiner who has had years of experience like John Reid and some of these other gentlemen; when they get done examining a person I would bank my last dollar on what they had to say as to whether that man was lying or not.

Q: All right. Perhaps I can phrase it this way then. Over the years, and considering only those examiners that you knew were skillful and qualified and sufficiently intelligent to operate this technique, how many times have you been confronted with a flatout error by a good examiner? Where he cleared a man who later confessed or he said a man was lying who was absolutely exculpated later on. Has it been a problem?

A: They're so few that—now, all the time that I was with the State Police in Michigan, and we were running people every day, I don't recall of a single person that was calibrated as being guilty that later turned out to be innocent. On several occasions innocent guilty people—wait, I'm getting twisted up. I don't recall of a single case of an innocent person being labeled as guilty. A few cases of guilty persons who were labeled as innocent. Of course, that is accounted for by the fact that some people just have such low key reactions that there just isn't enough of a variation on their chart to draw anything, it's too even all the way through.

MJ: But, if I understand that, the result of the examination could never be used to incriminate the individual.

WIT: No, no, never should.

MJ: Well, they couldn't be apparently because there wouldn't be sufficient reaction to even be able to reach a conclusion.

WIT: Yes, that's true.

Further questions by Mr. Bailey:

Q: Dr. Snyder, again relating to your entire experience in all three fields and having as our concern accuracy in litigation, if you had 20 criminal cases and divided them ten each, some innocent, some guilty, ranging from circumstantial cases to eyewitness identifications to confession cases, and you sent ten to John Reid and ten to jury trial, where would you expect to find the highest degree of statistical accuracy in the result as to who was guilty and who wasn't?

A: Well, I would—John Reid would be the person that I would rely on.

IC: All right, thank you.

ATC: No questions, Your Honor.

MJ: I don't have any questions either. I would like to thank you for appearing here, Dr. Snyder. I suppose like every other person, maybe these gentlemen and Mr. Bailey are different but, I am aware of your reputation and I am very honored to have you in the courtroom. I appreciate your testimony and your time, sir. Thank you very much.

WIT: Thank you, Your Honor, very much indeed.

MJ: Gentlemen, it's now 12:00. Let's recess until 1330. Would that be all right?

IC: Yes, Your Honor.

TC: Yes, sir.

(The court recessed at 1155 hours, 19 August 1971.)

(The court was called to order at 1331 hours, 19 August 1971.)

MJ: Court will come to order.

TC: Your Honor, all parties to the trial who were present when the court recessed are again present in court. Of course, there is no member of the court in the hearing room.

IC: Your Honor, may we have Mr. Clay Lowry, please.

MJ: Mr. Lowry.

(Mr. Clayborne A. Lowry, civilian, was called as a witness for the defense, was sworn, and testified as follows.)

DIRECT EXAMINATION

Questions by Major Eckhardt:

Q: Would you please state your full name?

A: Clayborne A. Lowry.

Q: Your residence, please, sir?

A: That's 2843 Cornelia Road, Augusta, Georgia.

Q: And your occupation?

A: Polygraph examiner.

TC: Your witness.

Questions by Mr. Bailey:

Q: Mr. Lowry, would you give the court some of your background in the field of polygraph examination and criminal investigation generally?

A: Well, I've been a criminal investigator in the United States Army from 19—approximately 1951 up until December of 1968. From 1961 until 1964 I was an instructor at the Polygraph Examiner Training School, Fort Gordon, Georgia. I had one year overseas assignment at which time I returned to the school where I remained until December of '68 when I retired.

Q: What kinds of courses did you teach at Fort Gordon?

A: Are you referring to polygraph or _____ .

Q: Polygraph and related courses; anything that's taught there.

A: It was primarily in the _____ I taught interrogation, pre-test interviewing, mechanics, operation of the polygraph, in-test procedures, practically everything except psychology and physiology which was left to the—our physiologists and psychologists that were assigned to us as instructors.

Q: Have you been active _____ .

MJ: I might inform you, he's also quite expert in the field of electronic surveillance.

IC: I see. I don't think we have any electronic surveillance in this case, Your Honor.

Further questions by Mr. Bailey:

Q: The people that you have known in the profession, I assume that includes some or most of the people that have been here today, or are still with us?

A: Yes, sir.

Q: Operate some other schools which I assume you're familiar with, Backster, Keeler and John Reid's school and so forth. Can you estimate for us, in your opinion at least, the standards at the Fort Gordon School and whether or not in your judgment that school has and is turning out now examiners who are competent and responsible?

A: The Fort Gordon School, of course I'm biased in my opinion, I feel that _____ .

Q: We'll accept your biased opinion.

A: It is the, as far as I'm concerned, one of the better polygraph examiner training schools in the United States. It utilizes techniques which are taught by all of the other schools, such as the zone comparison examination technique, the Reid's technique, the modified questions what we refer to it, peak of tension test, the relevant-irrelevant, et cetera, they are all covered within that particular school.

Q: Mr. Lowry, have you been involved as a result of your work in criminal investigation, generally, and polygraphs in particular, in cases that were litigated one way or the other in military courts?

A: Yes, over a period of time; however, the specific instances I don't recall.

Q: But you have some experience with the military judicial procedure?

A: Oh, yes, sir.

Q: And have you as a result of the exams that you have administered or supervised or been involved with on some personal level, been able to make an estimate of the reliability of an examiner's opinion as against the facts as they eventually turn out to be when there is a verification?

A: Could you repeat that just one more time, please?

Q: Yes.

Q: From your experience, have you been able to evaluate the reliability of this technique at doing what it's supposed to do, that is pick out liars from tellers of truth?

A: Oh, yes.

Q: And how do you regard it?

A: The polygraph technique?

Q: Yes.

A: It's very reliable. As a matter of fact, at one period at the school back in 1963 and '64 we ran a reliability test or check on cases that were examined by instructors and individuals at the school itself and of this particular grouping there was a 96 percent accuracy and 4 percent which was—which were unable to be evaluated due to physical defects or some mental problems of some kind.

Q: All right, then I take it there are physical defects or conditions in which a subject may find himself that makes it unrealistic to try and get a result in his test?

A: That is correct.

Q: Would you tell the court some of these cases where you have a man you just simply can't test?

A: Well, on occasion we had someone who was suffering perhaps from a broken limb.

Q: Yes.

A: Of course, these people are—we did not conduct any examinations on them at that particular time. Usually they're on medication and this affected some of the response criteria. So, we did not utilize these particular individuals. Some did not show adequate response criteria to the specific individual questions that were—was asked, and so these were inconclusive responses or charts. Whether the individual was a non-reactor or not, was actually not, at that particular period, determined. However, the cases were verified. The man apparently was responding properly but had no guilt complex to it or feelings toward this particular event.

MJ: Have you ever had a case involving amnesia?

WIT: I have never been involved in one like that.

Further questions by Mr. Bailey:

Q: Well, the polygraph is limited, is it not, to disclosing to the examiner what the subject believes and nothing more?

A: That is correct.

Q: If the man were guilty but by reason of mental disease thought he were innocent, he would test out that way, would he not?

A: That is correct.

Q: So that it is useful in evaluating candor or credibility, period.

A: Right.

Q: I take it that there are some classes of psychiatric diseases which would render a man unsuitable for testing?

A: Yes, sir, I—that is true.

Q: In the course of their training and in the experience that follows on after, are examiners alerted, in your experience, to the kinds of things to look for in order to eliminate unsuitable subjects?

A: That is correct.

Q: This is part of the training?

A: This—well, this—they receive instruction at the school by qualified psychologists and physiologists, actual doctors, et cetera, as to what to look for within the testing situation.

Q: Now, calling upon your recollection in the entire field of polygraph examinations, which I assume was until 1968, principally the military and since has expanded beyond.

A: Yes.

Q: In how many cases have you seen a responsible examiner make a demonstrable error, and by that I mean to call someone truthful later it is shown he's not, to call someone untruthful when it is later demonstrated that he must have been and thus mislead the investigators or lawyers who were relying on him, how often has that happened?

A: Very limited. I don't even recall a case of this, sir.

Q: In the military in your own experience, Mr. Lowry, when in the investigative section of the investigative process, a man who was judged by a recognized examiner to be telling the truth, how many of those cases do you know of when he was subsequently prosecuted formally in the military courts?

A: I can't recall any.

Q: Would you say that there was a practice or policy, admittedly unofficial, that the word of the military examiner was given considerable weight?

A: Oh, yeah, well, during the investigative phase, I recall when I was working primarily criminal cases and when we took an individual, a suspect, to the examiner, we usually followed his decision as to the procedures or the finalization of the investigation whether we eliminated that particular individual as a suspect or whether we looked for other people.

Q: Can you tell us whether or not, again in your experience, by reason of the polygraph innocent persons who might otherwise have been put to trial because of circumstantial or other evidence that seemed to incriminate them, have been eliminated almost solely on the polygraph examiner's opinion and thus avoided the need to stand trial in a military court? Have you seen that happen very frequently?

A: Oh, yes.

Q: Can you tell me whether or not it has been your experience that an examiner who is confronted apparently by very substantial evidence against the accused and very enthusiastic investigators who are in the midst of making a case, arrives at a result which is contrary to their expectations?

A: Well, this happens on numerous occasions.

Q: Sometimes the polygraph examiner winds standing up against the detective force?

A: Oh, yes.

Q: And in those cases where you have observed that to occur, who in the long run has in the main been correct?

A: The examiner.

Q: Now, have you ever been a member of a military court, Mr. Lowry? A court member?

A: No, I have not.

Q: All right. Have you seen the judicial process in action with witnesses testifying and judges and juries having to assess their credibility?

A: Yes, sir.

Q: If it were your responsibility to determine whether or not a witness, particularly an accused, were telling the truth, with all of the aids that we have—cross-examination and rebuttal evidence and so forth—would you think that your verdict as to who was telling the truth and who was not would be more or less accurate if you had the benefit of a polygraph examination to assist you?

A: Much more accurate with the polygraph.

Q: Would you think that if it were used as a matter of course under properly controlled conditions that this kind of evidence could enhance the overall reliability of our system of justice?

A: Yes, sir.

Q: By the way, were you on the faculty at the Fort Gordon School when Mr. Brisentine graduated from it?

A: Yes, sir.

Q: Then I take it you've known him not only personally but by reputation for a number of years?

A: That's correct.

Q: Do you have an opinion as to his professional competence and reputation for integrity?

A: Mr. Brisentine—I've known him for, well, it must be about 13, 14 years—something of this nature. I know him as a polygraph examiner. I've known him since he became the Chief of Quality Control. I know of no other individual within the military structure that's more qualified than he.

Q: You're aware I'm sure from your experience with court problems and criminal investigations of the occasional split in expert testimony, that is experienced whether it be psychiatrists or other kinds of experts.

A: Yes, sir.

Q: In your experience, Mr. Lowry, have you seen on many occasions or in any substantial numbers examiners arriving at different conclusions based on the same charts, the same subjects, the same issues?

A: Well, at the school—let me explain this particular area, if I may.

Q: Yes.

A: At the school, in the training process, all the student examiners conduct examinations which are then evaluated and supported by an instructor. Now, these particular—in dealing in hypothetical and live cases—actual events that transpired—on occasion, with a novice examiner—one that is the learning phase—there could possibly have been a minor error to some degree but it's very limited which is usually caught by an experienced examiner or one of the instructors. There's a very limited amount of error amongst qualified, experienced examiners especially at that particular school. You see, over a period of time, each instructor evaluates so many charts—well, it's up in the thousands—that they are forced to, through their instruction of the students, they evaluate, verify, and clarify any issues as far as the student is concerned. There's a very limited amount of error involved.

Q: Now, if an error were committed for any reason, either failing to recognize an unsuitable subject or a curious set of circumstances that caused a misdiagnosis, and the matter were to come to court so that you could expect there would be somebody supporting the examiner and somebody opposing him, do you have an opinion as to whether or not in all likelihood the error would be discovered and thrashed out before it misled either a court or jury? In other words, would qualified examiners, seeing a conflict _____ .

A: Well, within the military, this particular error possibility is minimized by the control factors that are involved. All examiners at the present time—this has been in effect since 1965—all examiners in the field forward all charts, everything, to the Quality Control Office which Mr. Brisentine and Mr. Presson are involved in. They in turn reevaluate all of the work that is done by the examiners in the field for clarification. And, of course, as to the amount of turnbacks or something of this nature or errors that were found by them, I am not knowledgeable in these areas. But I do know that it is very, very limited.

Q: Well, you are familiar, of course, with that phase of the judicial process which brings under close scrutiny any evidence which is contested. And what I am trying to find out, and I'm sure that the court and those who may at some point have to review this proceeding are interested in, is what is the likelihood that an error committed by an examiner at the time a test is run would be able to come through the witness stand, to the jury, past the court, past opposing counsel, and never be discovered or demonstrated and thus mislead the results?

A: Right now?

Q: Yes.

A: Maybe one percent, half a percent possibility. I even doubt that it would be that much. Of course, as I said, Mr. Brisentine and Mr. Presson could give you more better answers than that.

Q: I realize they can help us statistically. I'm calling only on your experience as to the safeguards within your profession because of the cross reading of charts coupled with the safeguards of the law where things are given a pretty tough look anyway.

A: It's a very small percentage.

Q: You would not regard it as a great danger?

A: No.

Q: I have only one other question. You mentioned, I believe, in passing that some other instructors, not examiners, were at the Fort Gordon school in various recognized fields of medicine. Can you tell us what kinds of people teach there and generally what kinds of courses they teach?

A: While I was attending—or was there on the faculty, we had Dr. Altshuler who was a retired Colonel, MD. He'd been in medicine on various fields for 30 years or more. On the instruction in psychology, we utilized Dr. Stewart Wiggens who's from the Medical College of Georgia at Augusta, Georgia, in the psych' phase of instructions.

Q: So, courses were taught in psychology?

A: Yes.

Q: And physiology?

A: And physiology, yes.

Q: And was there anything about psychiatry that was offered to the students that you can remember?

A: I do not recall, Mr. Bailey.

Q: Were they taught to recognize or at least be alert to recognize people with psychiatric problems that would interfere with the accuracy of the process?

A: Yes, sir, they were.

IC: Thank you, Mr. Lowry; I have no further questions, Your Honor, of this witness.

ATC: No questions, Your Honor.

MJ: I have no questions either. Thank you again for your attendance, Mr. Lowry. We appreciate your expertise. You're excused.

(The witness stepped down from the witness stand and resumed a seat in the courtroom.)

IC: Mr. Harrelson, Your Honor.

(Mr. Leonard H. Harrelson, civilian, was called as a witness for the defense, was sworn, and testified as follows.)

DIRECT EXAMINATION

Questions by Major Eckhardt:

Q: Would you state your full name, please, sir?

A: Leonard H. Harrelson.

Q: Your address, please?

A: 9067 Clifton Avenue, Niles, Illinois.

Q: And your occupation?

A: Polygraph examiner.

IC: Your witness.

Questions by Mr. Bailey:

Q: Mr. Harrelson, by whom are you presently employed?

A: Leonard Keeler, Incorporated.

Q: And what office do you hold in that business?

A: President.

Q: How long have you been at the Leonard Keeler, Incorporated address?

A: Since October 9th, 1955.

Q: What was your background prior to that time?

A: I'd been in law enforcement and intelligence work with the Federal Government.

Q: And by whom were you trained in the use of the polygraph?

A: Keeler Polygraph Institute.

Q: And who within the Institute? Anyone in particular?

A: Yes, at that time there was Colonel Ralph Pierce; Dr. LeMoyne Snyder was one of my instructors. Albert Brikesman who was a police officer at that time in Evanston.

Q: And how long have you been in charge of the operation of the Keeler school?

A: Since 1955.

Q: What kinds of classes do you conduct?

A: We conduct classes—well, now we're conducting two a year. We were conducting four a year. We teach the operation of the polygraph technique to various individuals from throughout the world.

Q: Is there any predominant group that is usually enrolled in the class?

A: Police and Government agents.

Q: And how many members in each class?

A: We have in our classes, Mr. Bailey, 12 to 14.

Q: And what is the duration of the basic course?

A: The basic course lasts for six weeks and after a year they have to return for two additional weeks.

Q: As an advanced course?

A: Yes.

Q: Do you exercise any supervision or review over those graduates who go into the field to start field operation?

A: Yes.

Q: In addition to the educational operation in the Keeler Corporation, do you do any actual examinations for agencies or individuals?

A: Oh, yes, sir.

Q: How many polygraph tests have you personally run or supervised since you began in the profession?

A: Well, I have conducted in excess of 30,000 and I would hate to guess at how many I've supervised.

Q: And what kinds of cases do you do on a daily basis at the Keeler school?

A: On a daily basis we do pre-employment type testing for various business enterprises, police departments around the area. We do the specific type of screening where we get involved in say homicide or larceny or whatever the case may be. And we do considerable work for various police departments and district attorneys throughout the whole United States.

Q: In how many different States would you say you have been a consultant in polygraph examinations to law enforcement agencies, just roughly?

A: Roughly, 40.

Q: And have you testified in court on numerous occasions?

A: Numerous occasions.

Q: Do you have some familiarity with the courtroom procedure and the rules of evidence as a result of that?

A: Yes, sir.

Q: Would you tell the court what it is?

A: Well, we can start with one of your first cases when you were out of law school where you defended or you represented an individual by the name of Dominic Bonomi who had been in prison at that time, as I believe, for in excess of seven years. He was convicted of uxorcide in Boston and he wanted a polygraph examination and he convinced you that he didn't do it and I gave him a test and the polygraph test did not agree with him and he subsequently confessed that he had, in fact, killed his wife.

Q: Yes, he did.

A: Then the other case, Mr. Bailey, is a case that took place in the State of Maine. A man was convicted and sent to prison in 1924. He was convicted of murder at that time. In 1958 everyone concerned officially had decided that they had made a mistake and that they had had this man in jail for all these years and he was the wrong man. So, they decided that they should free the man and give him a token check for the trouble that they had put him through for $250,000 and the Governor agreed with this but he said he should take a polygraph examination. He took a polygraph examination. The test indicated that he was not telling the truth, he had in fact committed the murder for which he had been convicted and he confessed.

Q: And the lapse of time between the murder and the test?

A: Well, from '24 to '58.

Q: 34 years?

A: Yes.

Q: Okay. Do you know the name of the man who ran that test and took his confession?

A: Parker Hennessey ran the test and he is the Superintendent of the Maine State Police.

Q: He was an examiner at that time?

A: At that time he was an examiner.

Q: And where was he trained?

A: At the Keeler Polygraph Institute.

Q: All right. Now, as to some of the other matters that have been covered, and I don't want to be redundant, but just as a matter of experience, have you had a problem in getting accurate results based on any chicanery such as the use of drugs or other efforts to so call "beat" the test?

A: No, sir.

Q: Do you think that with all of your experience you could devise a manner in which you could produce a truthful response when you were in fact being untruthful that would deceive a qualified examiner?

A: No, sir, I have personally tried that many times. I can't even deceive one that's not that well qualified.

Q: Now, in relation to the likelihood of litigation, we're concerned not only with reliability but whether or not this kind of evidence can be handled. In how many cases have you testified in court or been involved in litigation about the polygraph?

A: Well, Mr. Bailey, it'd be in excess of two hundred cases.

Q: Have you, as you are doing today, testified before as an expert laying matters of foundation and so forth?

A: Yes, sir.

Q: And have you testified as to specific results in specific cases?

A: Yes, sir.

Q: Do you feel that the process of cross-examination by an informed attorney is sufficient to guard the courts against either honest error or a dishonest examiner?

A: Yes, sir.

Q: Can you tell us anything about your view of the change, if any, in the status of the standardization of examiners and techniques during the past decade?

A: I've seen a tremendous change in our past decade and it's all been for the good.

Q: Is it fair to say that some years ago there were a number of different techniques that were advocated in various quarters of the profession?

A: Yes, sir.

Q: And, as of the present time, would you think that you ought to be able to read and form an opinion upon, for instance, Mr. Reid's charts or Mr. Backster's charts?

A: If I had the questions before me, yes, sir.

Q: And do you think that they could do the same with yours?

A: Yes, sir.

Q: Do you have any opinion to offer as to whether or not, from a point of view of accuracy of result, the polygraph could make any substantial contribution to the search of truth we call a trial?

A: Mr. Bailey, I think it could make a substantial contribution. Sometimes the tests do not even have to be conducted. I can remember when the President of the United States was a Congressman and there was a hearing called Alger Hiss. And Mr. Nixon had written to Keeler and asked him if he could conduct a polygraph examination on Chambers and Hiss and Keeler agreed that he would do it. But, when the two were asked by Mr. Nixon if they would take it, only Mr. Chambers agreed.

Q: Yes, I believe that's in the *Congressional Record.*

A: Yes, it is.

Q: Can you think of any reason or any subterfuge or deliberate effort on the part of knowing experts, should they in some way become perverted as to their integrity, that is likely to be able to mislead, deceive, or otherwise jeopardize the judicial process assuming competent counsel, a competent judge, and a halfway intelligent jury?

A: No, sir, I can't.

IC: Thank you, Mr. Harrelson.

MJ: I'd like the record to reflect that when Mr. Bailey stated, "a competent judge" he pointed in my direction. I appreciate that, Mr. Bailey. True or not, I appreciate it.

IC: I think that's been established, Your Honor.

MJ: Thank you very much for your testimony, Mr. Harrelson, and your attendance here. You may return to your seat, sir.

(The witness stepped down from the witness stand and resumed a seat in the courtroom.)

IC: All right. Mr. Berman, please.

(Mr. Milton A. Berman, civilian, was called as a witness for the defense, was sworn, and testified as follows.)

DIRECT EXAMINATION

Questions by Major Eckhardt:

Q: Would you please state your full name?

A: Milton A. Berman.

Q: Would you please spell your last name?

A: B-E-R-M-A-N.

Q: What is your residence, please, sir?

A: 1109 Ridgeline Drive, Louisville, Kentucky.

Q: Your occupation?

A: Polygraph examiner.

Questions by Mr. Bailey:

Q: Mr. Berman, are you a member of the American Polygraph Association?

A: Yes, sir, I am.

Q: How long have you belonged to it?

A: Since its origination—1966.

Q: Can you tell the court whether or not the American Polygraph Association is in essence the combination of a number of independent associations then in existence?

A: Yes, sir, in 1966 at the convention in Louisville the APA was formed from the other organizations, the Academy for Scientific Interrogation, the American Academy of Polygraph Examiners, and the National Board of Polygraph Examiners.

Q: As the result of that coagulation of associations into one, have you seen any appreciable change in the standardization of examiners and techniques?

A: Oh, yes, sir, we have.

Q: And what would your judgment be as to their current condition?

A: The current condition is much improved from what it was in '66.

Q: Now, do you hold any office in the Association?

A: I did when I left there this morning. I was a Member of the Board of Directors. I know I have been renominated, I don't know how the election came out.

Q: All right, reverting your testimony then to the expertise you had this morning in your official position, I wonder if you could tell us a little bit about the current membership requirements in the APA?

A: The requirements for membership in the APA require—well, there are several classes. It requires a college degree, graduation from an accredited school, a number of examinations having been completed prior to your application for membership. Now, some of these standards have been changed because of the number of examiners, for example in the military, who do not have college degrees but who have an equivalency, so exceptions were made. The number of examinations we're required to run was increased but the college requirement was decreased—the number of hours was decreased.

Q: What kinds of members are involved in the APA? In other words, what kinds of segments of the profession do they represent?

A: We have three classes—three divisions for which we have a Vice President for each division as a matter of fact. One is the private examiner, the police examiner, and the Federal examiner.

Q: Do you have a group of military examiners that belong and are affiliated with the association?

A: Yes, sir.

Q: Are they full-fledged members?

A: Yes, sir.

Q: Can you tell us generally from your experience the standards of competence that you would expect to find by one who is recognized by the military?

A: By the military, I would expect him to be very, very competent.

Q: Now, is there a code of ethics that is a part of your organizational structure?

A: Yes, sir, there is.

Q: And can you tell us essentially what it requires of an examiner in order to maintain his membership.

A: Well, I was chairman of the committee that wrote it. It took us three years to write it. I would have a little difficulty in giving you everything in it. I do have a copy if you want it entered into the record. I brought one with me.

Q: All right, then, I will ask to have it marked rather than ask you to recite it. But, can you tell me whether or not an effort is or is not constantly being made by the organization to protect against anyone who would pervert the considerable influence that examiners have?

A: Yes, sir, it is.

Q: Do you have any means of expelling members who for one reason or another might disregard their obligations?

A: Yes, sir.

Q: What kind of standards have been adopted by the American Polygraph Association?

A: Standards for schools?

Q: Yes.

A: We have established a required curriculum. This also was my committee. The Ethics and Standards Committee are one committee. Schools must teach a minimum of two hundred hours of actual instruction. This is a minimum, of course. They must make certain requirements as to the qualifications of the applicants before they're accepted to the school. There are requirements for the instructors in the schools. They must have certain experience and must qualify for membership or be eligible for membership in the organization so that we know that they are competent. They are requalified or reexamined—the schools are—every five years before they're accredited by the Association.

Q: Can you tell us whether or not all the people that you've seen testify today, and I believe you've seen them all, are presently active and accredited members of the Association?

A: Yes, sir, they are.

Q: And the only gentleman who's not testified but will follow hard on your heels, Mr. Brisentine is he in that category as well?

A: Yes, sir, he is. He serves on the Board with me. He remained on the Board.

IC: I see. Well, in the hope that you too have remained, I'll terminate the questioning.

ATC: No questions, Your Honor.

TC: I have no questions, sir.

MJ: I have one.

EXAMINATION BY THE COURT

Questions by the Military Judge:

Q: The only question I have is, to your knowledge are there licensing requirements by the various jurisdictions both State, Federal and local?

A: Yes, sir, happy to say. There are 11 States which have laws now for licensing, Kentucky having been the first.

Q Did you write that too?

A: Yes, sir. That law was passed in 1962. It's not nearly as complete as we should like it. However, we're going back to the Legislature in an effort to amend it. There are many other States which have laws in the hopper right now at the present time and we look forward to their successful passage.

Q: Are you aware now, this is really academic perhaps more than practical, but are you aware of any reasonably successful polygraph examiners or organizations that do not meet the standards of your organization? In other words, people that you would like to eliminate from the practice, if possible?

A: Yes, sir, I know that there are people I don't—can't think of anyone personally just off hand but I know that there are people who have made application for the Association and have not been admitted.

Q: So, I mean, there are some people that might not meet your qualifications that are in the business, sir.

A: Right.

Q: And I assume you're _____.

A: Private examiners.

Q: You're trying to eliminate these or bring them up to your standards?

A: Yes, sir, we are.

Q: All right. Do you foresee much success in this regard?

A: Oh, yes, the more State laws we have the fewer incompetent examiners we feel should not be licensed will be licensed.

Q: Well, just as a personal observation I would assume that, as Mr. Bailey has pointed out, an unqualified person would be exposed anyway.

A: Yes.

MJ: I don't have any further questions. Thank you very much, Mr. Berman, I thank you for your attendance here.

MJ: You're going to call Mr. Brisentine?

IC: Strictly for foundation matters and it'll be very brief.

MJ: All right, then, let's proceed.

IC: I will limit my examination to non-specifics so that if that's to be gone into he should be called again.

MJ: All right.

(Mr. Robert A. Brisentine, Junior, was called as a witness for the defense, was sworn, and testified as follows:)

DIRECT EXAMINATION

Questions by Major Eckhardt:

Q: Would you please state your full name?

A: Robert A. Brisentine, Junior.

Q: Your residence?

A: 12801 Chesney Lane, Bowie, Maryland.

Q: And your occupation, please?

A: Polygraph examiner.

TC: Your witness.

Questions by Mr. Bailey:

Q: Mr. Brisentine, you hold what position with respect to military polygraph examination?

A: I am, I guess you'd say, the Chief Polygraph Advisor to the CO, US Army CID Agencies.

Q: All right. And what day to day function do you perform in that office?

A: The function of that office requires the action as to certification and withdrawal of certification of polygraph examiners and to monitor, either by technical advice, and to personally review with my associate, Mr. Presson, all polygraph examination charts collected throughout the worldwide CID.

Q: I take it by that mention of certificates, there is some kind of licensing that's accomplished within the military for its examiners?

A: Very much so, sir.

Q: And that lacking such a license they're not permitted to run tests or give opinions unless they're in student status working their way up.

A: Unless they're in intern status, that is correct.

Q: All right. How long have you been giving tests in the military or supervising or reviewing them?

A: Well, I gave some tests prior to going to school; but since formal training, since 1961.

Q: All right. Have you known Mr. Charles Zimmerman, the gentleman to my left, whom I assume you can identify without difficulty?

A: Yes, sir.

IC: That's a leading question, Your Honor.

Further questions by Mr. Bailey:

Q: How long have you known him?

A: I've known Mr. Zimmerman since approximately 1957 I believe I first met him. I've known of him much longer.

Q: What was his duty and what was yours at the time of your encounter and where did it take place?

A: At the time I was not assigned to polygraph duties. I was a criminal investigator. Mr. Zimmerman was a polygraph examiner at the US Army Crime Laboratory at Frankfurt, Germany.

Q: Now, in connection with your services strictly as a polygraph examiner and taking in to account as well your experience as a criminal investigator relying on polygraph examinations to assist you in the function of your duties, can you tell the court just generally whether or not you have found a technique, assuming that it's in competent hands, to be a reliable day to day means of determining truth or deception?

A: Yes, sir, I'd have to say that or I'd have to find another occupation.

Q: Well, I assume you say it because it's been your experience as well?

A: Yes.

Q: Can you give us any recollection you may have of cases where persons, and I will restrict myself to the military with this question, where persons who have been cleared as to any criminal issue by a recognized, certificated polygraph examiner have subsequently been brought to trial or prosecuted?

MJ: On the same Charges.

IC: Yes.

Further questions by Mr. Bailey:

A: With the exception of one case that I'm not really sure of the Charges and Specifications. I know of no convictions by a trial of individuals who are found not to be lying during the polygraph examination.

Q: All right. In how many cases where you as an examiner have rendered an opinion that the man was telling the truth when he denied his guilt as to a specific Charge has that Charge later been put to trial? Can you think of any apart from this case?

A: None, apart from this—I'm not really sure on this particular case because I don't know the Charges and Specifications. I'm not really sure of it so I can't answer either way.

Q: Well, Im trying to elicit your information completely independent of this prosecution.

A: Independent of that I know of none, sir.

MJ: At the risk of invading the province of what Mr. Bailey—is the one case that you have cognizance of recent origin?

WIT: Yes, sir.

Further questions by Mr. Bailey:

Q: Is it another My Lai case, without specifying?

A: It's related, sir. I guess you maybe could refer to it as a My Lai case.

Q: Now, based on your experience as an investigator, and I assume that frequently you would follow through your investigations to see what the judicial result was as to acquittal, conviction, and so forth, in your experience as an examiner, which of course is interrelated, do you think that evidence of this sort can be adequately handled in the courtroom by lawyers, judges, and juries; that is, polygraph examiner's opinions on truth and veracity?

A: I'd have to answer that this way, Mr. Bailey, with the standardization existing within the Army, and I'm not at liberty except—that's why I've accepted the testimony of these other gentlemen here; but with the standardization presently existing within the Army, yes. I would say yes.

Q: All right. Do you think it could be an asset to the administration of military justice?

A: Well, as I previously testified, sir, I don't know of anyone who's been brought to trial with the exception of one case that was found to be innocent on a polygraph—using the literal term.

MJ: Well, I think the question, Mr. Brisentine, is not necessarily where the individual is shown to be innocent but what about when the individual is shown not to be innocent?

WIT: Yes, I think it would be—certainly on that side of the coin, Your Honor, that would certainly enhance the judge, enhance the court, or assist. I would have to answer that way.

Further questions by Mr. Bailey:

Q: Assume, as you could well be if a defense lawyer would ever let you get that far, assume that you became a juror, military or otherwise, would you think you could better reach a fair result to the accused and the Government if there had been a polygraph test and you knew about it and what the results were rather than just having to judge the man's credibility by listening to him testify?

A: Knowing what I know about the polygraph, I certainly would have to say that the polygraph in itself would certainly have a bearing. It would influence my judgment.

Q: All right. And perhaps to specifically highlight the question of the court, can you think of any reason why it would be unfair if a man volunteers to take a test and doesn't do well on it and it results in admissions or pretty obvious reactions why it would be unfair to use that evidence against him?

A: Definitely not, not a properly administered polygraph.

Q: Thank you, Mr. Brisentine. I take it then, I don't want to go through all these matters again, may I take it that you are in general agreement with the overall testimony that's been given here today?

A: Yes, I am, sir.

IC: Thank you.

ATC: No questions, Your Honor.

IC: I have nothing further, Your Honor.

MJ: Do you wish to pursue the second phase of this matter?

TC: Yes, sir, why don't we take a ten minute recess.

MJ: Yes, let's take a recess until 1430.

(The court recessed at 1415 hours, 19 August 1971.)

Index

Index

About the Author

Stanley Abrams is a clinical psychologist in private practice and associated with the Permanente Clinic in Portland, Oregon. Polygraphy has been one of his areas of specialization and he has published a considerable number of papers in this area as well as several chapters in books. He has employed this procedure in a wide variety of criminal and civil cases and has testified for both prosecution and defense. His research findings have been presented before legal, psychological, and polygraph groups and he has served on various polygraph boards and has held office in the polygraph associations.

Dr. Abrams received the B.A. degree in psychology from Wilkes College in Pennsylvania and the M.A. and Ph.D. in clinical psychology from Temple University. He completed an internship at Temple University Medical School in 1960 and in 1971 took a course in polygraph at the Gormac School in Los Angeles.